Historical Perspectives on Social Identities

Historical Perspectives on Social Identities

Edited by

Alyson Brown

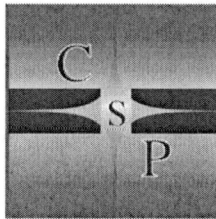

CAMBRIDGE SCHOLARS PRESS

Historical Perspectives on Social Identities, edited by Alyson Brown

This book first published 2006 by

Cambridge Scholars Press

15 Angerton Gardens, Newcastle, NE5 2JA, UK

British Library Cataloguing in Publication Data
A catalogue record for this book is available from the British Library

ISBN 1904303684

TABLE OF CONTENTS

CONTRIBUTORS

Martin Atherton is a Senior Lecturer in Deaf Studies at the University of Central Lancashire, Preston, having previously read for a degree in Deaf Studies and History at the university from 1994 to 1997. His particular area of interest is deaf history, particularly the place of leisure and sport in community cohesion. He was awarded his PhD by De Montfort University, Leicester in 2005 for his research into the activities of deaf clubs in north-west England.

Alyson Brown is a Senior Lecturer in History at Edge Hill College of Higher Education. She is on the management board of the Centre for Liverpool and Merseyside Studies and was organiser of the 'Identities' conference (2005) for this research centre. Her main research interest is English penal history and she has recently published *English society and the prison* (Willan, 2003). She has also published several chapters and articles on this subject area.

Mike Brennan is an ESRC Research Fellow in the Department of Sociology at the University of Warwick. His current research, which focuses upon issues of mourning and loss as central to the Israeli-Palestinian conflict in general, and to Israeli identity in particular, explores memory as a site of cultural narrative through which identities are performatively mobilised.

Angela Davis is currently completing a DPhil at St Cross College, University of Oxford, working on women's experiences of and attitudes towards motherhood c. 1945-1970. This research is based on an oral history project involving interviews with eighty women from around Oxfordshire. She has a wider interest in family and community history and her previously researched fatherhood in Britain in the first half of the twentieth century and married life in Britain between 1945 and 1970.

James Gregory is a Lecturer in Modern History at the University of Bradford. He is currently researching 'eccentricity' in British culture c.1760-1901, he has published essays exploring aspects of this topic (in *Northern History*, 2005; and in Waltraud Ernst, ed., *Social History of the Normal and Abnormal*, 2006). He is also completing a book-length study of vegetarianism in Victorian Britain, and a dual contextual biography of the Victorian statesman and reformer William Cowper-Temple and his wife Georgina.

Lynn Sorge-English is Associate Professor in the Costume Studies Programme at Dalhousie University, Halifax, NS, Canada, and is also a PhD candidate at Oxford Brookes University where her research is focusing on the British tailoring trade, stays and body transformation in eighteenth-century Britain. Part of this work can be seen in Lynn Sorge-English, "'29 Doz and 11 Best Cutt Bone': The Trade in Whalebone and Stays in Eighteenth-Century London," *Textile History* 36 (2005): 19-42.

Roger Spalding is Senior Lecturer in History at Edge Hill HE College. Initially his interests were primarily in the history of the British Left, in particular in the 1930s. More recently he has developed an interest in the history of cultural representations, again, in particular in and of the 1930s. This is not so much a linguistic turn, as a turn towards the sofa and the VCR.

Murray Steele was the former Head of Afro-Asian Studies (now retired) at Edge Hill College of Higher Education, where his main area of expertise was the colonial history of Southern Africa. He has taught and researched in Canada and Zimbabwe, as well as the UK. His publications cover a number of fields, including race relations, labour and missionary history, rural studies and comparative local government, predominantly in the last (twentieth) century. His contribution to this volume brings some of these perspectives to the development of post-war Liverpool as a multi-cultural society.

Andrew Walker is a Principal Lecturer in the Department of Humanities at the University of Lincoln. He is particularly interested in the articulation of local and regional identity. His current research interests include the nineteenth-century English provincial press and the social and cultural history of the Lincolnshire Show.

John Walton is Professor of History at the University of Central Lancashire and chairs the Research Committee of the Faculty of Cultural, Legal and Social Studies. He has published widely on the history of tourism, resorts, regions and identities in (especially) Britain and Spain, and his most recent book is (with Gary Cross), *The Playful Crowd: Pleasure Places in the Twentieth Century* (New York: Columbia University Press, 2005).

Tony Webster is Head of History at Edge Hill HE College. He studied for his PhD on the British empire in south east Asia at the University of Birmingham. A former tax inspector, he has published in the *Economic History Review*, the *Journal of Imperial and Commonwealth History* and the *Historical Journal*. His first book, *Gentlemen Capitalists: British Imperialism in south east Asia 1770-1890* appeared in 1998, and a second, *The Debate on the Rise of the British Empire* will be published in 2006. He is currently working on a full length biography of John Palmer.

INTRODUCTION: EXAMINING IDENTITIES

ALYSON BROWN

This collection of work on the theme of identities was the result of a conference held in the spring of 2005 at Edge Hill under the auspices of The Centre for Liverpool and Merseyside Studies (CLAMS). Whilst a significant proportion of the research focused on Liverpool and the North West, the theme of identities was sufficiently broad to entice scholars from diverse and varied fields. This collection, therefore, reflects the range of work presented and discussed at the conference and the multi-layered and multi-facetted nature of identity.

Contributors to the conference examined the concept of identity in Britain through a range of historical perspectives, concerning ourselves primarily with the later modern period. This is not to suggest that identity is a product of modernity but the relevance of, and the struggles around identity have been most overt over the last two to three hundred years.[1] Nineteenth and twentieth century British social, cultural and political change has given rise to pluralist, fragmented and fractured identities in which domestic, class, gender, religious and institutional frameworks have shifted continually. Recently, the July 2005 London bombings have heightened our awareness of fractured religious and cultural identities. Michael Howard, the Conservative Party leader, was reported in an article in *The Guardian* contrasting values of "decency, tolerance and sense of fair play" which he claimed were embedded in British identity to the "confusing" concept of multi-culturalism. On the other hand Will Hutton asked "Do the British even have a shared conception of what our identity is?"[2] The increasingly contentious nature of identities in the twenty-first century has stimulated extensive interest on the subject by historians and social theorists alike. Recent research into the concept has yielded numerous articles, chapters and books from across the disciplines of history, philosophy, cultural studies, economics and psychology.

Research on identities has often presupposed an individual, a "real inner self" that is "whole" and examined its origins, manifestation and impact. The individual since the eighteenth century has been "cast as the autonomous bearer of rights", "the basic building block" of political liberalism.[3] Of course, within this writers have debated the extent to which individuals are determined by social conventions, material and psychological constrained etc or have a measure of, or absolute, independence and free will. Norbert Elias suggested the "open personality" who had relative autonomy but is "fundamentally oriented toward and dependent on other people throughout his life".[4] Thus, for Elias, expanding social interdependence is one of the pillars of increasing civilisation and progress towards rational, reflective and self-restrained individuals who make up that society.

Postmodern theorists have, however, questioned the very existence of the individual, the subject. The deconstruction of identities by postmodernists has questioned the integrity and usefulness of this concept as a tool for analysis, has challenged the essentialist "notion of an integral, originary and unified identity".[5] Among the most important contributions to this field by postmodernist thinking has been the emphasis upon the negotiated and fluid nature of identity, that it is a process rather than a condition, in constant flux rather than static. This highlights that identities are not based in isolated individuals but in relationships. Stuart Hall has agreed with Foucault in his problematising of the self, of the individual, but instead of rejecting the subject, Hall instead advocates a "reconceptualization", a decentring of the subject in which identities are not unified.

Hall utilises the concept of "identification" which he describes as, "constructed on the back of a recognition of some common origin or shared characteristics with another person or group, or with an ideal, and with the natural closure of solidarity and allegiance established on this foundation."[6] But this identification is never complete, is persistently ambiguous and is consolidated by difference. Indeed, as is illustrated by the chapters in this publication difference, inclusion and exclusion, lie at the heart of identity and identification. Identity can be defined not only as being a part of something but also defined in negative terms as being unlike or apart from something else, some other. To give a specific example, Raphael Samuel highlighted as "an obvious point of contrast" between the 1940s and the 1980s the decline of public spirit. Positively it enshrined "a notion of duty, obligation and sacrifice in the interests of a higher cause" but negatively it stigmatised anyone who diverged from this as "anti-social" and served "as a paradigm for the conduct of everyday life".[7]

Crucially, identity and identification are contingent not only on material or physical factors such as housing, occupation and wealth but also on values, ideals and desires such as honesty, community and pleasure. The multiple identities that structure and are structured by the social world have histories, and historical analysis can help us to understand and evaluate them. The meanings attached to language, class, status, gender, race and sexuality for example, are not reborn with each generation they already exist, albeit in a state of constant flux. Whether they change very gradually or rapidly, they shape the lives of individuals, their expectations, opportunities and choices.

Examinations of identities have recognised this fluidity and instability but also a level of contingency in contexts which can be, or appear to be, relatively durable and stable,

"While many argue that an individual is always in the process of being formed… While it is important to recognize that identification is not a simple process, it is also important that 'identity formation' through which individuals incorporate certain characteristics and values is a process involving relatively durable attachments, obligations and promises".[8]

The range and diversity of the chapters in this publication is a testament to the complexity and quality of research on the subject of identity and the importance of identity formation for the development of social groupings, communities and social institutions. John Walton begins with a chapter which discusses the identity of resorts on the North West coast. Coastal resorts were constructed by numerous factors including location and their visitors and became strongly differentiated. Having different "place-myths"; these were towns that affirmed regional and class identities. There were several alternative versions of these towns that existed in parallel, although within a core, dominant identity. The examination of Blackpool especially reveals that while such pleasure resorts in many respects occupied liminal space, they were not without constraints as the workers from whole factories or industrial sectors had their holidays at the same time; rules were bent rather than broken. Blackpool came to epitomise both hedonism and respectability and working class behaviour there reflected, articulated and influenced changing expectations and civilising tendencies.

The theme of local identities is continued with Andrew Walker's analysis of identity as reflected through dialects. Nostalgia about custom and tradition permeated much of the dialect literature of nineteenth-century Yorkshire and Lancashire, the strength of which melded people to their locality and perhaps contributed to the development of a northern identity based on shared rhythms of work and play. In these sympathetic portrayals of traditional ways of life and the domestic ideal, outsiders were often the subject of humour and even abuse highlighting themes of insider and outsider groups. However, across the nineteenth-century dialect literature became less of a living link within communities and more an attempt to conserve dying cultures that were perceived to be under attack.

James Gregory takes up inclusion and exclusion as strategies in the formation of identities in his analysis of the place of local characters or eccentrics in nineteenth-century local, regional and national identities. One role of eccentrics was defensive. Some characters could be political radicals and/or wealthy but most were working-class, spoke in dialect and represented the survival of regional and even national identity in the face of a perceived rising cultural homogeneity. Gregory suggests that the identification of some individuals as different or "odd" served to promote a sense of place; that as much as location, "characters" were signifiers of identity, memorials of local characteristics.

In a shift of emphasis in the book to individually constructed identities, Tony Webster observes how John Palmer consciously constructed an identity suited to operating his agency house in India. John Palmer's identity as a wealthy, noble, compassionate civic and political leader, based predominantly on the aristocratic mores of his day, brought him tangible commercial advantages and opportunities. However, in the face of an increasingly competitive and unpredictable economic and political context some aspects of this identity, especially his lavishness and tolerance became liabilities and perceived as naïve within the changing business environment of 1820s and 1830s.

A particular professional identity was also crucial to the operation of Richard Viney's eighteenth-century staymaker business. Lynn Sorge-English discusses the multi-layered and inter-linked commercial and personal identity of a moral, educated and religious man and also of the identities of his clients. In an occupation that required intimate contact with his customers Richard Viney's high moral conduct was an indispensable aspect of his work and in combination with his education enabled him to cross class and gender boundaries and to meet his customers on a social level. The staymaker and his stays helped to define the identity of his clients as fashionable people, the person and performance individuals presented to the public.

The remaining chapters explore more diverse manifestations of identity, namely political identities, motherhood, disability, race and loss. In his chapter on "Imagined Solidarities", Roger Spalding highlights the ways in which cultural identities diverge and how class identities are defined, often in a very conscious manner. His work concerns the inter-war period and the ideology and activity of upper middle class socialists whose political beliefs necessitated a re-appraisal of their social identity. On one level the resolution of their political problems is presented as an ability to reconcile themselves to the working class body and its smells!

Angela Davis examines locality and class as well as gender in the context of young mothers in two rural villages in Oxfordshire. Her chapter on the construction of maternal identities 1954-1970 concludes that the women interviewed constructed their identities primarily in terms of their motherhood, although many undertook some kind of paid employment, and despite the 1960s re-evaluation of the theoretical work of Bowlby and Winnicott by feminists. This analysis emphasises the extent to which different facets of social identities over-lap but retain a perceived hierarchy of importance to the individual. This element of hierarchy evident within identities is not only self-constructed but is also constructed by others. This process is analysed by Martin Atherton in his research on Britain's deaf community. Atherton asserts that the deaf community itself has rejected deafness as a disabling factor in their lives and notes that it is the attitude of the hearing majority towards deaf people that is the disabling factor. Rather than living together as a location-based community, deaf people have found ways of coming together and sharing the life and culture of a community. Referring to the period

1945 to 1995, Martin Atherton examines one of these ways; the network of deaf social clubs. Involvement in this network helped many deaf people to accept their deafness as an important part of their identity, that these clubs constructed a form of normality and positive shared experience.

The next chapter concerns the way in which identities are manipulated or unconsidered and the impact of this. Murray Steele contends that until well into the twentieth century the minimising of Liverpool's role in the slave trade was representative of general attitudes to the city's black community. According to Steele, this was in part a function of the New Imperialism of the late-nineteenth and early twentieth centuries which effectively submerged recognition of the slave trade. It is only in the later twentieth and early twenty-first centuries that this situation has begun to change significantly and the first steps have been made to reintegrate the history of Liverpool's black community and to recognise the extent to which tension has been a consequence of an alienation from the majority white culture.

The final chapter also focuses on Liverpool. This is an analysis of a tragic event and its aftermath which has had a profound and lasting impact on local identity on Merseyside; the Hillsborough disaster of 1989 in which 95(6) football supporters died. In this chapter, Mike Brennan asserts that condolence books tell us not only about the way people mourn but also about the discursive practices through which the social identities of those who mourn are formed and by which people can work through their emotions. As a kind of "empirical marker" and public forum, condolence books denote linguistic, social and cultural practices around death and the way that it is experienced, marked and understood. In the case of the Hillsborough condolence books, people were not only mourning the victims of the tragedy but also mourned "for the loss of selves and for people and places gone before".

---

[1] For an interesting overview of the historiography of the self and self-realization see See R.Porter (ed.), *Rewriting the Self: Histories from the Renaissance to the Present* (London: Routledge, 1997), especially Porter's introduction.

[2] 17 August 2005, "Promote British values to stop terror says Howard" and *The Guardian* "Our Britishness can beat the bombers" 31 July 2005. Also see, for example, *The Guardian,* "Race and faith post 7/7" 30 July 2005.

[3] R.Porter, "Introduction", in R.Porter (ed.), *Rewriting the Self: Histories from the Renaissance to the Present* (London: Routledge, 1997) 5-6. In Adam Smith's *Wealth of Nations* (1776) the "hidden hand" of individual self-interest was the foundation of classical economics.

[4] Elias' "civilizing process" is discussed in J.Carter Wood, *Violence and crime in nineteenth-century England* (London: Routledge, 2004) 15-20. See E.Norbert, *The Civilizing Process: The History of Manners and State Formation and Civilization* E.Jephcott (trans.) 1939)

(Oxford: Blackwell, 1994); also see J.Fletcher, *Violence ad Civilzsation: An Introduction to the Work of Norbert Elias* (Cambridge: Polity Press, 1997).

[5] S.Hall, "Introduction: Who Needs 'Identity'?", in S.Hall and P.du Gay (eds), *Questions of Cultural Identity* (London: Sage, 1996) 1.

[6] *Ibid*, 2.

[7] R.Samuel, "Introduction: exciting to be English", in R.Samuel (ed.), *Patriotism: The Making and Remaking of British National Identity Vol.1, History and Politics* (London: Routledge, 1989) xxi-xxii.

[8] E.F.Isin and P.K.Wood, *Citizenship and Identity* (London: Sage, 1999) 19.

RESORTS AND REGIONS: BLACKPOOL, SOUTHPORT, LANCASHIRE AND BEYOND

JOHN WALTON

Seaside resorts might be assumed to be peripheral to regional identity. They are often seen as liminal, "places on the margin", where freedom from the constraints and conventions of everyday life in the liberating atmosphere of the debatable zone where land meets sea enables a shedding of the carapace of custom and the temporary emergence of a more hedonistic self.[1] This conception of the seaside resort immediately despatches this kind of place beyond the external realms of the serious, the workaday and the political. But such assumptions are over-simplified and misleading. If resorts are of any size and complexity they bring people together from different kinds of place, both within and beyond the regional hinterland, and from contrasting class and cultural backgrounds. Like the shopping and entertainment centres of great cities, or the eighteenth-century spas and county towns of the 'urban renaissance', or contemporary shopping malls, they are places where people are working at their leisure, conscious of being on display, promenading, preening, flirting and playing the *flaneur*, wanting to demonstrate an appropriate command of resources and to lay claim to that difficult combination of being fashionable and distinctive.[2] They are therefore sites of cultural innovation, exchange and conflict, although they also need enough consensus and control to be able to function as, or contain, spaces of shared enjoyment that stimulate or relax without threatening or challenging.[3] This perception of the resort raises cultural and social questions of obvious general relevance, although it might seem to challenge notions of regional identity rather than to affirm them.

This is also too simple an assumption, and we need to look more closely and directly at relationships between resorts and regions. Can seaside resorts also, despite their physical marginality and the divisive and potentially cosmopolitan, transnational or at least metropolitan aspects highlighted above, be places that affirm regional identities, or act as alternative regional capitals, celebrating the shared characteristics of provinces, counties (in the British usage) or economic regions against the "otherness" of those "elsewheres" that may also be present, especially when resort catchment areas transcend regional or national boundaries? Can different resorts within a region encapsulate different aspects of ascribed regional character, bringing out the internal "otherness" that lies within broader definitions of regional experience and consciousness (in the neglected formulation of J.D. Marshall), whether the fault-lines follow locality, sub-regional divisions, class or culture?[4] It is perhaps significant that no British seaside resort (not even Brighton) can lay claim to encapsulating *national* identity in the way that San Sebastián did (for a time), at least for a Spanish elite, or Ostend did for Belgium (despite its additional and perhaps more important role as international playground), or Manly claimed to do for inter-war Australia.[5] If resorts do represent or even distil external identities in Britain, those identities are necessarily regional ones.[6]

What, in any case, do we mean by a region in this context? This is a serious problem, especially in Britain, if we want to go beyond administrative lines drawn on maps, or statistically convenient building blocks, and try to delineate shared territorial cultures and characteristics. An approach through the old administrative counties is the most promising line for historians, especially in the light of the etiolated development of regional identities on a broader canvas in Britain, certainly as compared with other European nations, and especially if we assume that the four elements of the United Kingdom are "nations without a (full-blown) state" of their own, as opposed to regions in the usual sense. Even the North, the English region with the strongest discursive identity, is at its most coherent when set stereotypically against an external "other", the metropolitan "south". Moreover, its sub-divisions dissolve as soon as they are carefully interrogated. Even "Northumbria" or "the North-East", despite its black and white regional flag, disintegrates into rival linguistic and cultural enclaves when we look beyond its Geordie heartland, while the imagined "North-West" proves to be largely a discursive construction of the late 1960s onwards, with hardly anyone using that label to talk about any of its incarnations before then.[6]

Regions elsewhere in Britain, and especially in England, are even harder to define; but we cannot manage without the concept, if only as a shorthand way of generating generalisations on a manageable scale below the level of a notional "nation as a whole", providing a jigsaw with few enough pieces to generate internal comparisons that offer some depth of field. So the word will feature in what follows, denoting a geographical entity with some degree of recognition and coherence below the level of the nation-state and above that of the county, but without assuming that British regions can be precisely delineated with universally agreed boundaries or characteristics. This chapter deals with the region as heuristic device and discursive construct, not as an objective reality on the ground and "out there". Rather than grapple with the various configurations of counties and parts of counties that have gone to make up versions of the English "north-west", I shall be treating the (pre-1974) county of Lancashire as if it were a region. Charles Nevin's recent book on aspects of contemporary Lancashire identity contains a useful map showing how the county has been dismembered and realigned over the last thirty years or so; and here as elsewhere, in what presents itself as a whimsical piece of journalism based on an admittedly preposterous premise, a valid point is made almost by stealth.[7] Here as elsewhere, it was the more extensive pre-1974 county, whose territory included Liverpool and Manchester and extended across Morecambe Bay into the southern Lake District, that was the focus of lasting attachment, especially against rival "others"; and this chapter deals with the last two centuries of its existence, when the Industrial Revolution and the Lancashire seaside resort coincided in a symbiotic relationship that has persisted beyond the demise of what had become the "traditional" manufacturing economy itself.

This chapter brings those experiences together, and in so doing challenges assumptions about the peripheral (and, therefore, "beyond the mainstream") nature of the seaside resort itself. The focus of the argument is on the British experience of seaside resorts with largely regional and national catchment areas, in what might still be called "the age of the railway" which lasted up to the 1950s in Britain, before or alongside the issues that were to be raised by the advent of (for example) the seaside university or the language school; and the argument homes in especially on northern England and, within that, on Lancashire and its coastline. At the outset, however, we must emphasize the diversity within the "first industrial county", where the cotton industry was only the most conspicuous identifying marker and was itself divided and sub-divided between spinning and weaving and a diversity of local specialities; where Manchester was more regional capital than industrial town; where coal and chemicals dominated much of the south-west of the county; where contrasts between the small pastoral farms of the Pennine uplands and the broad arable acres of the great estates of the coastal plains remained important; and where Liverpool was genuinely exceptional, an international gateway city and cultural melting-pot in its own right, to a much greater extent than any of the county's seaside resorts, from the slave trade to the "Cunard Yanks" and, of course, beyond.[8]

Here are some questions that we might consider as we approach the theme of seaside resorts and regional identities in this context, and with special reference to the experience of Lancashire. What do resorts look like in regional terms? Do they express regional architectural styles, for example? Is their scenery "typical" of the region? Where do resorts draw upon for their visitors? How "regional" is their catchment area? Where do their migrants come from, whether as business people, commuters or retired people? What myths of resort development are propagated in their propaganda? To what extent do they actually lay claim to representing or expressing regional identity? How "regional" are their entertainment menus and accommodation offerings? Do they pull regions together, or emphasize divisions within them, or dilute regional identity by bringing people into temporary but telling contact with other customs, attitudes, and ways of life? Are these really binary oppositions, or should we view their likely resolutions as points on a spectrum or continuum?

Further questions follow from recognition of the fault-lines and complexities that cut across imagined regional identities. Do resorts express class (and other) identities, and conflicts, within regions? Class remains important as a theme, and certainly for the period under review, which was in no sense post-industrial. This point is reinforced by the way in which leisure and tourism became industries with their own workforces, and leisure preferences followed class lines while sometimes crossing them. Gender is a particularly important theme here, too, especially when we consider the distinctive employment history of the cotton industry, and especially the unusual earning power of women, whether as individuals or as contributors to family incomes, in the weaving industry, and the scope for independence and assertiveness that popular culture ascribed to women from this background. The complex, shifting, inescapable category of "respectability" haunts this territory, taking different dominant forms for different social strata and for men and women, but also taking on identities of its own that offered vertical linkages across the class and gender divides, as value systems coalesced around churches, chapels and secular voluntary organizations or leisure and sporting cultures in ways that brought the classes and the sexes together in partial or contextual dissolution of differences that might persist in other settings. In this context religious cultures within Christianity were particularly important as potential fault-lines, especially those between Catholic and Protestant, and (even more so for present purposes) between easy-going nominal Anglicanism and earnest Nonconformity, whether in middle-class puritan guises or in those where a more proletarian Nonconformity met up with the socialism that traced its cultural roots to Ruskin, Morris and even Carpenter, although increasingly from the early twentieth century many such people preferred to avoid the commercialised seaside altogether. The rise of the Co-operative Holidays Association, Holiday Fellowship, Clarion Cycling Clubs, and less formally organised rambling groups (especially those that went out from Manchester into the Derbyshire Peak District), expressed a conscious rejection of the generic Blackpool holiday with its rush to spend time and money on artificial attractions, sensual excitement and intensive industrial entertainment.[9] Ethnicity is a further issue, though of limited salience in this setting before the 1950s. We should note the conspicuous Jewish presence in the larger Lancashire resorts by the early twentieth century, which was highlighted by popular novelists; but we should also acknowledge the (enduringly) limited extent and impact of ethnic diversity among the Lancashire coastal resorts, even as regards the Irish, despite the eventual export of the Liverpool processional cultures of St Patrick's Day and 12 July to Southport.[10]

Without seeking to follow the extensive agenda outlined above in a slavish, mechanical or exhaustive way, we now develop these themes with reference to the

Lancashire coast and especially its two biggest resorts, Blackpool and Southport. We also draw attention to the anomaly that is Morecambe, and muse over whether the Isle of Man and other resorts beyond the county can be regarded as part of an extended "Lancashire" for these purposes.

Lancashire was early in developing a resort system. It was a little behind the metropolitan coastlines of Sussex and Kent, and it was mainly a product of the railway age, from the 1840s and 1850s onwards; but its origins lay in the eighteenth-century stirrings at Blackpool and Southport, and by the late nineteenth century, as some of its resorts began to cater for working-class visitors on an impressive and pioneering scale, its coastline provided something for all social groups and preferences except seekers after international high society or picturesque solitude. By 1911 its seven main seaside resorts, with varying degrees of specialization (Blackpool, Southport, Lytham St Anne's, Morecambe, Thornton-Cleveleys, Fleetwood and Grange-over-Sands) had accumulated a combined resident population of 184,525, as enumerated at an early spring census. By 1951 this already impressive figure had nearly doubled, to 344,580.[11] Seaside resort Lancashire, imagined as a combined urban entity stretching along the littoral, would have added up to the third largest city in this very heavily urbanised county, behind Manchester and Liverpool. This may be seen as special pleading; but the fluid, volatile nature of resort populations also means that far more Lancastrians would have experienced seaside living as a life-cycle stage, as temporary migrants for the summer season, as holidaymakers (Blackpool laid claim to seven million visitors per annum in the 1930s), or as any or all of these at different times.[12] The Lancashire seaside also attracted very large numbers of migrants and visitors from beyond the county boundary, of course, but there is no doubt that it came to be fully integrated into popular notions of Lancashire identity, not least through media like the music-hall song, dialect and other popular literature, the monologue and, by the inter-war years, radio and regional cinema. By the late nineteenth century there was already widespread awareness of the status gradations between and within resorts; and such awareness extended beyond the county boundary, to other resorts (especially New Brighton, on the Cheshire side of the River Mersey, Douglas on the Isle of Man, and a string of destinations along the North Wales coast) that were busy each summer with Lancashire visitors and contributed to an extended version of the county's extra-territorial spheres of influence and expressions of holiday identity.

Blackpool and Southport dominated this picture. Southport made the early running, primarily as a resort for middle-class Manchester and Liverpool, but Blackpool overtook it in terms of popularity in the 1870s (it could already claim around three million visitors per annum in the early 1890s) and in the early twentieth century as regards resident population: Southport, including recently-annexed Birkdale, still held the lead in 1911 but failed to match the sustained dynamism maintained by an innovative and resourceful Blackpool during the inter-war years. Southport faltered in the development of its "popular" side beyond the smallpox epidemic of 1876 and the retreat of the sea from its extensive shoreline from the early 1880s, which coincided with a great acceleration in the growth of Blackpool's popularity: by the 1930s the latter's visitor numbers stood at three or four times the Southport figure, though the statistics are notoriously "soft". Southport's large landed estates, with their intrusive planning regimes, ensured that pubs would be few and far between and cheap housing hard to find, while providing a favourable environment for respectable Nonconformist commuters and comfortably-off retired people, with an ostentatious scattering of opulent Victorian and Edwardian churches and chapels.[13] Blackpool, on the other hand, was "open", secular and receptive to pleasure seekers of all classes.[14] By 1951 its official population, standing at 147,184, had increased more than tenfold over seventy years, while that of Southport lagged behind at 84,039, and had multiplied itself less than fourfold over the same period.

But even these flagship resorts, which it would be so easy to identify with contrasting puritanical and hedonistic incarnations of a notional "Lancashire character", were never monolithic. Blackpool's North and South Shore were always dominated by middle-class respectability, despite the compromising presence of the Pleasure Beach at the southern end of the promenade from the turn of the nineteenth and twentieth century, while Southport had its own fairground in the form of "Pleasureland", and kept a working-class presence in its visiting public. Further to the north, Morecambe, which was less of a "Lancashire" resort as such because of its heavy dependence on Leeds, Bradford and other West Yorkshire textile centres, concentrated on a narrower social stratum of skilled, supervisory and clerical workers, with the accent on an orthodox version of respectability, although this did not prevent a good deal of cheerful horseplay from permeating the Mitchell and Kenyon films of holiday crowds at this resort in Edwardian times.[15] Morecambe was particularly popular during the inter-war years, overtaking Lytham St Anne's in population terms as it became one of the most dynamic of British resorts; and the other Lancashire seaside resorts fitted into the pattern as respectable venues for middle-class family holidays, with a growing admixture of commuting (especially at Lytham) and retirement (especially at Grange-over-Sands). Apart from Grange, an isolated outpost on Morecambe Bay which like Morecambe itself drew as much on industrial Yorkshire as on Lancashire, the smaller resorts of the Fylde coast remained within Blackpool's orbit in the sense that people could base themselves there while taking what they wanted of the fleshpots and excitements of Blackpool when it suited them, just as Blackpool visitors in search of a quiet day in a less commercial leisure environment could take the tram to one of its doubly suburban satellites and enjoy a rest from the commercial whirl of the larger resort centre.[16]

The key point is that the Lancashire coast, like those of (especially) North Wales, Kent, Sussex, Essex and the Clyde estuary, developed a genuine resort *system* between the 1850s and the 1950s: one that catered, somewhere, for all the seaside holiday demands of its catchment area, from the upper middle classes (though not, in Lancashire's case, the gentry or aristocracy) to those lower-paid or otherwise disadvantaged elements in the working class who could only just afford an irregular day excursion. The mix changed over time as well as varying between destinations, seasonally and by day of the week; and the changes and variations involved geographical origins as well as social standing and cultural preference. The Lancashire coast was unique in the early rise of popular holidaymaking, as part of the rise of the first working-class consumer society in the 'cotton towns' of the late nineteenth century (professional football, music-hall, popular musical culture, fish and chips, the Co-op...), and in the dominance of 'cotton town culture' in its accents and entertainments, reinforced by the Wakes system whereby whole towns went on holiday in the same weeks, staggered through the summer, from the Bolton holidays at the end of June and Burnley fair in mid-July to Oldham wakes in early September.[17] But this was not the whole story, and the Lancashire coast was reaching out to draw in working-class holidaymakers from the West Riding and the West Midlands by the 1890s, and from across most of Britain by the inter-war years.[18] Blackpool predominated in this regard, while the surviving 'popular' side of Southport became more narrowly 'regional' in the composition of its crowds; but the other resort systems mentioned above, North Wales apart, were metropolitan rather than provincial in their main catchment areas (if we count Glasgow as a metropolis), and only the later-developing popular side of the Devon resorts could match Blackpool (in particular) for national reach, on a much smaller scale in terms of sheer numbers (even in the 1960s). By the early twentieth century (and even in the 1890s) the Lancashire cotton towns were already exporting some of their more prosperous and adventurous working-class citizens not only to North Wales but as far afield as Devon, as the accents of Rochdale and Oldham could be heard and remarked upon in Torquay and Ilfracombe, while in the 1920s and 1930s they could be found at Ostend and the nearby battlefields, and in 1934 William Holt tracked them across Belgium and France for Manchester's *Daily Dispatch*.[19]

By this time, however, each of Lancashire's own resorts had long developed strongly differentiated identities and "place-myths" of their own, within the overall shared idioms and conventions of the British seaside holiday, but with a distinct set of regional flavours.[20] Blackpool's was the strongest, but even as it emerged as "working-class regional" or "Lancashire at play" in the late nineteenth century it developed cross-currents and apparent contradictions *within* this core identity as well as between it and alternative versions of the town. Its visitors worked in coal mining (though this was a later developer in generating holiday demand), engineering, transport and many other industries and services as well as in cotton, though most working-class Lancastrians from the "cotton towns" would have "been through the mill" with all the associated disciplinary acculturation, and in the predominant "cotton district" most coal miners (for example) lived alongside the mill workers rather than in separate settlements with their own distinctive cultures, as was more often the case south and south-west of Wigan.[21] From the 1870s onwards, as real family incomes rose for most people in the "cotton towns" and investment in popular attractions and cheap accommodation grew in step, Blackpool became the world's first working-class seaside resort, although this was always a dominant rather than an exclusive identity, and the towns rulers were always trying to propel its image up-market. Its chief rival contender, New York's Coney Island, attracted greater numbers of poorer people by the early twentieth century, but these were overwhelmingly day, half-day and evening trippers to the beaches and amusement parks, and Coney Island lacked the stability, infrastructure and permanence that soon became hallmarks of the big Lancashire resort.[22] Late Victorian and Edwardian Blackpool was sometimes likened to an American city for its grid-pattern streets, its rapid growth and openness to down-market development, its air of enterprise, drive and "push", and its eager civic boosting; but these were as much Lancashire as American characteristics in the heyday of the cotton industry, and the predominant image was one of "Lancashire at play". This entailed, as Patrick Joyce argues, something more than just the proletariat: it was a broader slice of "the popular", as the Mitchell and Kenyon films strongly suggest, extending to embrace those of the lower and even the substantial middle classes who put pleasure and fun before the tighter interpretations of respectability, and characterised by the energy, vitality and good humour that accompanied temporary release from workaday constraints, a democratic lack of pretension, a characteristic openness and friendliness (but with a caustic tongue when deemed appropriate), and an openness to the rude and the ribald within the limits that unspoken consensus prescribed, and that were reinforced by the known presence of local authority figures and potentially censorious neighbours in a setting where whole towns went on holiday at once. Notions of liminality and the carnivalesque, the world temporarily turned upside down, thus have to be tempered in the Blackpool setting by awareness of the constraints provided by a regional popular culture which, from perhaps the 1880s up to the 1950s and beyond, never lost sight of the values of workaday respectability that kept the system going. Thus it was that holiday crowds observed factory hours at mealtimes, when the promenade would suddenly empty and the boarding houses and cheap restaurants would fill up with hungry customers.[23]

At the height of the holiday season Blackpool's bustling centre and teeming promenades had an air of the popular and boisterous, like the shoreline itself, with its accommodating sands, lively waves and, sometimes, boisterous breezes. Its red brick terraces, built piecemeal (but on a basic grid pattern) on relatively small estates to meet the imagined preferences of the lowest common denominator, looked like those of the "cotton towns" writ large, with a couple of extra storeys and, in the summer lodging house districts close to the old railway stations and the promenade, a great multiplication of hidden bedrooms at the back. The famous landladies who ran these establishments were themselves drawn largely from the "cotton towns", many being weavers who had saved enough to try out a small business in a familiar but desirable setting, and they also tended to be represented as larger than life in the jokes and stories of almanacs, dialect sketches and comic postcards. They made their own contribution to the stereotype of the strong and potentially fearsome Lancashire woman, which also made its presence felt in entertainments that transgressed gender boundaries, in sexual innuendo that (most people thought) rarely found physical expression and was almost an escape from it, and in jokes about suffragettes that had a special Lancashire dimension in the Manchester origins of the Pankhursts and in the radical working-class suffrage campaigners of the Edwardian cotton towns. The "homeliness" that was their stock in trade extended its embrace to the temporary extended family of guests that renewed itself week by week during the summer season. The virtuous landlady in Arthur Laycock's morality tale of the Blackpool seaside occupied "Homely House".[24] Blackpool looked like a Lancashire mill town without the chimneys or the clogs, and by the late nineteenth century it reconstituted, serially, substantial samples of the populations of each of them week by week through the summer, in their best clothes but not necessarily on their best behaviour, sampling energetically from a range of entertainments and food outlets that were not unfamiliar in style and content, but more diverse and, at the top end, on a much grander scale than at home. But Blackpool also looked like a Potteries town without the kilns, or a Black Country town without the mines and smoky workshops, and it attracted visitors from across the industrial Midlands and from Yorkshire as well as from its own county, some of whose towns were built in stone rather than brick. Moreover, it was not until the inter-war years that Liverpool and the chemical works and coal mines of south-west Lancashire began to send significant contingents. Blackpool was both more and less than working-class Lancashire at play (and at work, for the same applied to the recruitment of those who serviced the holidaymakers). Indeed, an enduring middle-class presence, coupled with the absence of the poorest strata of the cotton towns as visitors (and even the better-paid families while the children were young and dependant), meant that it catered for both more and less than the working class itself.

Blackpool's achievement was to express and put on display a set of characteristics that many of those who wrote about the county claimed to be salient and distinguishing. Lancastrians proverbially both worked hard and played hard; they were prepared to accumulate through the year to enjoy their hard-earned savings to the full when the time came, over and above any opportunities that might come their way at an ordinary week-end, whether at the pub or the music-hall, the cinema when that appeared, the football match or the street bookmaker; and the womenfolk were represented as strong and assertive, powerful in and out of the home, strident, independent and taking no prisoners.[25] Commentators from outside the culture were impressed and appalled by turns at the high-pressure way of life that Blackpool magnified and intensified, as a place for letting off steam, releasing accumulated tensions (and, some thought, acting as prophlyactic against revolution), and proudly spending a year's holiday savings in a hectic week (at least, so the enduring legend ran). This was a resort primarily for adults–it was beyond the means of working-class families with young children, as the visual evidence confirms – until the 1950s, and the lack of family responsibilities (and escape from the necessary internalised disciplines of the workplace) perhaps helped to promote an atmosphere of childish horseplay. Front stage and back stage, in Goffmann's terms, were more integrated than in most resort settings, and behaviour that would have been frowned upon (and might have led to arrest) in the close-knit small towns of the cotton industry was accepted here as part of the holiday spirit.[26]

But Blackpool was also a disciplined place, and could be seen as a site for the civilization of the working-class holiday crowd, although it responded to the attitudes and expectations that people brought with them as well as moulding them on its own account. Early working-class invasions using the new trains in the late 1840s and early 1850s generated moral panics about assertive behaviour, noise, nudity on the beach, and the ill-treatment of donkeys, and provided an important impetus to establishing formal local government institutions. But here Blackpool was at one with its Lancashire hinterland, as more general unease about working-class behaviour in public places also prompted new initiatives in policing and the provision of "counter-attractions" in places like Bolton.[27] The much faster-flowing tide of working-class visitors from the 1870s, on a larger scale, provoked further critical comment about inappropriate attire (mufflers, clogs, shawls) and behaviour (smoking clay pipes, spitting, shouting, horseplay, litter and again the inevitable cruelty to donkeys). Within a decade, however, the focus was shifting from criticism to praise, for the orderly and acceptable presentation of the collective working-class self as it now appeared even to potentially censorious Nonconformist observers. This transition was associated with the rising living standards that enabled working-class Lancastrians to buy "best clothes" for holiday wear, as is evident in the Mitchell and Kenyon films of the early twentieth century, not least by contrast with representations of the workaday streets of Rochdale or Oldham. The sense of occasion (and need to look after expensive purchases) that accompanied the wearing of such garb might well have led in itself to the modification of public behaviour, but contemporaries offered plenty of alternative or additional explanations for the perceived transition, from the self-discipline inculcated by compulsory schooling to the tighter disciplinary codes of workplaces in which trade unionism itself set great store by respectable demeanour. Here, and enduringly (until the post-war generation), Blackpool reflected, articulated and influenced the changing expectations about the presentation of self, approximating to a version of the "civilising process" of Norbert Elias, that marked the behaviour of (to use another value-laden phrase) the mature industrial working class. This was not a purely Lancashire phenomenon, but just as rising living standards and disciplined saving for unpaid seaside holidays were first in evidence here, so Blackpool might be thought to distil and embody in concentrated form a set of recognisably Lancashire (or at least "cotton Lancashire") social characteristics.[28]

So Blackpool came to epitomise both the hedonistic and the respectable elements of working-class industrial Lancashire. Its rulers, whose approach to the provision of municipal services and amenities was in tune with the active, interventionist civic traditions of the Victorian industrial towns of Lancashire (but also of, for example, Birmingham and Leeds), took pride in its orderliness, while winking at amiable infractions that would not have been tolerated elsewhere; and they tacitly went along with its growing reputation as a "seaside sex capital", while professing alarm when any specific investigations were undertaken, as with Mass-Observation's prurient but rather bathetic findings in the late 1930s.[29] The rules of everyday conduct were relaxed and bent rather than being subverted or broken; and the journalist Graham Turner, writing as late as the 1960s, argued that Blackpool was at bottom a puritanical place, with the prevailing atmosphere of innuendo a smokescreen for a normative culture of repression and self-control.[30] Despite cross-currents and eccentricities, its dominant ethos in this period was heterosexual and heterosocial, as the popularity of decorous dancing underlined. The Tower Ballroom was a social melting pot, where mill-owners' sons might forge acquaintanceship with working-class young women; but this did not mean that promiscuity was rampant, under the gaze of landladies, workmates and neighbours; and in Stanley Houghton's scandalous play *Hindle Wakes* (1912, and a popular basis for inter-war films) such a relationship had to be moved to Llandudno to be consummated. Marriages, usually hometown ones, were made in Blackpool.[31]

If we direct our gaze away from the seething popular crowds around the Tower and "Golden Mile", and look towards the urban periphery where new municipal investment was directed during the 1920s and 1930s (promenade extensions, Stanley Park, South Shore swimming baths. North Shore gardens...), we see a much more middle-class (though still open and permeable) version of Blackpool that approximates it more closely to the mainstream middle-class family experience of the British seaside in the railway age. Here, the Lancashire element was diluted: Anthony Burgess commented of the 1930s that, "A lot of Blackpool's residents had posh accents, as though they were carpetbaggers from the south". The other resorts of the Lancashire system were much closer to that norm, inflected as they were by local peculiarities as well as broader regional influences. In some ways the nearest approximation to Blackpool in its guise as Lancashire playground was probably the Isle of Man, and especially the capital Douglas. This Manx setting was doubly liminal by virtue of being on an island as well as by the sea, reached by boat from Liverpool or Fleetwood (but also from Glasgow). Its reputation was more bound up with dancing and the open air, with young couples and early holiday camps, as the poor in time and money were filtered out by the sea voyage. Here a (mainly) Lancastrian playground was grafted on to a strong local culture which was busily inventing and reinventing traditions in defence against the influx of commercial culture on the mainland, a kind of negotiated globalization in miniature, although there was no saving the living language.[32] But this was a much more artificial, external tourism imposition than was the case at Blackpool, which was itself in Lancashire and whose original agricultural population had been tiny. Here and in North Wales, where Rhyl and other resorts also had an incarnation as Lancashire resorts beyond the county and linguistic and other cultural issues, including Sabbatarianism, were very much alive, there were cultural tensions that were absent from a Blackpool whose population was already, by the 1870s, dominated by migrants from inland Lancashire.[33] Much closer to Lancashire in geographical terms was New Brighton, on the Cheshire side of the Mersey a ferry crossing away from Liverpool. Here was Liverpool's Coney Island, a day and half-day playground with a wider Lancashire hinterland for its boarding-houses until catastrophic decline set in during the 1960s, again in parallel with Coney. New Brighton had its own Tower, which was actually higher than Blackpool's and also built in the 1890s, but was unable to sustain it for more than a single generation, as the countervailing drive to Merseyside suburbanity won out against the trippers and longer-stay visitors. My grandfather, when a platelayer in north Derbyshire with access to privilege tickets on the London, Midland and Scottish Railway around 1930, used to take his family to New Brighton and Blackpool in alternate years; but this is a reminder that, here too, Blackpool was one among several options. And Liverpool was, of course, a very different version of Lancashire from the "cotton towns", with its own exceptional migration flows, economy and cultures. Scousers were not industrial Lancastrians: they never built up the holiday traditions of the textile district; and it showed.[34]

In a sense, Southport, with its Liverpool as well as cotton Lancashire commuter population and its easy image as the polar opposite to Blackpool, may have been closer to it as an emblem of regional identity than any of these extra-territorial rivals. Its dominant "social tone" and reputation were overwhelmingly middle-class, and, whether Nonconformist or Church of England, it took its religion seriously in ways that Blackpool could not claim to match. Where Blackpool had magnificent pleasure palaces and an abundance of pubs, it had imposing (and expensively endowed) churches and chapels. It was increasingly a residential suburb and place of genteel retirement for Lancashire industrialists, perhaps more so than Liverpool merchants, who were often tempted southwards and westwards. It did anticipate Blackpool's inter-war move towards up-market municipal investment by two generations and more, with its Victorian parks and marine lakes. It was planned from almost its earliest beginnings, by two contrasting landowning families who achieved similar results by different routes. Blackpool, by contrast, was a testament to the limitations of the free market, and could never have laid claim to Southport's preferred label of "seaside garden city". Southport's publicity had always put health and improvement ahead of pleasure and entertainment. On this basis, Southport could claim to represent an alternative Lancashire, that of the sober, serious, frock-coated, Nonconformist, prosperous entrepreneur and businessman (and this was a much more "masculine" society in its dominant representation than that of Blackpool), who enjoyed his profits here while his employees spent their annual savings so liberally at Blackpool, although his family were also perfectly capable of shopping in their own expensive style on elegant Lord Street. But, and predictably, this contrast (or complementarity) is too simple.[35]

On the one hand Blackpool, in its official publicity material, also routinely prioritised health and outdoor exercise, the promenade ahead of the pleasure palace, eagerly laying claim to its own version of Southport's regional middle-class mantle, and promoting it assiduously, as we have seen, on its planned urban fringes; while Southport had its own, more family-oriented fairground to set alongside Blackpool's Pleasure Beach, in the form of Pleasureland, which became part of the municipality's leisure portfolio alongside more obviously up-market offerings. Southport also had its working-class trippers, though they were drawn more from Wigan, Bolton and Manchester than from the weaving towns that formed the traditional core of Blackpool's constituency. Moreover, it had its own enclave of boarding houses for the working-class holiday market, tucked away between the shopping Mecca of Lord Street and the municipal Marine Lakes; and it had its working-class suburbs, on the "wrong side of the tracks" or tucked away at a discreet distance, to house necessary but unsavoury services and those who operated them.[36] None of these cross-currents invalidates the overarching idea that Blackpool and Southport represented contrasting sides of a distinctive "Lancashire character", the free-spending frivolous popular and the serious religious entrepreneurial; but they draw attention to the overlaps between the resort experiences, which underline that the tempting stereotypes are not the whole story.

It was Blackpool, however, that really became identified as the resort *par excellence* of the Lancashire working class at play: a popular regional identity that was much more persuasive, if not convincing, than the middle-class version. This was enduringly more convincing than the alternative representations of Blackpool as a more broadly Northern resort, an energetic opposite pole to the languor of the metropolitan South, or as representing a national working-class or popular leisure identity from, say, the 1930s onwards.[37] In both ostensible guises it had too many rivals to hold the field convincingly, for its towering lead in visitor numbers owed a great deal to the sheer quantity and spending power of its core visiting public, the four and a half million Lancastrians on its doorstep who came to form a loyal market of multiple repeat visitors. It was never the resort for the whole of Lancashire, and nor was it ever exclusively a Lancashire resort. As Burgess put it, "The town was for Lancashire, but it constituted a sort of extraterritorial enclave." But it was, for example, where Frank Randle, whose humour did not travel beyond the county, was always most at home, and the dominant accents on its streets were those of whichever Lancashire towns held their Wakes in that particular week.[38] From these and other perspectives, Blackpool was Lancashire at play; and as such it distilled the essence of something that deserves to be represented as Lancashire identity, however we might wish to qualify and complicate that initial, but revealing, bold statement. What was to happen after the 1950s to complicate matters further is, of course, another story.

---

[1] R. Shields, *Places on the Margin* (London: Routledge, 1991); and on related issues see now D. Webb, "Bakhtin at the Seaside: Utopia, Modernity and the Carnivalesque", *Theory, Culture and Society* 22 (2005) 121-38.

[2] P. Borsay, *The English Urban Renaissance* (Oxford: Clarendon, 1988); P. Borsay, *Bath 1700-2000* (Oxford: Oxford University Press, 2000); L. Nead, *Victorian Babylon* (New Haven: Yale University Press, 2000).

[3] J.K. Walton, "Policing the Alameda", in S. Gunn and R.J. Morris (eds.), *Identities in Space* (Aldershot: Ashgate, 2001) 228-41.

[4] J.D. Marshall and J.K. Walton, *The Lake Counties from 1830 to the Mid-Twentieth Century* (Manchester: Manchester University Press, 1981), Introduction.

[5] J.K. Walton, "Tourism and Politics in Elite Beach Resorts: San Sebastián and Ostend, 1830-1939", in L. Tissot (ed.), *Construction of a Tourist Industry in the Nineteenth and Twentieth Centuries* (Neuchatel, Switzerland: Alphil, 2003) 287-301; P. Curby, *Seven Miles from Sydney: a History of Manly* (Manly: Manly Council, 2001) Chapter 12.

[6] J.K. Walton, "Blackpool and the Varieties of Britishness", in S.A. Caunce *et al.* (eds.), *Relocating Britishness* (Manchester: Manchester University Press, 2004).

[6] D. Russell, *Looking North: the North in the National Imagination* (Manchester: Manchester University Press, 2004).

[7] C. Nevin, *Lancashire, Where Women Die of Love* (Edinburgh: Mainstream, 2004) facing 160.

[8] J.K. Walton, *Lancashire: a Social History 1558-1939* (Manchester: Manchester University Press, 1987); J. Belchem, *Merseypride: Essays in Liverpool Exceptionalism* (Liverpool: Liverpool University Press, 2001).

[9] H. Taylor, *A Claim on the Countryside* (Edinburgh: Keele University Press, 1996).

[10] D.L. Murray, *Leading Lady* (London: Hodder and Stoughton, 1947).

[11] G. Shaw and A. Williams (eds.), *The Rise and Fall of British Coastal Resorts* (London: Mansell, 1997) 27-9.

[12] J.K. Walton, "Seaside Resorts and Maritime History", *International Journal of Maritime History* 9 (1997) 125-47.

[13] J. Liddle, "Estate management and land reform politics", in D. Cannadine (ed.), *Patricians, Power and Politics* (Leicester: Leicester University Press, 1982).

[14] J.K. Walton, *Blackpool* (Edinburgh: Edinburgh University Press, 1998).

[15] R. Bingham, *Lost Resort? The Flow and Ebb of Morecambe* (Carnforth: Cicerone, 1991); J.K. Walton, "The Seaside and the Holiday Crowd", in V. Toulmin *et al.* (eds.), *The Lost World of Mitchell and Kenyon* (London: *bfi* Publishing, 2004) 158-68.

[16] J.K. Walton, *Wonderlands by the Waves* (Preston: Lancashire County Books, 1992).

[17] J.K. Walton, *Lancashire: a Social History 1558-1939* (Manchester: Manchester University Press, 1987) Chapter 13.

[18] J.K. Walton, "The Demand for Working-Class Seaside Holidays in Victorian England", *Economic History Review* 34 (1981) 249-65; G. Cross (ed.), *Worktowners at Blackpool* (London: Routledge, 1990).

[19] D. Nield Chew, *The Life and Writings of Ada Nield Chew* (London: Virago, 1982); *Daily Dispatch*, 3-12 August 1934.

[20] J. Urry, *The Tourist Gaze* (London: Sage, 1990).

[21] T. Griffiths, *The Lancashire Working Classes, c. 1880-1930* (Oxford: Oxford University Press, 2001).

[22] J.K. Walton, "Popular playgrounds: Blackpool and Coney Island, *c.* 1880-1970", *Manchester Region History Review* 17 (2004) 51-61; idem., "The transatlantic seaside: Blackpool and Coney Island", in N. Campbell, J. Davies and G. McKay (eds.), *Issues in Americanisation and Culture* (Edinburgh University Press, 2004) 111-25.

[23] P. Joyce, *Visions of the People* (Cambridge: Cambridge University Press, 1991) 165-71; Walton, "The Seaside and the Holiday Crowd"; Cross, *Worktowners*; G. Cross and J.K. Walton, *The Playful Crowd: Pleasure Places in the Twentieth Century* (New York: Columbia University Press, 2005) Chapters 1-4.

[24] J.K. Walton, *The Blackpool Landlady: a Social History* (Manchester: Manchester University Press, 1978) especially Chapters 1, 3-6; J. Liddington and J. Norris, *One Hand Tied Behind Us* (London: Virago, 1977); Rose Collis, *Colonel Barker's Monstrous Regiment* (London: Virago, 2001); Anthony Burgess, *Little Wilson and Big God* (London: Penguin, 1988) 130.

[25] Nevin, *Lancashire*, is good on the stereotypes as they have endured.

[26] Cross and Walton, *Playful Crowd*, Chapter 3; J.K. Walton *et al.*, "Crime, Migration and Social Change: England and the Basque Country, *c.* 1870-1930", *British Journal of Criminology* 39 (1999) 90-112.

[27] J.K. Walton, "The Social Development of Blackpool, 1788-1914", Ph.D. thesis, Lancaster University, 1974, pp. 382-7; P. Bailey, *Leisure and Class in Victorian England* (London: Routledge, 1978).

[28] Walton, "Demand for Working-Class Seaside Holidays"; Walton, "The Seaside and the Holiday Crowd"; Joyce, *Visions of the People*; H.J. Perkin, *The Structured Crowd* (London: Routledge, 1981); J. Golby and W. Purdue, *The Civilisation of the Crowd* (London: Batsford, 1984).

[29] Cross, *Worktowners*; Burgess, *Little Wilson and Big God*, 127-8.

[30] G. Turner, *The North Country* (London: Eyre and Spottiswoode, 1967) 134-5.

[31] L. Jolly, "Blackpool: Seaside Sex Capital?", B.A. dissertation, University of Central Lancashire, 1999.

[32] Burgess, *Little Wilson and Big God*, 129; J. Belchem, "'The Playground of Northern England": the Isle of Man, Manxness and the Northern Working Class", in N. Kirk (ed.), *Northern Identities* (Aldershot: Scolar Press, 2000) 71-86.

[33] G. Parry, "'Queen of the Welsh Resorts": Tourism and the Welsh Language in Llandudno in the Nineteenth Century", *Welsh History Review* 21 (2002) 118-48.

[34] M. Hope, *Castles in the Sand* (Ormskirk: Hesketh, 1982); Belchem, *Merseypride*.

[35] Liddle, "Estate management".

[36] S. Copnall, *Pleasureland Memories: a History of Southport's Amusement Park* (London: Skelter Publishing, 2005); H. Foster, *Crossens: Southport's Cinderella Suburb* (Birkdale: Birkdale and Ainsdale Historical Research Society, 2002).

[37] J.B. Priestley, *English Journey* (London: Heinemann, 1934) 266-7; T. Bennett, "Hegemony, Ideology, Pleasure: Blackpool". In T. Bennett *et al.* (eds.), *Popular Culture and Social Relations* (Milton Keynes: Open University Press, 1984).

[38] Burgess, *Little Wilson and Big God*, p. 129; Jeff Nuttall, *King Twist* (London: Routledge and Kegan Paul, 1978).

"'MY NATIVE TWANG': IDENTITIES AND THE WEST RIDING NINETEENTH-CENTURY DIALECT LITERATURE OF JOHN HARTLEY AND 'THE SHEVVILD CHAP'"*

ANDREW WALKER

"'My Native Twang'
Fowk tell me aw'm a vulgar chap
An owt to go to th' school
To leearn to tawk like other fowk
An neet be such a fooil;
But aw've a noashun do you see
Although it may be wrang
The sweetest music is to me
My own, my native twang

An when aw'm away throo all my friends
I'other tooans aw rooam
Aw find ther's nowt can make amends
For what aw've left at hooam;
But as aw hurry throo ther streets
No matter tho aw'me thrang
Ha welcom if my ear but greets
My own, my native twang."[1]

This extract from the Yorkshire dialect writer, John Hartley's work "My Native Twang", suggests the centrality of dialect in individuals' own self-construction of identity. Over 50 years later, another dialect writer, Allen Clarke, from west of the Pennines, in his poem "In Praise o' Lancashire", declared that the "good owd dialect, warms eaur hearts [and] sawders us together". Clarke announced in his work that "Lancashire folk an their dialect/ Are as fayther an as son".[2]

During much of the nineteenth century a flourishing literature celebrated local dialect, its speakers and the district in which it was spoken. Dialect literature prospered most conspicuously in the manufacturing districts of northern England.

The popularity of dialect literature in the counties of Lancashire and Yorkshire, especially the West Riding, needs some consideration. Evidently dialect was not confined to the industrial north of England. However, a market for such material was present in this part of the country which perhaps was less readily so elsewhere. As the nineteenth century advanced, a commercial market for dialect literature was produced in Lancashire and Yorkshire as a consequence of the presence of a literate population with substantial spending power. The growth of these manufacturing districts was largely effected by migration: in 1851 less than half of the population of Manchester had been born in the town[3], and, in Sheffield, 49 per cent of the population over twenty years of age had been born outside the borough boundaries.[4] At first sight, therefore, it might seem that such circumstances were unpromising ones in which dialect literature would flourish. However, much of this migration took place over short distances and allegiances to specific localities were often cemented by residential clustering of migrants.[5] Indeed, according to the 1861 census findings, Lancashire and Yorkshire were the English counties which retained the largest proportion of their indigenous populations, with 90.96 per cent and 88.03 per cent of their natives respectively living within their county of origin.[6] According to Patrick Joyce, the combination of a relatively tight community structure and radical social and economic change proved particularly fertile ground in which dialect literature flourished.[7]

Over the past thirty years or so, a significant amount of historical scholarship has examined the work of Lancashire dialect writers. Brian Hollingworth's anthology, *Songs of the People: Lancashire Dialect Literature of the Industrial Revolution*, published in 1977, drew attention to this rich vein of writing. Other historians who have focused upon Lancashire dialect writing have included Martha Vicinus, in her work, *The Industrial Muse*, and Patrick Joyce, who dedicates a significant amount of his book, *Visions of the People*, to nineteenth-century dialect writing. According to Joyce, the pan-class appeal of such works and the constant references within the texts to "people" and "folk", which were contained even within the work of avowed socialist dialect writers such as Allen Clarke, can be viewed as evidence that class as an analytical tool has limited application in industrial Britain.[8]

In much of the historical scholarship in nineteenth-century dialect literature, the principal focus has been directed at Lancashire writers, such as Rochdale-born Edwin Waugh (1819-1890), whose dialect poetry according to Martha Vicinus, "reminds his predominantly city audience of a happier past" and which sought to give his readers "a lift on the way".[9] Another prominent Lancashire dialect writer was Ben Brierley, (1825-1896) who produced dialect prose and became famous for his comic sketches of working-class urban life, most notably involving his fictional character, "Ab' o' th' Yate", who lived near the centre of Manchester.[10]

However, besides such Lancashire exponents of dialect literature, there also existed a number of significant dialect writers in the West Riding of Yorkshire who have, broadly speaking, received rather less attention by historians (though they have been appropriately commemorated by the Yorkshire Dialect Society).

Yorkshire dialect writers such as Tom Treddlehoyle, who from 1838 to 1875 wrote the *Barnsla Foaks Annual*, and Bradford-born Ben Preston (1819-1902), who produced mainly work about the plight of the poor, enjoyed a wide audience.[11] However, perhaps the most successful of the Yorkshire dialect writers was John Hartley, whose annual publication, *The Original Illuminated Clock Almanack*, first published in 1867, was still reputedly selling 75,000 copies annually in 1931.[12] In the preface to *The Clock Almanack* in 1879, Hartley claimed that the first volume had sold 5000 copies and that "last year's sale bids fair to be 100,000."[13] A testimonial, which was signed by a wide range of Yorkshire worthies in 1907 in an unsuccessful attempt to award John Hartley a civil list pension, noted that since its first publication in 1867, *The Clock Almanack* had "given delight amusement and enjoyment to many millions of people throughout the whole world."[14]

Despite the obvious sales success of his work, John Hartley's career mirrored that of many other dialect writers. He made little money from his dialect writing alone. He supplemented his earnings in a variety of ways. Hartley was born in 1839 in Halifax, the son of a tea merchant and died in 1915 in relative poverty.[15] He trained as a pattern designer in Halifax and became inspired to write dialect literature at the age of 23 when he read Edwin Waugh's "Come Whoam to thi Childer An' Me".

Waugh's poem, first published as a broadside in 1856 was a sentimental piece which championed the domestic and familial over the counter-attractions of the public house.[16] The work details a wife's successful attempts to entice her errant husband back into the home. The poem reached a wide audience: within days of its publication, 20,000 copies had been sold.[17] Its moral message led Mrs Burdett Coutts to buy between ten and twenty thousand copies of Waugh's work for distribution amongst the London poor.[18] The work also prompted a number of parodies, including the dialect writer, Ben Brierley's "Go Tak the Ragg'd Childer An' Flit".[19] The sentimentality and unimpeachable morality of "Come Whoam to thi Childer An' Me" informed the content of John Hartley's first published poem, "Bite Bigger", which described a scene suffused with pathos and selflessness, in which a half-starving ten-year old waif discovered a discarded apple in the snow and shared it with his younger brother:

> "'Here's an apple, an't moast on it's saand,
> What's rotten, I'll throw into t'street
> Wern't it gooid to lig theer to be faand?
> Naa boath on us can have a treat.'

So he wip'd it an rubb'd it, an then
Said 'Billy, thee bite off a bit:
If tha hasn't been luck thisen
Tha sal share un me such as I get.'

So t'little un bate off a touch
T'other's face beam'd in pleasure all through
An't he said 'Nay, tha hasn't taen mich
Bite agean, an bite bigger, naa do.'

I wanted to hear nowt no more;
Thinks I there's a lesson for me
Thaas a heart i' thy breast if th'art poor
T'would were richer no more sich as thee."[20]

As John Hartley became established as a dialect writer, he was appointed editor of *The Original Illuminated Clock Almanack* in 1867 by Charles Wilson, a member of a prominent family of Halifax hatters. The title of this dialect almanack was derived from the fact that the Wilsons' hat shop was located under an illuminated clock.[21] Hartley produced the almanack until his death, apart from several years when he sought his fortune unsuccessfully in North America working as a painter-decorator and theatre manager.[22]

Upon returning to Britain, Hartley supplemented his dialect writing, like many of his peers, with live performances of his work. Public readings by dialect writers were particularly prevalent in the mid-Victorian period and some of these readings took place outside the locality in which the particular dialect was spoken. Both Edwin Waugh and John Hartley, for instance, undertook readings in the United States. Edwin Waugh, the Rochdale-born dialect writer regularly gave readings in the West Riding of Yorkshire. Waugh performed in Bradford in 1863 and 1866. Following one of two readings in the West Riding town of Bingley, a proposer of a vote of thanks "said that the dialects of Lancashire and Yorkshire were sufficiently closely akin to enable us to claim Edwin Waugh as pretty much our own".[23] A prestigious double-reading took place at St George's Hall Bradford by both Waugh and Yorkshire-born dialect writer Ben Preston in 1867.[24]

For many, no doubt, the opportunity to see and hear writers interpret their own works helped to enhance later performances of these texts within the audience members' own homes. Clearly, dialect literature lent itself to being performed, and in this sense can be linked to the oral tradition which, although much-derided by many Victorian cultural commentators, still permeated much popular print culture in the second half of the nineteenth century.[25] In many of John Hartley's printed works, a significant number of references were made to his availability to recite his works. On several occasions, *The Clock Almanack* proclaimed that the forthcoming season of performances, usually from October to Easter, was to be the last. In announcing his season of "farewell public readings" in 1880, *The Clock Almanack* noted that:

"This is Mr Hartley's fifteenth annual tour and his success as a Reader is too well known to require advertising. Owing to the increase in his literary labours, he is reluctantly compelled to make this his farewell season as a public entertainer ... Mr Hartley takes this opportunity to return his sincere and grateful thanks to the many thousands who have ever received him with such cordial kindness and to assure them that the happy memories associated with them will never fade from his heart until death."[26]

Two years later, however, Hartley was again accepting invitations to perform and was employing a family member, Riley Hartley, as his Theatrical Agent.[27] He was still accepting "a limited number of engagements" in the 1908-09 season at the age of 70.[28]

"Opinions of the press" on John Hartley's readings, which were included in the 1871 *Clock Almanack* indicated that he had recently performed in London, Craven, Bradford, Keighley, Halifax, Bacup, Cleckheaton and Todmorden. Whilst invariably such press extracts were inclined to hyperbole, some indication of the nature of these performances can be obtained. According to the *London Review*:

> "Each of the pieces is the outcome of a real impulse, distinguished by a genuineness of feeling, not a particle of which seems to be simulated."

The *Halifax Guardian* declared that "Mr Hartley deserves to be remembered for he has given us something more than amusement, his poems having matter in them for reflection." The critic of the *Bradford Daily Telegraph* warned readers that John Hartley's performances "occasioned such intense merriment that the heartiness of the laughter became almost dangerous."[29]

A recurring feature of Hartley's work, as with that of other dialect writers such as Waugh and Brierley, was his affectionate representation of place and the people who lived there. These evocations invariably offered a good-humoured gentle ridiculing of the town and townspeople in question. This undoubtedly, especially at recitals, would have been well received, particularly by those from neighbouring communities. In 1892, for instance, in *The Clock Almanack*, Hartley wrote of a fictitious Huddersfield resident, Ben Baystay. He was:

> "a Huthersfield chap, an like all th' rest on em he fancies at he's
> wonderful clivver. He's steady an works hard ivvery day, an
> when he's had his drinkin he dons hissen up, leets his pipe-
> parades throo the principle [sic] streets (ther's nobbut one,
> an that's a principle at yields varry little interest) an thanks
> his stars that he war soa lucky as to be born i' th' cleanest,
> praadest an tames taan i' Yorksher."

Having built up Huddersfield inhabitants, Hartley then proceeded gently to knock them down:

> "It's true there's some varry daycent fowk exist thear
> (yo can hardly say they live, butt hey get along). They're
> a class o' honest fowk at believe i' aitin, workin an sleepin,
> mooastly sleepin, but they can be depended on to pay ther
> way."[30]

Similarly, Hartley sought to capture the nature of his home town, Halifax, two years later when he reported on the laying of the foundation stone of the town's new hospital. He wrote:

> "All hail! Old Halifax! Some fowk say at th' grand old taan is slow.
> Wel – maybe it isn't as fast as some but if it's slow it's sewer [sure].
> It may tak a long time to consider abaat things, but when it's once
> made up its mind what out to be done, it does it an it does it
> reight."[31]

Much dialect writing during the nineteenth century passed comment on the development of the townscape, particularly the substantial civic building projects which were undertaken and that, in the formal public rhetoric at least, sought to embody the spirit of the locality.[32] Dialect writers often took delight in advancing an alternative viewpoint of such construction work, and those who were responsible for undertaking it. In the 1868 *Clock Almanack*, for instance, Hartley poured scorn on recent civic building projects in the West Riding. In his "Rambling Remarks" for March 1868, he noted that:

> "The Bradford Exchange wor oppened this month, 1867, an' aw luk
> on it that wor a disappointment to some.' "Exchange is noa robbery"
> they say, but if some foak knew what it had cost, they might think
> that it had been a dear swap. Ther are fowk at call it "a grand success"
> -but then awve heard some call Th' Halifax Town Hall a "grand
> success", but they havent made me believe it."[33]

Warming to his theme, Hartley went on to make further critical remarks about Halifax Town Hall, which had been designed by Sir Charles and E.M. Barry, built between 1859 and 1862 and cost approximately £50,000.[34] Hartley commented on the motto over the door of the Halifax Town Hall, which read "Act wisely". He noted: "Its summat like tellin a chap to be honest at th' same time yo're pickin his pocket." In conclusion, he remarked,

> "a chap cannot help longin for th' time when brain an' not brass shall
> fit a man for Toan Caancillor. But fowk mun get consolation aght o'
> summat; soa they try to fancy th' Taan Hall lucks handsome."[35]

In many ways, this extract is characteristic of much mid-Victorian dialect writing. Those in authority are gently challenged and the "folk" are represented as long-suffering but largely uncomplaining. The stoicism of the people is indirectly celebrated and there is no sustained call for radical change.

Perhaps the principal attraction of dialect literature to its readership was the essential celebration of the quotidian contained within it. Hollingworth, in *Songs of the People*, wrote of dialect literature that "its subject matter was always 'homely' … [and] avoided the conventional and grander subjects of poetry to record the life of 'simple' and unregarded men."[36] Martha Vicinus, in *The Industrial Muse*, also noted that much dialect literature "was set in a pub or around a hearth."[37] In Lancashire examples of the genre, Brierley's Ab' showed contentment with his wife, affectionately calling her "me owd rib". Samuel Laycock and Sam Fitton respectively in "Bowton's Yard" and "Cotton Fowd", wrote about the ordinary people in their home streets.[38] Similar themes can be detected in the work of their Yorkshire peers. Two recurring characters in John Hartley's work are husband and long-suffering wife, Sammywell and Mally Grimes. This fictional couple lay at the heart of much of Hartley's writing–and feature prominently on the front cover of the annual almanack.

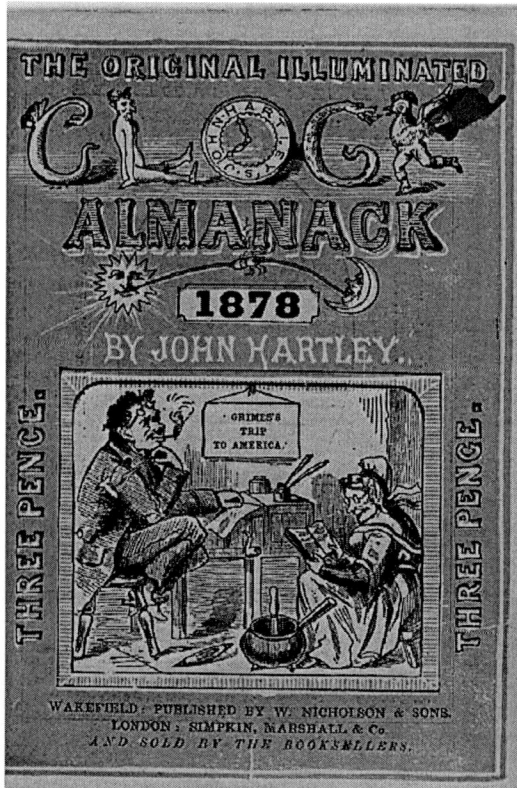

Here, Sammywell and Mally are pictured sitting together comfortably in a modest domestic environment, with Sammywell looking on contentedly, nursing his pipe, whilst Mally is immersed in a book. Beside the two of them on the floor are the tools of their trades, a shuttle next to Sammywell and a cooking pot at Mally's feet. Nailed to the wall, in the place of a homely motto, was displayed the title of one of Hartley's latest publications: in 1878, "Grimes's trip to America" was posted; in 1907, it was "Mally an me by John Hartley, price 2s". In all other respects, the illustration produced by Hartley remained unaltered over this twenty-nine year period. By apparently freezing these two aged characters in time, as the unchanging illustration suggests, this enabled Sammywell and Mally Grimes to comment with some bewilderment upon the transformations taking place around them.

Nostalgia permeates much of the dialect literature and has the effect of anchoring readers to their locality, reminding them of changed landscapes and altering customary ways. Inviting readers to share common memories arguably helped knit the readership and audience together. Such subject matter suggests that dialect literature's principal market was likely to be an older readership, though through performance in the home, the young became familiar too with dialect literature. Undoubtedly, such material helped enrich cross-generational relationships.[39] Brian Hollingworth has suggested that, in the second half of the nineteenth century, dialect literature "moved away from a living expression of the 'songs of the people' to an antiquarian and rather nostalgic attempt to conserve a dying culture and language."[40] Certainly, within the work of John Hartley, there is evidence of a wistful reminiscence of a colourful local customary culture under threat from homogenising cultural forces. In 1877, for example, in the "November–Ramblin' Remarks" section of *The Clock Almanack*, Hartley commented on the declining observation of local custom, particularly the consumption of local delicacies:

"This month isn't as mich thowt on nah as it wor when aw wor a
lad. Ther isn't as mitch traitle [treacle] parkin etten bi monny a
booat looad as ther wor then ... Th' moor police ther
is an th' fewer bunfires. Young fowk at this day have a deeal o'
things 'at we knew nowt abaht when we wor childer. We'd noa
short-timers, noa schooil boards, noa skatin' rinks, raand th'
bunfires at plot neet rooastin puttates, burnin' 'em to a cinder
o' one side an leeavin 'em raw o' tother, but they used to get
etten for all that ... They tell me it's an age o' progress, but
aw think it's an age o' growless as far as happiness is consarned.
Awm nowt ageean 'improving the intelligence of the rising
genrration' but aw think when they're stockin' ther heeads

soa full they shouldn't forget to fill ther bellies."[41]

Local customs and, by implication, local identity, it seems, therefore, according to
Hartley, were under attack in part from national schooling and over-zealous
policing.

A collection of stories by John Hartley involving the Grimeses, entitled "Mally
an me" was advertised as "A very choice selection of humorous and pathetic
incidents from the life of Sammywell Grimes and his wife, Mally."[42] Hartley's
verse, *Sammy an Mally*, published in the 1881 edition of *The Clock Almanack*,
paints a sympathetic portrait of this elderly couple, to which clearly readers were
expected to relate:

"*'Sammy an Mally'*
   ...Young fowk point ther fingers an' grin as they say,
   'Sich old fogies, we nivver did see'
   An it hurts me becoss aw remember the day
   When they lukt up to thee an to me

   Why Sammy, what ails thee aw cannot mak aght
   For awm sewer we're a reight gradely pair
   An th' young ens at laff are but fooils aw've noa doat
   Aw havn't much gumpshun to spare
   We've been laft at befoor yet we toddle along
   An aw think we booath thankful should be
   At altho we've grown old, we are hearty an strong
   An that is a blessin, sewerlee..."[43]

Various exploits arc recounted by which means Sammywell escapes his work
place. Many of these strategies involve his observation of the strange ways of
others on his various trips away from the bosom of his own family, in various tales
such as "Grimes's trip to America"; "Seets i' Lundun"; and "Seets i' Paris". A
widely advertised work, produced by John Hartley, chronicled Sammywell
Grimes's journey along the Leeds-Liverpool canal. In 1878, it was announced that
"Seets i' Yorkshire and Lancashire, or Grimes's Comical Trip from Leeds to
Liverpool in a Canal Boat" was on sale.[44] The travelogue was a common form of
dialect literature and was a means of extending the audience for the work. In the
case of "Seets i' Yorkshire and Lancashire", Sammywell's comical observations
were generally complimentary towards the places along the route, including those
in Lancashire, as the following extract illustrates:

   "We'd left Yorksher behind an' wor havin' th' first taste o' Lancasher.
   Peter sed Nelson had sprung up like a mushroom but that's hardly
   a fair illustration: for although mushrooms spring up varra sharply,

they're allus varry tender an barely oughtlast a day.

Nelson's noa longer a ramblin village on a hill top, but a big thrivin'
bustlin taan. Ther's a covered market at wodn't disgrace onny
Lancasher city, a theatre far handsomer aghtside nor what Leeds or
Bradford can booast. Mills at employ hundreds an' rows or
substantial dwellings, a peep into many on 'em enough to show
at ther inside comforts are well cared for ..."[45]

Such works, which in many ways demonstrated the similarities between the
Yorkshire and Lancashire manufacturing districts, it has been argued, could be
regarded as playing a contributory role in the knitting together of a broader
northern identity.[46]

Yorkshire admirers of dialect literature, as has been shown already, were keen
to embrace the output of Lancashire writers, both through reading the work and
also attending recitals. John Hartley regularly paid generous tribute to Lancashire
writers. This was particularly evident upon the deaths of both Edwin Waugh and
Ben Brierley, which were marked by verses written by Hartley and published in
The Clock Almanack. Hartley, in "Lines on the death of Edwin Waugh, the
Lancashire poet" wrote of Waugh , the "rural minstrel", whose work "shalt live
long in our memories" and "shall endure longer than mortal's breath."[47] On the
death of Ben Brierley, Hartley declared magnanimously that "All Yorkshire joins
with Lancashire to weep/ The sense of loss hangs heavy o'er our hearts". The lines
of "In Memoriam – Ben Brierley" continue:

"How many firesides did he deck with mirth?
How many tales he told to while the hours?
'Twas him who gave old 'Ab-oth-Yates' his birth
'Twas him who cheered the heart with 'Moorland Flowers'
A jovial soul he loved to sit and chat
With kindred spirits and he ne'er forsook
His native twang, which made his jokes come pat
He will be missed from many an inglenook"[48]

In celebrating the lives and work of his fellow dialect writers, it is perhaps
curious to discover Hartley writing largely in Standard English. In each case,
perhaps the gravity of the occasion was thought to necessitate the use of an
authoritative, humourless language. Nevertheless, as well as demonstrating the
close interlinkage of Lancashire and Yorkshire dialect literature, its exponents and
consumers, Hartley's valedictory poem in honour of Ben Brierley also offered a
clear insight into the idealised environment in which dialect writers thought their
work should be consumed, in the comfort of the reader's own home.

The quotidian was also favoured as a subject by another Yorkshire dialect
writer, Abel Bywater, (1795-1873), who produced dialect literature under the

pseudonym, "The Shevvild Chap". Like John Hartley, Bywater's writing did not form his sole means of income: Bywater was a Sheffield pharmacist, though his roots were modest. Many of the tales told by "The Shevvild Chap" sought to appeal to a popular audience. Bywater was perhaps best known for *The Shevvild Chap's Annual*, which was published between 1836 and 1856.[49] Some of his vignettes, such as *The Gossips Tea Drinking* were set in a working-class street and were based upon rituals familiar to his readers. Other stories produced by "The Shevvild Chap" were based in the workplace, usually "uppa are hull arston", at our hull hearthstone, in a grinder's workshop, where the conversation usually involved two workers, Jack Wheelswharf and Bil Heftpoip. These two characters were representatives of Sheffield's "little mesters", who were portrayed as being answerable only to their wives.

In both Lancashire and Yorkshire, work, particularly the staple industries of textile production and, in the case of Sheffield, cutlery and associated trades, was a recurring motif used to represent local community within the dialect literature. Whilst the workplace may not have been the setting for much Lancashire dialect writing, because of the noise of the cotton mills, where often gurning was the favoured means of communication, its centrality to people's lives was recognised in the names given to the key *dramatis personae*, such as "T'owd weyver"; "Owd Throstle"; and "Tim Bobbin". Similarly, principal characters' names employed by "The Shevvild Chap" were often drawn from trade words: Bil Heftpoip's surname for instance was a dialectal noun meaning a temporary wooden handle used by grinders to hold the tang of a knife during grinding, and Dame Flatback, another regular character in the output of "The Shevvild Chap" was named after a cheap, poorly-made knife.[50]

By concentrating upon the "homely" and the "familiar" aspects of the lives of their readers, and by making use of the often very particular vocabulary of the district's staple industries, the writers of dialect literature gave a legitimacy to, and some type of acknowledgement of, the way of life led by urban industrial workers and their families. However, just as local identity was celebrated through sympathetic portrayals of domestic life and workplace conviviality, so much dialect literature featured an opposing element to the integrative championing of community. Often contained within the dialect writing were references to outsiders whose "otherness" was invariably the subject of humour, often generated by misunderstanding. In an early edition of *The Clock Almanack*, an example of such confusion featured in a piece in which one young women, Betty told another, Nancy, about her new husband:

> "'Oh, aw've gotten wed to a forriner at comes throo Staffordsher.'
> '…An what does he do for a livin'?' 'Why, it's a rayther queer trade,
> but he stails pots.' 'Stails pots, Betty! A'a wonder how tha could

bring thisen doan to wed a chap o' that sooart ... noa chap gets his
livin honestly at stails ...' 'Why Nancy, aw thowt tha'd moor sense
aw did for sure – aw mean his trade is to put stails on to pots.'
'Oh! A'a! E'e! tha min forgi mi this time, Betty, aw see what tha
meeans, he puts hanels on to pots: that's it isn't it?' 'E'ea'."[51]

Where outsiders do appear, their linguistic differences and variations in
manners are highlighted. Where outsiders are of a superior standing in society to
the local characters, invariably the latter are shown holding their own – to the
delight of the readership. John Hartley, for instance, wrote of the visit of a school
inspector:

"Aw heard a bit sin abaat a school inspector up i' Scammonden,
who war hearin chidder ther geography. 'What are the names
of the principal English lakes?' he axed. 'Football laikin', nur and
spell laikin, pitch an toss, an prize feightin' sed a lad abaht eight
year owd."[52]

Elsewhere, awkwardness at social events forms the focus of humour. In the
1868 *Clock Almanack's* "January Ramblins", a worker tells of his experiences
attending a "posh do" in which he confused waiters for guests and other
misunderstandings occurred:

"'Shall I pass you a little soup?' said the maister. 'Noa thank yo''
aw said, 'aw washed me afoor aw coom.' 'Not soap my good friend,
I mean soup', he said. 'Oh! Broth is it, aw didn't know what yo ment.
Each aw'll tak a soop o' broth if yo' please ...'"[53]

The royal family featured regularly within the dialect literature, both in
Lancashire and Yorkshire. Though undoubtedly outsiders, however, invariably the
royal family members were granted the status of honorary insiders, suggesting both
an unlikely homeliness and accessibility on the part of the monarchy, and a
nobility and generosity of spirit on the side of the local community. The Lancashire
dialect writer Ben Brierley wrote of the visit of the young Prince of Wales to
fictitious Walmsley Fold, where attempts were made to feed-up the heir to the
throne. As one character noted, "If the Prince had bin browt up i' Walmsley Fowt
an had to feight for his buttercakes, he'd ha takken more cloth for his cloas nur he
does neaw ..."[54]

In John Hartley's work, a number of encounters are recorded between the
Queen and his colourful Halifax characters, the Grimeses, including "Grimes's visit
to th' Queen"; and "Sammywell at Sheffield to see the Queen".[55] Perhaps the most
striking interaction between Victoria and a fictional Yorkshire dialectal figure takes

place, though, in the work of "The Shevvild Chap". For many years, in *The Shevvild Chap*'s *Annual*, letters of advice were included which were produced by a fictitious elderly wise Sheffield woman, Dame Flatback. In the 1842 annual, for instance, Dame Flatback, following the birth of the queen's first daughter, gives "advice to't Queen for't present and future welfare o' lass". Dame Flatback explains to the Queen that "she should be thankfull at it worn't a lad."[56]

Following the birth of the Prince of Wales in 1842, Dame Flatback, again wrote to the Queen giving her detailed advice about breast feeding.[57] Indirectly, perhaps, such works can be read as defences of tried-and-tested customary, mutual support networks upon which communities relied and from which it was felt that the royal family was unfortunately detached.

In the evocation of neighbourhood contained within much of the dialect literature, women's voices appear to be prominently presented, though female dialect writers seem conspicuously absent. In the W. Halliday and A. S. Umpleby's *White Rose Garland: An anthology of Yorkshire dialect verse*, of 79 listed authors, only 14 were women.[58] Both Martha Vicinus and, more recently, Susan Zlotnick have identified the absence of female dialect writers.[59] According to Zlotnick, who draws heavily upon Edwin Waugh's work, the working-class world constructed in dialect literature was one in which women were restricted to the home. She argues that this representation of domesticity was one which dominated working-class culture despite the fact that much evidence suggests working-class women often continued to work outside the home after marriage. She asserts that "in the cotton districts of Lancashire, the centre of dialect activity, a long tradition of married women's work existed. But this is a truth one would never grasp from reading dialect poetry."[60] Zlotnick concludes that "in their single-minded devotion to the domestic ideal, dialect poets robbed working-class women of the realities of their lives as workers"[61]

Closer analysis of the output of the work of John Hartley suggests, though, that Zlotnick's view is somewhat unnuanced. Undoubtedly, there is evidence to suggest that Yorkshire dialect literature sought to represent the domesticated women as the ideal. However, there is significant evidence to suggest that dialect writers were aware of, and were prepared to represent, the disquiet that many working-class women clearly felt about this. In John Hartley's dialect verse "Women's Work", published in 1886, the monotony and hard physical labour associated with working-class housewifery in an industrial setting was made very apparent:

> *"'Women's Work'*
> Aw cannot tell why aw gate married
> Sed Mary one morning in May
> Aw reeally do wish at awd tarried
> A bit for aw've never noa play –
> It's toilin an tewin and workin

Thro Sundy to Satterdy neet
Aw'm not one at's given to shirkin
Mi wark if it's easy an leet ..."[62]

In 1888, in "A Wife's Tribbles", Hartley outlined a working-class woman's
reservations on marriage:

"It's all right for them 'ats long purses
To wed an have childer bi' the scooar –
But them 'at's to be their own nurses
Can happen stand two, but not mooar.
Aw wish aw'd mi time to coom ovver
Aw'd not be i' this hoil yo'd see –
They've to wed befooar lasses discover
Hah bad thear dear husbands can be."[63]

In contrast to the apparently passive, accommodating behaviour of the ill-
treated wife which Zlotnick refers to in Edwin Waugh's "Come Whoam to thi
Childer An' Me", alternative interpretations of women's attitude towards
housework and husbands can then be discerned in the dialect literature. Some fifty
years before Hartley's "Women's Work" and "A Wife's Tribbles" were published,
The Shevvild Chap's Annual of 1836 included a piece entitled "The Gossips Tea
Drinking", which highlights a rather more feisty spirit expressed by women than
that evoked in Waugh's work. One of the female characters in the piece by "The
Shevvild Chap" complains of monotonous domestic work: We're smothered up it
hail throo morning to neet, hardly niver gooas twenty yards throo us own door
stooan..." Instead of the stoical wife's behaviour celebrated in "Come Whoam to
thi Childer An' Me", the story by "The Shevvild Chap" reveals a very different
response to a husband's misbehaviour. One of his characters, Mally, told of how
she treated her husband upon his return from a heavy drinking session. Having
returned home and demanded a beef steak, Mally's husband fell asleep. Whilst he
slept, Mally prepared the food, ate what she wanted and then discarded the rest. She
then rubbed some fat on her husband's lips. When he awoke, she declared "thah's
had thee supper ... nebbut o havent, he say." Mally replied "feel if the lips izznt
greazy, thah's forgotten, mun; sooa he felt: wa suz he o thout o haddent had me
supper; but o feel hungry yet."[64]
    Clearly, this piece reveals that women could, in their domestic settings, on
occasions, gain the upper hand over their menfolk. The work of "The Shevvild
Chap" portrays these characters with humour, but these strong women were
labelled as being outside conventional and acceptable norms. They are referred to
as "gossips" and are given alliterative names such as Dinah Dubbletung and Dolly
Doolittle, registering disapproval of their actions.

Contrary to the assertion by Susan Zlotnick that women's identities in dialect literature were constructed entirely within the domestic sphere, there is some evidence in dialect writing to suggest that the work place outside the home was recognised as a crucible of identity formation for women as well as men. In 1843, for instance, in *The Shevvild Chap's Annual*, an article was published entitled "Dame Flatback's Annual Epistle to t'Queen" in which Dame Flatback wrote on behalf of her fellow workers in the cutlery industry urging the Queen to make use of Sheffield-made knives in order to improve the trade. Dame Flatback pleaded: "if yo' nobbut begin a paring an cooking ... we ahr flatback knoives, o kno' varra well, we'st sooin have plenty a wark."[65] Occasionally, women workers were also represented in the dialect writing of John Hartley in the textile industry. In 1876, he commented upon the passing of the working week and how it affected the appearances and moods of women en route to their work at the textile mills. By Thursdays, he noted, "They luk cross on' ther heeads are abaat hauf a yard i'advance o' ther tooas. Ther clogs seem to ha made up ther mind not to goa." By contrast, on Saturdays, which were half-days, "yo can tell the difference as sooan as yo clap een on 'em. They're all i' good spirits ..."[66]

Whilst Hartley's representation of working-class women demonstrates a certain sympathy towards their plight, nevertheless he took a socially conservative stance on several occasions when the idea of extending women's rights were given short shrift. Significantly, when commenting on attempts to extend women's rights, the criticisms advanced by Hartley were invariably expressed through his female characters. In 1897, for instance, the New Woman forms the subject of an exchange between Sammywell and Mally. As Mally observes wryly,

> "It's noan new wimmin, it's new men at we want. But it's noa use me
> saying owt, for tha art an awst ha to put up wi thi. Here's th' sixpence
> si thee an see at tha gets full messur an doan't sup hawf on't befoor
> tha lands hooam."[67]

One aspect of dialect literature closely associated with identity is its preoccupation with rhythm. Central to this literary genre of course is the representation of particular dialectal speech rhythms, which will be examined shortly. However, rhythm prevailed in other forms within both Yorkshire and Lancashire dialect writing. The dialect almanack, for example, laid out the predominant calendar customs observed by inhabitants in the region in which it was targeted. Many of the dates mentioned in these works related to national occasions, such as Christmas and the births and deaths of prominent Britons. But there was a local dimension too: in some works, district worthies were also celebrated. For instance, in the 1868 *Clock Almanack*, the death in 1857 of the Halifax sculptor J.B. Leyland was marked on 27 January.[68] In addition to these dates, though, the almanacks and annuals also drew attention to forthcoming events which composed the characteristically local temporal landscape. As Bob Bushaway has observed: "The local customary calendar provided a frame of reference in which was expressed a perception of the social structure of the community, and also of its physical delineation."[69] References to the June fairs, which took place across the West Riding textile district feature regularly in *The Clock Almanack*, where their longevity and continued significance are emphasised. In 1878, for instance, Hartley declared:

> "They say th' fairs are deein aaght an' a few years'll see th'end
> on 'em and ther's some 'at say 'The sooiner an th' better' ...
> Be hanged to fowk 'at praich such a shallow selfish doctrine!
> Let th' youngens enjoy thersens! They''ll nivver be young
> but one!"[70]

In addition to the celebration of the annual rhythms, which arguably helped provide an anchor in a rapidly changing world for many people, dialect literature also regularly evoked the rhythms of the working day and week which so many of its readers shared across the manufacturing districts, especially in times of prosperity. In Brian Hollingworth's anthology of Lancashire dialect poetry, titles such as "The Factory Bell" by Edwin Waugh and the rather later poems of William Baron, "Hawf Past Five at Neet" and "Six O' Clock at Mornin'" relate directly to the rhythms of the working day.[71] Similarly, as has been shown, John Hartley's output regularly explored the pace of the working day and week, both in the workplace and at home. Such works, perhaps rather romantically at times, also reminded readers of the sensory as well as the limited pecuniary pleasures to be enjoyed in the workplace. In "Wayvin' Mewsic", for example, Hartley explored this:

> "Ther's mewsic i' th' shuttle,
> i' th loom an i' th frame
> Ther's melody mingl'd i' th noise ...
> At th' clank o' the tappet, the hum o' th' wheel
> Sing this plain unmistakeable song:-
>   Nick a ting, nock a ting,
>   Wages keep pocketing
>   Workin for little is better nor laiking
>   Twist an twine, reel an wind
>   Keeps a contented mind
>   Troubles are oft ov a body's own making."[72]

Such works clearly encouraged an appreciation of the communal rhythms of work and play and it was through this emphasis upon such commonly shared cultural virtues that local and regional identities could be fostered.[73]

However, leaving aside the subject content of this dialect literature, of course its representation of dialect lay at the heart of its success. Dialectal differences, sometimes over short distances, could be marked. The nineteenth-century antiquarian Sidney Addy, for instance, cited the case of a migrant from Derbyshire who moved to Sheffield in the 1830s. According to Addy, "The cutler came, when a boy, from a village in mid-Derbyshire to live at Crookes in the parish of Sheffield. He says that he lived there many months before he could converse with people whose dialect differed so much from his own."[74] Dialect, then, was clearly an effective badge of identity, marking out effectively those who belonged from those who did not. The skill of the successful dialect writer, though, was to evoke dialect but to ensure that it could be understood over a commercially viable territory. The most popular dialect literature produced in either Lancashire or Yorkshire was enjoyed on both sides of the Pennines. Edwin Waugh's Lancashire dialect writing for example was well-regarded in the West Riding, where he performed his work on a regular basis.

In order to ensure maximum comprehensibility, many dialect writers compromised in their representation of dialect. Adept writers could represent their chosen dialect through skilful use of syntax, grammar and the occasional employment of dialectal words. Most, though, moderated the capturing of the accent, or did so inconsistently in order to aid comprehension. Accurate phonetic representation of dialect would have made much of the literature impenetrable to the lay reader. However, for some, dialect writers' attempts to represent vernacular speech did not go far enough. Sidney Addy, for instance, wrote critically of attempts by the "The Shevvild Chap" to represent the city's dialect. He commented that: "If people in Sheffield had been free from the idea that acquaintance with a provincial dialect is a thing to be ashamed of, better specimens might have been available …"[75]

Arguably, though, such criticisms rather missed the point of dialect literature, which played an important role in the development of English popular culture. Undoubtedly there was a "homely", "nostalgic" dimension to much of this literature which sought to celebrate neighbourhood, family and the rather nebulous notion of "community". But there was also another side to this genre of writing which was marked by intolerance to difference. In much of his work, "The Shevvild Chap" hurled volleys of abuse at strict teetotalism, Owenism and Catholicism.[76] In *A Popish Discussion*, for instance, a regular character of "The Shevvild Chap", Jack Wheelswharf remarks of a Catholic neighbour:

"Wa Bil, lad, he's a genuine specimen of a priest-ridden Irishman

whose faith is in his priest an whose ignorance of the plan of
salvation by Jesus Christ is as a the darkness that might be fact."[77]

The determined attempts by "The Shevvild Chap" to construct and represent a
restricted ideal type of Sheffielder prompted some exasperation within the town.
One critic, "A. Silversmith" resorted to responding in dialect prose and declared:

"He's neer been nowt bur a slaundering skandalashon pest
to't taan ivver sin he began a publick loife. Nobuddy kan
blawah ther nooas bur he starts a blaiting."[78]

This rather more potent, partisan dialectal output has tended to be somewhat
overlooked in the consideration of this cultural form. Such examples make clear the
dangers of assuming that dialect literature constituted a straightforward cultural
product which articulated consensual notions of local and regional belonging.

However, perhaps a more positive note to end on is to reflect upon the legacy
dialect literature has left in the development of popular culture in the twentieth
century and beyond. Although it could be argued that local and regional cultural
identities have been threatened by developments in mass communications, such as
the coming of the music hall, cinema and, later, a largely centralised broadcasting
system, nevertheless, the robustness of dialect literature as a popular commercial
product, which survived into the early twentieth century, demonstrated that there
was cultural space for the championing of the quotidian and the local. The
popularity of characters such as Sammywell and Mally Grimes arguably have
inspired later performers of stage and screen such as George Formby and Gracie
Fields. The ancestry of soap opera stalwarts such as *Coronation Street's* Hilda and
Stan Ogden, Jack and Vera Duckworth and *Emmerdale's* Dingle family can also be
traced back to the vividly drawn characters whose regular appearances in print
made the work of Yorkshire and Lancashire dialect writers so popular.

* I would like to thank staff based in the Local Studies sections of the Hull, Leeds and Sheffield central libraries for their assistance in consulting the dialect literature referred to in this article.

1. John Hartley, *The Original Illuminated Clock Almanack* (Halifax: Wilson, 1868) 38-39. The title of this annual work is referred to hereafter as *The Clock Almanack*.

2. Patrick Joyce, *Visions of the People: Industrial England and the Question of Class, 1840-1914* (Cambridge: Cambridge University Press, 1991) 290-291.

3. Peter Mathias, *The First Industrial Nation: Second Edition* (London: Methuen, 1983) 178.

4. Sidney Pollard, *A History of Labour in Sheffield* (Liverpool: Liverpool University Press, 1959) 6.

5. See for instance Michael Anderson, *Family Structure in Nineteenth-Century Lancashire* (Cambridge: Cambridge University Press, 1971).

6. *Parliamentary Papers: 1861. Census. Vol. III*, 1863, 162.

7. Joyce, *Visions*, 280-283.

8. Joyce, *Visions*, 290.

9. Martha Vicinus, "Literary Voices of an Industrial Town", in H.J. Dyos and Michael Wolff (eds), *The Victorian City: Images and Realities, Volume Two* (London: Routledge and Kegan Paul, 1973) 752; and Martha Vicinus, *The Industrial Muse: A Study of Nineteenth Century Working-Class Literature* (London: Croom Helm, 1974) 227.

10. Joyce, *Visions*, 284-287.

11. Vicinus, *The Industrial Muse*, 196; and K.E. Smith, "Ben Preston in his Time and Ours" *Transactions of the Yorkshire Dialect Society*, Part LXXV, Vol. XV (1980) 34-46 .

12. Dave Russell, *Looking North: Northern England and the National Imagination* (Manchester: Manchester University Press, 2004) 119.

13. Hartley, *Clock Almanack* (1879) 2.

14. C. Forshaw, *John Hartley, Poet and Author: An Appreciation* (Bradford: Thornton and Pearson, 1909) 19.

15. John Hargreaves, "John Hartley", in H.C. G. Matthew and Brian Harrison (eds), *Oxford Dictionary of National Biography, Volume 25* (Oxford: Oxford University Press, 2004) 617-618.

16. Patrick Joyce, *Democratic Subjects* (Cambridge: Cambridge University Press, 1994) 40.

17. Vicinus, *Industrial Muse*, 210.

18. Joyce, *Visions*, 274.

19. Vicinus, *Industrial Muse*, 212.

20. John Hartley, *Yorkshire Ditties* (Halifax: Wilson, 1870) 7-9.

21. Vicinus, *Industrial Muse*, 197.

22. Forshaw, *John Hartley*, 9-14. In 1873 and 1874, during the absence of John Hartley, Edmund Hatton was editor of the *Clock Almanack*.

23. Ian Dewhirst, "The Public Readings of John Hartley, Benjamin Preston and Edwin Waugh." *Transactions of the Yorkshire Dialect Society* Part XCIII, Vol. XVIII (1993) 18.

24. Dewhirst, "The Public Readins", 20. This double-reading occurred a week before the same venue played host to Charles Dickens. Cheapest tickets for the dialect performers were priced at one quarter of the cost of equivalent tickets for Dickens, which perhaps reflects the relative prestige accorded to dialect literature.

25. See for instance David Vincent, *Literacy and Popular Culture, 1750-1914*, (Cambridge: Cambridge University Press, 1989) 193-195.

26. Hartley, *Clock Almanack*, 1880.

27. Hartley, *Clock Almanack*, 1882.

28. Hartley, *Clock Almanack*, 1909, 32.

29. Hartley, *Clock Almanack*, 1871.

30. Hartley, *Clock Almanack*, 1892, 35.

31. Hartley, *Clock Almanack*,1894, 49.

32. James Vernon, *Politics and the People: A Study in English Political Culture, c. 1815-1867* (Cambridge: Cambridge University Press, 1993) 48-55; Colin Cunningham, *Victorian and Edwardian Town Halls* (London: Routledge and Kegan Paul, 1981) 34-55.

33. Hartley, *Clock Almanack*, 1868.

34. Cunningham, *Victorian and Edwardian Town Halls* , 45 and 75.

35. Hartley, *Clock Almanack*, 1868.

36. Hollingworth, *Songs of the People,* 1.

37. Vicinus, *Industrial Muse*, 191.

38. Joyce, *Visions*, 395-399.

39. Joyce, *Visions*, 264.

40. Hollingworth, *Songs of the People,* 5.

41. Hartley, *Clock Almanack*, 1877, 25.

42. Hartley, *Clock Almanack*, 1909, 44.

43. Hartley, *Clock Almanack*, 1881, 42.

44. John Hartley, *A Rolling Stone: A Tale of Wrongs and Revenge* (Wakefield: W. Nicolson and Sons, 1878) 308.

45. John Hartley, *Seets i' Yorkshire and Lancashire*, (Wakefield: W. Nicolson and Sons, c. 1878) 116-7.

46. Russell, *Looking North,* 128.

47. Hartley, *Clock Almanack*, 1891, 47.

48. Hartley, *Clock Almanack*, 1897, 16.

49. John Widdowson, "From Hunter to Newspeak: Dialect Study in Sheffield, 1829-1984," *Lore and Language* 11 (1992-1993) 220.

50. Dyson, *A Glossary of Words and Dialect Formerly Used in the Sheffield Trades. Part One*, (Sheffield: Sheffield Trades Historical Society, 1936 [Reprinted 1979]) 21.

51. Hartley, *Clock Almanack*, 1868.

52. John Waddington-Feather, *Yorkshire Dialect* (Clapham, North Yorkshire: Dalesman, 1970) 47.

53. Hartley, *Clock Almanack*, 1868.

54. Ben Brierley, "The royal visit", in *Ab' o' th' Yate Sketches, Vol. III*, reprinted in Joyce, *Visions*, 391.

55. See for instance John Hartley, *Grimes's Visit to th' Queen: A Royal Time Among Royalties*, c. 1878, and Hartley, *Clock Almanack*, 1898, 43.

56. Abel Bywater, *The Shevvild Chap's Almanack* (Sheffield: Chaloner, 1842).

57. Abel Bywater, (writing as "The Shevvild Chap"), *The Prince of Wales Almanack*, 1842.

58. Wilfrid Halliday and Arthur S. Uppleby, eds. *White Rose Garland: An Anthology of Yorkshire Dialect Verse* (London: J.M. Dent and Sons, 1949).

59. Susan Zlotnick, "'A Thousand Times I'd Be a Factory Girl': Dialect, Domesticity and Working-Class Women's Poetry in Victorian Britain," *Victorian Studies* 35, no. 1 (1991) 9.

60. Zlotnick, "A Thousand Times", 12.

61. Zlotnick, "A Thousand Times", 16.

62. Hartley, *Clock Almanack*, 1886, 12.

63. Hartley, *Clock Almanack*, 1888, 47.

64. Abel Bywater (writing as "The Shevvild Chap"), "The Gossips Tea Drinking", in *The Shevvild Chap's Annual,* (Sheffield: 1836).

65. Abel Bywater (writing as the "The Shevvild Chap"), *The Shevvild Chap's Annual and Winter Fireside Almanack for the Year 1843* (Sheffield: 1842).

66. Hartley, *Clock Almanack*, 1876, 17.

67. Hartley, *Clock Almanack*, 1897, 39.

68. Hartley, *Clock Almanack*, 1868.

69. Bob Bushaway, *By Rite*, (London: Junction Books, 1982) 34.

70. Hartley, *Clock Almanack*, 1878, 15.

71. Hollingworth, *Songs of the People,* 86-93.

72. Hartley, *Yorkshire Ditties* 22.

73. John Langton, "The Industrial Revolution and the Regional Geography of England", *Transactions of the Institute of British Geographers* 9 (1984) 159-162.

74. Sidney Addy, *A Glossary of Words Used in the Neighbourhood of Sheffield* (London: English Dialect Society, 1888) xviii.

75. Addy, *A Glossary of Words,* xviii.

76. See for instance the following works by Abel Bywater, writing as "The Shevvild Chap": "A Popish Discussion", in *The Shevvild Chap's Christmas Present* (Sheffield: 1850); *A Conversation Between The Shevvild Chap and a Freethinker* (Sheffield: 1858); and *Reasons for Drinking Ale (Moderately) and Wine (When He Can Get It)* (Sheffield: n.d.)

77. Abel Bywater, *A Popish Discussion.*

78. "A. Silversmith", *A Balus For a Chap i't Park What Isn't Habel to Buy Water Wee Ahr Filosofikal Hoppingons Uppa't Parsons, Kristianity etc* (Sheffield: n.d.).

'LOCAL CHARACTERS' AND LOCAL, REGIONAL AND NATIONAL IDENTITIES IN NINETEENTH-CENTURY ENGLAND AND SCOTLAND

JAMES GREGORY

The early-nineteenth century antiquarian, J.T. Smith observed that: "every age produces at least one eccentric in every city, town and village".[1] This chapter investigates the role of such people- often called "characters" or, with some irony, "worthies"-in constructing or fostering local, regional and even national identities. Though eccentricity is a topic that has had little scholarly attention, "singularity of conduct: oddness", to quote one contemporary definition, was no minor matter.[2] It was, amongst other things, a component of "Englishness" according to many contemporaries.[3] I have explored elsewhere a national dimension through eccentric biographies organised on a *British* basis, here the focus is the local and Scottish interest in the strange or odd character, which the English aspect has tended to obscure.

The study of eccentrics concerns *identity*: the cultivation or acceptance of an "odd" identity; its bestowal by community or by commentators, and its role in creating local knowledge or characteristics, leading to a sense of place. In recent research on mad or deviant characters in Italian piazzas, Sara Bergstresser argues that "marginal" figures who live in the centre of a community, actually exemplify Italian cultural norms of localism, a strong attachment to home, and a heightened sense of place. The locality's distinctive character is partly derived from such people. This interpretation is suggestive for nineteenth-century Britain too.[4] In life and memory, the characters that animated townscapes and villages, were signifiers of identity as much as the places. Yet their part in the "symbolic construction" of a community is neglected by British historians and folklorists.[5]

Robert Colls is therefore unusual when he suggests of early-nineteenth-century Tyneside ballads, that their eccentric heroes helped express localism.[6] Eccentrics demonstrated regional individuality and "character". Local-centred pride meant that they were remembered as, in the words of one Tyneside ballad collection, "memorials of the peculiar characteristics" of a locality.[7] Colls studied their place in humorous and satirical songs by proudly "local poets". They also appeared in portraiture (which advertised itinerant or newly-established purveyors of likeness), private memoirs and local historiography.[8] The focus here, is on certain printed genres dealing with eccentrics: local or regional histories, "dictionaries", guidebooks and reminiscences; though their authors often alluded to other media (such as ballads and three-dimensional representation) in their works. If every parish had its tale o' men, overall local historians preferred tales about "characters" who were true worthies;[9] but those that did discuss eccentrics were following in the steps of the pioneers of county history such as Robert Boyle who had been interested in those "remarkable by some accident, or other particular affection of their bodies".[10] Inevitably, too, antiquarians and local historians in pursuit of entertaining stories turned to "local characters".[11]

A few of these writers acknowledged interest in eccentrics in the titles of their works: such as John Briscoe in Nottingham or John Sykes in north-east England.[12] In other cases, as in *Clitheroe in its Railway Days*[13] these appeared unheralded. Histories of village and parish, often seeking to evoke a picturesque rural past, presented real or fictional "characters".[14] Fictionalised accounts, perhaps most notably Thomas Miller's *Our Old Town*, also depicted "queer characters".[15] The adjective was not necessary, for the word "character" was certainly understood to refer to eccentricity. William Abram in Blackburn, helpfully glossed it as "one who is not cast in the common mould, who has a form and method and manner of his own".[16]

Inevitably, the material studied here is provincial and parochial in the main. But some were marketed at a national audience fascinated by "wonderful characters" and which, through publications emanating from London or pirated from metropolitan models, consumed biographies of "local characters" from across Britain.[17] One such work was the popular *Every-Day Book*, a compendium of calendar folklore and local traditions which the radical London publisher William Hone assembled in the late 1820s. It provided the model for Chambers's later *Book of Days*.[18]

Eccentric characters in England

One concentration of coverage was in the north-east, where media depicting eccentrics ranged from ballads, newspapers and local histories to artefacts such as mugs. Historians such as John Sykes (*Local Records*, 1833) and Moses Richardson (*Local Historian's Table Book*, 1841-46) recorded eccentrics. The late-Victorian popular journal *Lore and Legend*, based on contributions to the leading provincial paper, *Newcastle Weekly Chronicle*, gave a conspicuous place to characters. Building on this prominence, Charlton's late-Victorian *History of Newcastle* devoted a chapter to them. Attention transcended the local: in the late 1820s, Hone's *Every-Day Book* and his *Table Book* received anecdotes about several north-east characters, who were presented as the subject of celebration by expatriates in London.[19]

Elizabeth Gaskell's *Life of Charlotte Bronte* had discussed the odd character of Yorkshire, "the remarkable degree of self-sufficiency" the "strange eccentricity" fostered by isolation and distance from public opinion.[20] Sabine Baring-Gould, introducing his collection of strange Yorkshire folk in 1874, noted a friend's comment: "Every other Yorkshireman is a character", and agreed that the county did contain a unique extent of originality. The cliché of rugged individuality meant that eccentricity could seem a natural development of Yorkshire character and offered one characteristic in the attempt to describe Yorkshire identity.[21] Several other works of Yorkshire anecdote collected eccentrics. Taylor's *Anecdota Eboracensis* (1883 and 1887), included eccentrics amongst its "professions". The characters were standard oddities already represented in Baring-Gould's collection, or national collections (such as Jemmy Hirst, Peg Wharton, Richard Dickinson of Scarborough).[22] Yorkshire characters such as Peg Wharton featured in county histories, dictionaries and pamphlets.[23]

Another, more specific contribution to local lore was *Reminiscences of Old Sheffield,* which originated in a local newspaper in 1872-3, featured discussion of many eccentrics of the 1830s and earlier. "[H]ow many eccentrics formerly we had about the town," it reflected, "now any that we have seem to be hidden." Recalling characters such as "Silly Luke", a contributor commented: "we had no Idiot Asylums then in which they might have been trained to more usefulness". But contributors shared the common view that folly could be combined with shrewdness, as in the case of Luke, many of whose sayings were handed down.[24] Some people classed as eccentric in nineteenth-century collections were political radicals whose enthusiasms gave them an eccentric reputation. In Sheffield one character (one of several eccentrics across Britain called "Lord John Russell", after the diminutive Whig politician), was a brush maker whose speciality was making political reform speeches to a large following of boys.[25]

Writers from Lancashire produced several collections. They focussed on Rochdale and Blackburn; perhaps surprisingly, none came from Manchester or Liverpool despite noted eccentric inhabitants such as Joseph Williamson, "Mole Man of Edge Hill".[26] The reporter William Robertson was the chronicler of Rochdale's eccentrics. In his *Rochdale Past and Present*, a chapter of eccentrics followed more typical subjects for a local guide: information on government, institutions and ancient families. Like many eccentrics in local histories, his characters were all working-class and spoke in dialect. Their nicknames were associated by Robertson with the era before "the progressive spirit of manufacturing industry"; geographically confined to the "lower parts of the town and especially in the surrounding villages".[27] His characters were mostly described as simple-minded: barefooted but strong simpletons. One was a lazy character whose craziness was part pose, another was a virago who preferred male company and politics, and who insisted on heading up tory processions. Some characters had emblematic roles: such as the one-legged "Maltoot", a conservative noted for his military or scholastic garb and wit "of no ordinary character." Others appeared as burlesque figures: "Crazy Michael" who presented himself as a parliamentary candidate and led a counter-yeomanry. In Bradford, William Abram presented twenty five characters, many identified as eccentric, in a posthumously-published collection drawing on the East Lancashire dialect tales of "Jack" Salisbury the auctioneer and humorist, whose stories as "Tummus Carter" had many references to local "odd or notorious" characters. Such characters became proverbial, thus the combing of his hair by the dirty early Victorian socialist Harry Barker represented an impossibility.

Hone's work publicised recent and living characters in Nottingham such as David Love and Benjamin Mayo.[28] Mayo was the subject of a tract derived from a local newspaper account of his sayings and doings and depicted in three other published portraits.[29] His admirers erected a memorial in the general cemetery when he died in 1843 (he was also immortalised in a pub name). Wylie's *Old and New Nottingham* (1853) and Briscoe's *Nottinghamshire Facts and Fictions* (1877) rehearsed the lives and anecdotes of Mayo, Love and other eccentrics.[30]

"Derby has been prolific in noted and also in eccentric men". So claimed Pendelton in his *History of Derbyshire* in 1886.[31] They certainly had lavish attention in the stone mason/ antiquarian Joseph Robinson's *Derbyshire Gatherings* of 1866 which included biographies and engraved portraits of local characters and eccentrics such as the shrewd lunatic Samuel Eyre, guide of Castleton.[32] He noted that such portraits were gratifying to their locality, "not so much for any useful lesson to be derived therefrom, as for their being objects of curiosity."[33] Perhaps Robinson was encouraged by the fact that the local antiquarian journal, *The Reliquary*, had been featuring local characters, such as Pheobe Bown: "A maid of mutable condition, /A jockey, cowherd and musician".[34]

Other regional collections came from the west country, a place like the north east, feeling strongly the charm of local attachment. Baring-Gould produced two popular works.[35] His eclectic Cornish collection included a politician, crazed radical, wrestler, regicide, astronomer, eighteenth-century dramatist, and the last speaker of Cornish. The existence of eccentrics was taken by Baring-Gould to indicate the survival of regional identity and individuality.[36] Its Celtic population set Cornwall apart from English culture, its isolation tended "to develop in it much originality of character". Religious enthusiasm was associated with the effects of working in the cramped and strange environment of mines.[37] His Devonian collection was well-reviewed by the national press as attractive to those interested in (to quote the *Westminster Gazette*) "human documents which are out of the ordinary".[38] Unlike the Cornish collection there was no reflection on the link between region and character.[39] Plymouth characters appeared in the *South Devon Monthly Museum* in the mid-1830s. Characters such as Jack O' Diamonds, the "Lord of the Isles" and the itinerant seller of radical-literature Tom Hynes (the latter introducing a series of "public characters" [40]), were plebeians. Their lawlessness and appearance rendered them exotic according to this local literary miscellany.[41]

"Notes and queries" journals such as the *Western Antiquary* [42] and *Cornish Notes and Queries* noted Hynes and others.[43] Similar journals, and newspapers for counties and localities across England also reported eccentrics. London oddities certainly were reported and depicted, as Hone noted.[44] Wits and artists also depicted those whom "spleen or mirth usher into notice" [45] in Oxford and Cambridge, the latter having the whimsical Jemmy Gordon, reported in Hone and university guides.[46]

Southern eccentrics and characters lacked the same publicity. Yet they existed, as a roving artist, John Dempsey, demonstrated, by his portraits from Portsmouth, Winchester and elsewhere, in the 1840s.[47] There was a similarly limited coverage in English-language Welsh and Irish histories.[48]

II. Scottish Eccentricity

There were prominent attempts to claim eccentricity as characteristically Scottish.[49] With the fame of Walter Scott's eccentric characters in the nineteenth century, this was credible. Moreover the eighteenth-century Jamie Fleemin, Lord Udny's fool (1713-78), was a national celebrity, and probably an important influence on the depiction of the Scottish eccentric. His biography had reached a twenty-sixth edition by 1829 and a monument was erected in 1861.[50] Daft Jamie, another half-wit, gained a British fame for a tragic reason: as a victim of Burke and Hare he was recalled in a biography and several ballads.[51]

As in England, anecdote and biography linked eccentricity to claims about originality and individualism, whether Highland, urban, or national. An important general treatment was the Episcopalian dean Edward Ramsay's *Reminiscences of Scottish Life and Characters*, in which the demise of eccentrics was integral to an argument about the trend of increasing sameness. Anecdotes were meant to record elements of national life and "national eccentric points of character" which were fading within a lifetime through Anglicisation of language and humour.[52] His eccentrics ranged from domestic servants, beadles, professors and judges, to naturals and feigning idiots. Parochial idiots, now in asylums, had been accorded a place in parish life, and "many odd sayings which emanated from them were traditionary in country localities". Viewing such characters as the living versions of Scott's David Gellatley, he recounted anecdotes about people such as Rab Hamilton ("a well-remembered crazy creature of the west country").

According to Henry Grey Graham's *Social Life of Scotland in the Eighteenth Century*, published at the end of the Victorian era, "In no other country, surely, did there exist such marked individuality of character... The country swarmed with 'originals' in every rank, in town and village."[53] Graham's comments on the past ubiquity, and recent loss of the "originals" and demise of the "natural" could be found elsewhere.[54] For Archibald Geikie, they had disappeared with the increasing decencies of communities and the Lunacy Board, but thereby "a little of the picturesqueness of village life" was lost.[55]

Peculiar Glaswegians were well-chronicled. The last volume of Peter Mackenzie's *Reminiscences of Glasgow and the West of Scotland* (1857) included the lives of street vendors, hawkers, beggars and the mentally deficient: such as "Hawkie", "Blind Alick", "Jamie Blue". The volume was sufficiently commercial to be reprinted. It also became a source for histories such as Andrew Wallace's *Popular Traditions*.[56] Edinburgh also had its characters, drawn most eccentrically in the late-eighteenth century by John Kay, his engravings were reproduced in the nineteenth century for instance in *Old Edinburgh Pedlars* (1886), and Gray's *Edinburgh Miscellany*.[57] Characters such as Cuddie Willie also featured in ballads.[58]

Similar works devoted to "characters", came from Jedburgh (in Roxburgh), Dundee and Brechin (in Angus) and Aberdeen. Jedburgh eccentrics surfaced in several editions of *Jethart worthies* and in photographs in the later-nineteenth century. A poem on Dundonian characters reached a third edition by 1893.[59] Neish's Brechin characters were "fixtures" who "seemed part and parcel of the quaint old town", such as innocent and counterfeit fools, itinerant bookseller, characterful war veterans, miser and drunks. Others were periodic incomers: pedlars and farmers coming to market.[60] Aberdonians were collected in the late-nineteenth century, with Blin Bob (Duncan Mackinlay) described as the "last of the Aberdeen Characters".[61]

Ayrshire, Perthshire, Sutherland, Caithness and other counties had literary memorials to eccentrics in scattered anecdotes or book chapters. [62] In early-nineteenth century Kirkcudbrightshire, the engineer John Mactaggart's *Scottish Gallovidian Encyclopaedia* (1824) featured eccentrics as part of his effort to display a rich individuality against encroaching English culture.[63] His dictionary included entries on "Naturals" in general,[64] dialect words for various behavioural and physical oddities, and entries on particular characters, who were equated with characters in Scott John Sinclair's effort to publicise the depressed extreme north as a place of untouched beauty in the late-nineteenth century, included Thurso eccentrics of the 1830s-1840s. Anecdotes about "Peelans", "Boustie" and "Mouzie" demonstrated how integrated these foolish or colourful characters were in the cultural identity of this northernmost town.[65] The Caithness originals of this era and later years were celebrated in an extensive collection in the Edwardian era.[66]

Perhaps the most charming collection of eccentrics appears in Isabel Anderson's *Inverness before Railways* (1885). Her work reiterated that common association between erosion of local and strongly-marked character and the railway, in this case, in the "quiet exclusive" capital of the Highlands in 1850.[67] The Inverness and Nairn railways brought in southerners, a new competitiveness which stimulated progress and activity, and social complication where previously there had been few classes.[68] Anderson recalled genteel and working-class characters,[69] and crazy or lazy mendicants.[70] She noted that before the railway, "any one who was a 'character' was eagerly sought after, in order to prevent formality, and promote the amusement of the guests".[71] Many mendicants, she said, would now be incarcerated, whilst others who only had a "want" had fulfilled useful roles or obtained precarious livings. Some entered the folklore as proverbial figures, though if they were not pleasant characters, this could be as the local bogeyman/woman used to frighten children into silence or good behaviour.

Conclusion

How should this fascination with local eccentrics, as expressed in histories and other records, be interpreted and contextualized? Obviously there are histories of physical deformity and disability, social nonconformity, and mental illness, to which this material ought to be related. Their role in endorsing or destabilizing cultural norms should be considered. I wish to draw out some conclusions about the eccentric in relation to the identity of place, and say something further about the question of "class".

The "place-oriented loyalty" which helps create identity, generated and was produced by local authors, who could incorporate eccentrics and characters. Reminiscences of oddities could even be offered by expatriates: whose sense of communion with their homeland was reinforced by such reminiscences.[72] Thus, there were, according to Neish of Brechin, many "in far-off lands, whose early memories still cherish the familiar figure and character of Drummer Wood".[73]

Their decline marked *changing* identity, and their place in local history, which was stimulated by a sense of loss, was natural.[74] As Tennyson said, "The individual withers, and the world is more and more", or as Thomas Hardy wrote, "progress and picturesqueness do not harmonise".[75] In the mid and late-Victorian period a decline in local nicknames, "local individualism" and the rise of uniformity were identified by chroniclers of characters. When Blackburn had less than half its present population, William Abram wrote: "it would have been easy for a person well acquainted with the town to name ten or a dozen men and women in the place who were recognisable by their neighbours as real originals... How many such can be mentioned now?'"[76] Such observations were replicated elsewhere.[77] So those who chronicled eccentrics were alert to the transformation of local cultural and social peculiarities through wider change, often identified with technological developments. Local characters symbolised the consequent passing of bygone or quaint customs, lost individuality and community spirit.[78] Alternatively, their demise signified a more enlightened response to mental illness and fecklessness. Whatever the perspective, social transformation made them rare.

How far is there a "class" dimension to the treatment of characters? Few genteel and aristocratic eccentrics figure: eccentric identity, according to the material collected here, generally marked one as plebeian or pauper. Thus eccentrics contributed a demotic side to local biography- quaint peasants, plebeians and indigents balancing the great and the nationally important: providing a comic slant on localities which could not be allowed in relation to "worthies". The authors examined here often treated poor and deformed people as quaint, picturesque, grotesque and humorous, as Sean Shesgreen has shown was the case with the popular genre depicting *Cries of London*.[79] Though this meant objectification and commodification by their "betters", there was also the possibility that the eccentric was a mascot.[80] They contributed in life and memory, to the sense of a *community's* identity.[81]

There is a national dimension. Eccentrics and characters collected across Britain fell into common categories: hermits and secluded misers, and public characters like viragos, naturals, drunks, bellmen and hawkers. Nineteenth-century local records reflected an awareness of national models; and parallels in the guides and histories of other communities. Correspondence in national journals, allowed the local to contribute to a national sense of characters and quaintness. Eccentric characters represented the "picturesque past" in *general*: their importance was partly as a symbol of rapid change in *national* identity too.[82]

The memory that created local identity and "local past", was created by journalists, local historians, correspondents and readers. Pursuit of a good story and "human interest" obviously help explain the interest in strange characters. If tales about them were collected as acts of local piety, it was also hoped that their recollection would animate dry local annals.[83] In our internet age, eccentrics foster community, regional and national memory, in school projects, BBC sites, projects such as Scran.ac.uk (devoted to Scottish culture), and websites devoted to "unofficial" viewpoints on tourist sites.[84] Evidently they contribute to those "cultural and mythological maps" needed to create identities.[85] A commercial imperative is also clear in attempts to sell places through "characters", and in a continued demand for writings on area-specific eccentrics.[86] Several of these are prefaced by reflections on the decline in eccentricity, a decline which always seems to be happening and is usually lamented.

[1] J.T. Smith, *Life and Times of Nollekens* (1828).

[2] For an attempt at a "scientific" study of eccentricity, see D. J. Weeks and J. James, *Eccentrics: A Study of Sanity and Strangeness* (London: Weidenfeld and Nicolson, 1995). See J. Gregory, "Eccentric Lives: Character, Characters and Curiosities in Britain, *c.*1760-1900", in W. Ernst (ed.), *Ab/Normal. A Social History of the Normal and Abnormal* (Routledge: forthcoming) on literary treatments of eccentricity in the context of a wider cultural interest in the "abnormal". Other studies of eccentricity are generally confined to English literature, e.g., R. Emig, "Eccentricity Begins at Home: Carlyle's Centrality in Victorian Thought", *Textual Practice*, 17 (2) 379-390. The definition quoted comes from *Chambers's Etymological Dictionary of the English Language* (1882)

[3] See P. Langford, *Englishness Identified. Manners and Character. 1650-1850* (Oxford University Press, 2000) 301-10.

[4] S. Bergstresser, "Deviant roles, Normal lives: Why every piazza needs its own "madman" ", in W. Ernst (ed.), *Ab/Normal.*

[5] On this, see A. Cohen, *The Symbolic Construction of Community* (Chichester: Ellis Horwood, 1985), ch.4. Local characters can be related to the "local legend", see J. Simpson, "The Local Legend: A Product of Popular Culture", *Rural History*, 2:1 (1991) 23-35. The "local-character anecdote", a short legend depicting characteristic action by a noted local individual, has been studies by folklorists, see for instance D.I. Tye, "Local Character Anecdotes: A Novia Scotia Case Study", *Western Folklore* 48:3 July 1989.

[6] R. Colls, *The Collier's Rant. Song and Culture in the Industrial Village* (London: Croom Helm, 1977),.50.

[7] Prefatory remarks to *The Newcastle Song Book; or Tyne-Side Songster. Being a Collection of Comic and Satirical Songs, Descriptive of Eccentric Characters, and the Manners and Customs of a Portion of the Labouring Population of Northumberland and the neighbourhood* (Newcastle: W and T. Fordyce, 1842).

[8] W.D. Lawson, *Tyneside Celebrities* (Newcastle, 1873) 5-17, identifies "Northern character" with decisiveness, self-reliance, independence and superficial peculiarity; K. Wrightson, "Northern Identities; the Longue Duree", *Northern Review*, 2 (winter 1995) 25, sees "defining characteristics of a northern identity" as "pride and truculence".

[9] E.g., Anon., *The Harwich Guide to which are added Biographical and Historical Notices of EXTRAORDINARY CHARACTERS* (Ipswich: J. Raw, 1808); J. Fotheringham, *Carnoustie Sketches. The Village, Its Character and Customs* (Arbroath: Brodie and Salmond, 1889). The inclusion of "mediocrities...those by accident and birth...and Unworthies" in W. B. Gerish, *A Handlist of Hertfordshire Worthies (together with some Unworthies)* (Bishops Stortford, 1916) was the result of the lack of any really great men.

[10] For the context of county histories, histories of local communities and individual places, see C.R.J. Currie and C.P. Lewis (eds), *A Guide to English County Histories* (Stroud: Sutton, 1997). On Boyle, see J. Reed, "Monstrous Knowledge: Representing the Natural Body in Eighteenth Century Ireland", in H. Deutsch and F. Nussbaum (eds), *'Defects' and Engendering the Modern Body* (Ann Arbor, Michigan: University of Michigan Press, 2000) 154-176.

[11] There are parallels with modern tourism, where the peculiar and characterful are often emphasised. Theorists of tourism such as J. Jafari, J. Krippendorf, J. Urry have argued that at the heart of the tourist experience is the pursuit of the unusual or distinctive, to make the experience different form ordinary life: see P. Thornton, 'Cornwall and the Tourists Gaze', in P.Payton (ed.), *Cornish Studies One* (University of Exeter Press, 1993) 82. For stimulating thoughts on places, tourism and identity, see J. Urry, *Consuming Places* (London: Routledge, 1995).

[12] J.P. Briscoe, *Nottinghamshire facts and fictions.* Second series. *Eccentrics and Eccentricities* (Nottingham: Shepherd Brothers, 1877); J. Sykes, *Local Records; or historical register of remarkable events which have occurred exclusively in the counties of Durham and Northumberland, town and county of Newcastle upon Tyne, and Berwick upon Tweed; with an obituary of persons of talent, eccentricity and longevity* (first edition: Newcastle: Sykes, 1824)

[13] For instance, W.H. Wylie, *Old and New Nottingham* (London: Longman, Brown, Greens and Longman, 1853) ch.9, is devoted to eccentrics, impostors and others.

[14] See J. Arthur Gibbs, *A Cotswold Village or Country Life and Pursuits in Gloucestershire* (London: John Murray, 1898) ch.3, "Village Characters", which included "quaint hamlet folk"; and D.D. Dixon, *Upper Coquetdale* (Newcastle upon Tyne: R. Redpath, 1903). An example of real characters, see the anecdotes on characters of Catwick in the parish of Holderness, selected on the basis of their "comic corner", by their rector, William Smith, *Brazzock* (London: A.Brown and Sons, 1905). They included beggars, prophetess, and peculiar parsons

[15] T. Miller, *Our Old Town* (London: J and C. Brown, 1857). See the chartist Thomas Cooper, *The Life of Thomas Cooper*, ch.2 (London: Hodder and Stoughton, 1872) for references to Miller and another character from their shared childhood.

[16] W.A. Abram, *Blackburn Characters*, VII (Blackburn: J and G. Toulmin, 1895): James Brogden.

[17] An edition of 1842 from the North Riding of Yorkshire added local eccentrics: see G.H. Wilson, *Wonderful Characters* (London: Walker and Co., 1842). This copy, in the British Library collection, belonged to H.S. Ashbee. The printer was W. Braithwaite of Stokesley, Yorkshire.

[18] W. Hone, *The Every-Day Book, or the Guide to the Year: Relating to the popular amusements, sports, ceremonies, manners, customs, and events, incident to the three hundred and sixty-five events in past and present times; being a series of five thousand anecdotes and facts; forming a perpetual key to the almanac*, 2 vols. (London: W. Tegg, 1827).

[19] See J. Gregory, "Local Characters": Eccentricity and the North East in the Nineteenth Century', *Northern History* 42 (1) (March 2005) 163-186.

[20] E. Gaskell, *The Life of Charlotte Bronte* (London: Smith, Elder, 1857) ch.2.

[21] Not, of course, that a single Yorkshire identity, let alone a "northern" identity, exists or existed. On this point, see S.A. Caunce, "Is there a separate northern English identity", abstract of a paper given at the conference "Regional Identities: Shifting Boundaries and Contested Meanings", Manchester Centre for Regional History, 13-14th September 2000.

[22] A few local characters appear in the Sterne-esque *Anecdotes and Manners of a few Ancient and Modern Oddities. Interspersed with deductive inferences and occasional observations, tending to reclaim some interlocutory foibles which often occur in the common intercourses of society* (York : Printed by W. Storry; and sold by J. Wolstenholme, York; Scatcherd & Letterman, London; and Constable & Co., Edinburgh, 1806); Richard Vickerman Taylor, *Yorkshire Anecdotes, or, Remarkable incidents in the lives of celebrated Yorkshire men and women: compiled from various sources, and arranged in alphabetical order, with brief biographical particulars, and a copious index* (London: Whittaker; Leeds: R. Jackson, 1887). Peg Wharton is referred to in other works, for instance J.W. Ord, *The History and Antiquities of Cleveland* (London: Simpkins and Marshall, 1846) 258-259.

[23] Langdale, *A Topographical Dictionary of Yorkshire* (1809; Northallerton: J.Langdale, 1822); W. Grainge, *Three Wonderful Yorkshire Characters* (Pately: Thomas Thorpe, 1864).

[24] R.E. Leader, *Reminiscences of Old Sheffield. Its Streets and Its People* (Sheffield, Leader and Sons, 1876) 225-226.

[25] See the online "Sheffield Forum Archive" for 20th century characters who are being recalled now.

[26] Only a few eccentrics appeared in *Local Notes and Queries from the Manchester Guardian* over the period 1874-1876, there are references only to Jonathan Hulme, Viper Killer, and Moss of Ringway, both from Hulbert's *Memoirs*. On Williamson, see for instance, *Recollections of Old Liverpool, by a Nonagenarian* (Liverpool:J.F.Hughes, 1863). A sketch or engraving supposedly of Williamson is reproduced in G. Chandler, *Liverpool* (London: B.T. Batsford, 1957) 359: without any details on the source. See portraits of local characters in G. Chandler, *Liverpool*, 404-405. See R. Whittington-Egan, *Liverpool Characters and Eccentrics* (South Wirral: Gallery Press, 1985) for eccentrics or characters including Williamson, "Skittles" the Victorian courtesan, the armless artist Sarah Biffin and others.

[27] W. Robertson, *Rochdale. Past and Present. A History and Guide* (Rochdale: Schofield and Hoblyn, 1875) 225.

[28] *Every-Day Book,* vol.2, 14 February, p.113, 22 November, p.788. Love was depicted by the itinerant artist John Dempsey, with his portrait from Hone's work.

[29] *Every-Day Book,* vol.2, 22 November, 785-788. For other portraits, see three different lithographed portraits, over the period 1840-1880, reproduced by the North East Midland Photographic Record.

[30] J.P. Briscoe, *Nottinghamshire Facts and Fictions...Eccentrics and Eccentricities* (Nottingham: 1877) 12.

[31] J. Pendleton, *A History of Derbyshire* (London: Elliott Stock, 1886) 16. Pendleton mentioned Jacky Turner, Rowland Millington and John Hallam, 20.

[32] J.B.Robinson, *Derbyshire Gatherings* (London: J.R. Smith, 1866). Published by subscription, *Notes and Queries* noted Robinson was a "prophet honoured in his own land", vol.10, 3rd series, 251, 20 October 1866, 325. Robinson, a stone mason, published designs and guides for stone masons, antiquarian guides and work in the Derbyshire dialect.

[33] Robinson, *Derbyshire Gatherings*, 102.

[34] *The Reliquary of depository of precious relics, legendary, biographical and historical* (London vol.2, 1861-2). Pendleton also refers to Phoebe Bown, 60. On Bown, see *The*

Reliquary, vol.2, no.7, January 1862, 137-140. On Molly Bray, see July 1863, 40-42; on centenarians, see vol 8, 1866, 113

[35] *Strange Cornish Characters and Strange Events*; *Devonshire Characters and Strange Events* (London: John Lane/Bodley Head, 1908). Baring-Gould disparaged the fantastic details in earlier sketches produced by the R.S.Hawker, *Footprints of Former Men in Far Cornwall* (London: Russell Smith, 1870). Morwenstow, himself an "identity-conscious" eccentric, was biographised by Baring-Gould and is the subject of a modern study stressing this identity, see Piers Brendon, *Hawker of Morwesntow. Portrait of a Victorian Eccentric* (London: Cape, 1975) who notes that Baring-Gould admitted that he had exaggerated Hawker's eccentricities. See also A.M. Kent, *The Literature of Cornwall. Continuity, Diversity, Difference, 1000-2000* (Bristol: Redcliffe Press, 2000) 104-111.

[36] On the subject of individuality, independence and Cornish identity see B. Deacon and P. Payton, "Re-inventing Cornwall: Culture Change on the European Periphery'" in P. Payton (ed.), *Cornish Studies 1* (Exeter: University of Exeter Press, 1993) 69.

[37] 'Preface', S. Baring-Gould, *Cornish Characters and Strange Events* (London: John Lane/Bodley Head, 1909).

[38] See the comments printed in the advertisement in the catalogue at the back of the 1909 edition.

[39] S. Baring-Gould, *Devonshire Characters and Strange Events* (London: John Lane/ Bodley Head, 1908). Eccentric and strange characters included Princess Caraboo, Joanna Southcott, and the mysterious sisters called the "Ponies of Alphington". The latter were the subject of Staffordshire ware pottery, and lithographs by the local bookseller Edward Cockren of Torquay.

[40] "The Life of Tom Hynes. From his own Narration", *The South Devon Monthly Museum*, 1 April 1835, vol.5, no.28, 85-192.

[41] G and J. Hearder, *The South Devon Monthly Museum*, vol.VI: no.33, 1 September 1835, 97-102.

[42] *Western Antiquary or Devon and Cornwall Note-book* (1881-1894), vol.1 (1881-2), 3, 6; vol.6 (1886-7) 244; and vol.7 (1887-8) 44. a Mr Kearley wanted information on Hynes, Billy the Button Boy, the King of the World, the Admiral (Hot Pieman), Van Daggeran, Mother Fortycats, Bob Cowley, Joe the Newsman and "Dr" Budd, see vol 6, no.10, March 1887, 244. *Devon Notes and Queries* (vol.2, 1903) featured a discussion on Joanna Southcott.

[43] Peter Penn, ed., *Cornish Notes and Queries* (Penzance: Cornish Telegraph Office/ London: Elliot Stock: 1906) 277-280. On one of the characters mentioned in this work, Henry Quick, see Kent, *The Literature of Cornwall*, 96-99.

[44] Hone, *Every-Day Book*, vol.2, 22 April, 267.

[45] J. Caulfield, *Portraits, Memoirs and Characters* 4 vols. (London: T.H. Whiteley, 1819-1820) 38.

[46] Hone, *Every-Day Book*, vol.1, 23 May, 353-354.

[47] My thanks to David Hansen, formerly senior art curator at the Tasmanian Museum and Art Gallery, Hobart, for information on the collection of watercolour studies of British characters, identified as the work of the miniaturist John Dempsey.

[48] See the collection of eccentrics and the brief discussion on Irish eccentricity compared with English, in P. Somerville-Large, *Irish Eccentrics. A Selection* (London: Hamish

Hamilton, 1975). There were eccentrics of wide fame in Ireland, these included Michael Moran (*c.*1794-1846), the blind ballad seller whose fame was perpetuated decades after his death in a short-lived comic magazine using his title, "Zozimus" (Dublin, C.Smyth: 1870-2) and a short essay, "The Last Gleeman", by W.B. Yeats. The categories used by Somerville-Large are the same as those to be found in England and Scotland, and there is a similar body of visual record. But there was not the same volume of printed literature on eccentrics. Somerville-Large argues that the concentration on the Anglo-Irish, if partly stimulated by their environment creating eccentrics, is also the result of the prejudices of writers, who did not class the behaviour of the poor native Irish as eccentric.

[49] Hugh MacDiarmaid's *Scottish Eccentrics* (London: G.Routledge, 1936) is the most famous twentieth-century collection of Scottish characters, literary and national figures such as Lord George Gordon, Lord Monboddo, William McGonagall and "Christopher North". MacDiarmaid explored the "Caledonian *Antisyzygy"* which blended order and fantasy, see N. Gish, "An Interview with MacDiarmid'" *Contemporary History*, 20 (2) (spring 1979) 152, for the poet's comments on "that complexity of character, that interest in a diversity of ideas, and particularity in language, quite un-English. It's been bred out of them to a very large extent".

[50] J. B. Pratt, *Life and Death of Jamie Fleeman* (1831). "Fleemin Bob" has given his name to a pub and cookery book in modern times. On his monument, see F.H. Groome, *Ordnance Gazeteer of Scotland: A Survey of Scottish Topography, Statistical, Biographical and Historical* (T.C. Jack: George Publishing Works, Edinburgh, 1882-1885). He is mentioned in Bram Stoker's short story "Crooken Sands".

[51] See ballads in the National Library of Scotland, for instance "Elegiac Lines on the Tragical Murder of Poor Daft Jamie", Ry111.a.6 (017). The editor of this ballad, William Smith of 3 Bristol Port sold an illustrated life of Jamie, see the British Library collection of Smithiana, 840.m.33, 1 (1-14), which also included an illustrated chapbook life of Boby Awl (Robert Kirkwood), "An Idiot who strolled about Auld Reekie and its Vicinity" (1829).

[52] E.B. Ramsay, *Reminiscences of Scottish Life and Characters* (Edinburgh: Edmonston and Douglas,1874). First published in 1857, Ramsay expanded his work until his death, when the twenty-second edition was published (1874). See the Preface to this edition.

[53] Henry Grey Graham, *The Social Life of Scotland in the Eighteenth Century* (1899). Cited in H and M. Evans, *John Kay of Edinburgh. Barber, miniaturist and social commentator* (Aberdeen: Impulse Publishers, 1973) 11.

[54] An important treatment appears in W. Harvey, *Scottish Life and Character. In Anecdote and Story* (Stirling: E. Mackey, 1899), where a whole chapter, 'The Worthy', 235-267, is devoted to the different types of odd character and their transgressions from kirk to work.

[55] Sir A. Geikie, *Scottish Reminiscences* (Glasgow: Maclehose, 1904) 331. See R.A. Houston, *Madness and Society in Eighteenth Century Scotland* (Oxford: Clarendon Press, 2000) ch.8: "The Language of Insanity. I: Words about the Insane", 332-347, for reference to the colloquial words which were often applied to "characters": such as "daft", "mad", "idiotic" and "silly". As Houston notes, 347, the word "daft" with a contraction of the subject's name, "while implying familiarity and even fondness, compounded the belittling implicit in the term 'daft'"

[56] See A. Wallace, *Popular Traditions of Glasgow: Historical, Legendary and Biographical* (Glasgow: T.D. Morison, 1889) ch.12 (quote at 242-243). Alick appeared in the appendix to John Strang, *Glasgow and its Clubs*. Hawkie, Bob Dragon and others appeared in R. Alison, *The Anecdotage of Glasgow* (Glasgow: T.D.Morison, 1892).

[57] See also *Geikie's Etchings. Illustrations of Scottish Character and Scenery* (Edinburgh: W. Paterson, 1885) for early nineteenth century depictions of characters including 'Show Jamie' and 'Blind Aleck'. For a modern collection, see J.K. Gillon, *Eccentric Edinburgh* (Edinburgh: Mowbray House, 1990).

[58] These ballads are accessible via digitised images at the National Library of Scotland. Hawkie was the subject of a biography: J. Strathesk, *Hawkie. The Autobiography of a Gangrel* (Glasgow: David Robertson, 1880).

[59] Norrie's *Dundee Celebrities of the Nineteenth Century* (Dundee: W.Norrie, 1873) 224-6.

[60] J.S. Neish, *Reminscences of Brechin and its Characters. A Series of Sketches of Well-Known Brechin Worthies* (Dundee: Weekly News Office, 1878).

[61] M. Gregor, *Album of Aberdeen Characters. Ye album of 31 rare and curious portraits* (Aberdeen: Granite City Portrait Gallery); *Life of Blin' Bob (Duncan Mackinlay) Last of the Aberdeen Characters. Sketch of His Life and Times*.

[62] A.R. Adamson, *Rambles through the Land of Burns*, ch.5 (Kilmarnock: Dunlop and Drennan, 1879); J. Monteath, *Dunblane Traditions. Being a series of warlike and legendary narratives, biographical sketches of eccentric characters etc.* (Stirling: E. Johnstone, 1835); A. Mackay, *Sketches of Sutherland Characters* (Edinburgh: James Gemmell, 1889), on the characters William Aberach and Seamas Brochd; and J. Sinclair, *Scenes and Stories of the North of Scotland* (Edinburgh: James Thin/ London: Simpkin Marshall and Co., 1890).

[63] J. Mactaggart, *The Scottish Gallovidian Encyclopaedia. The Original, Antiquated, and Natural Curiosities of the South of Scotland; containing Sketches of Eccentric Characters and Curious Places, with Explanations of singular Words, Terms and Phrases; interspersed with Poems, Tales, Anecdotes, etc and various other strange matters; the whole illustrative of the ways of the Peasantry and manners of Caledonia* (London, 1824) 45. It was reprinted in 1876 and in 1981. See H.C.G. Matthew's entry on Mactaggart in the *Oxford Dictionary of National Biography* (2004), where the author is described as an "independent and piquant character".

[64] "Human beings who want a part of the mind that seemingly they ought to have; who move about, as it were, partly by the dictates of nature, such creatures are common in all countries, and attract the attention of man by their wild and out-of-the-way eccentricities", 361.

[65] Sinclair, *Scenes and Stories of the North of Scotland*, Preface, vi.

[66] J. Horne, *Caithness Originals. With Sixteen Portraits* (Wick: W. Rae, 1906). I am grateful to Sara J. Richardson of Caithness for access to a copy of this work.

[67] I. H. Anderson, *Inverness before Railways* (Inverness: A & W. Mackenzie, 1885), 118.

[68] *Inverness before Railways*, 3.

[69] *Inverness before Railways*, ch.3, 'The Characters of Old Inverness', 118-170. Other chapters featured people of "marked individuality", ranging from ministers to well-known market traders. The publishers, A and W. Mackenzie, who specialised in works of Scottish folklore, and Celtic culture, which catered to the growth of Scottish nationalism in the 1870s-1880s.

[70] *Inverness before Railways*, ch.4, "The Wanderers of Old Inverness", 171-193.

[71] *Inverness before Railways*, 140-141.

[72] See K. Schurer, "Regional Identity and Populations in the Past", in D. Postles (ed.), *Naming, Society and regional Identity* (Oxford: Leopard's Head Press, 2002) 201-227.

[73] Neish, *Reminscences of Brechin and its Characters*, 39. *Kircudbright Advertiser*, 14 September 1888, in its obituary of Johnny Sinclair, wrote of "[m]any a heart in many a place in all quarters of the world" being touched by the news of his death. See transcription in the Kirkcudbright Community Website: http://oldKirkudbright.net/people/worthies/note48a.htm.

[74] See A.J. Kidd, "Between Antiquary and Academic: Local History in the Nineteenth Century", in R.C. Richardson, ed., *The Changing Face of English Local History* (Aldershot: Ashgate, 2000) 94-109.

[75] Alfred. Tennyson, "Locksley Hall", quoted in W. Forsyth, *In the Shadow of Cairngorm. Chronicles of the United Parishes of Abernethy and Kincardine* (Inverness: The Northern Counties Publishing Company, 1900) ch.33. T. Hardy, "The Dorsetshire Labourer", *Longman's Magazine*, July 1883, reprinted in J.M. Golby, *Culture and Society in Britain. 1850-1890* (Oxford: Oxford University Press, 1992), 301.

[76] W.A. Abrams, *Blackburn Characters*, 2.

[77] E.g., W. Forsyth, *In the Shadow of Cairngorm. Chronicles of the United Parishes of Abernethy and Kincardine* (Inverness: The Northern Counties Publishing Company, 1900) ch.33; and the preface to a new edition of G. Beattie, *John o Arnha*.

[78] For the hymning of lost rural individuality and character, and the pursuit of the quaint or "Old English" stylism, see M. J. Wiener, *English Culture and the Decline of the Industrial Spirit. 1850-1980* (Reading: Penguin, 1985).

[79] S. Shesgreen, *Images of the Outcast: the Urban Poor in The Cries of London from the Sixteenth Century to the Nineteenth Century* (Manchester: Manchester University Press, 2002).

[80] They could perform the function of the "in-group deviant" identified by the sociologist Erving Goffman, see Goffman, *Stigma: Notes on the Management of Spoiled Identity* (Englewood Cliffs, New Jersey: Prentice Hall, 1963) 141-45.

[81] Memories are always cultivated: but some are more authentically 'popular' than others. Ballad makers of the North East England used a demotic language, and presented the exploits of eccentric poor people, but were not necessarily "of" the people, nor were their works consumed solely by the people. But collectors of eccentric lives would have argued that they were presenting them as worthies of a *community*.

[82] See for instance the depiction of picturesque London, as discussed in L. Nead, *Victorian Babylon. People, Streets and Images in Nineteenth-Century London* (New Haven and London: Yale University Press, 2000) 32. Some of the characters included as eccentrics and characters- beggars and gypsies- were part of the tradition of the picturesque figure, see P. Garside, "Picturesque Figure and Landscape: Meg Merrilies and the Gypsies", in S. Copley and P. Garside (eds), *The Politics of the Picturesque: Literature, Landscape and Aesthetics since 1770* (Cambridge: Cambridge University Press, 1994).

[83] One observation on this point, albeit from 1919, will suffice. J. Affleck in the *Kirkcudbrightshire Advertiser* observed of the "galaxy of outstanding characters and worthies" that although their failings might be amusing, "yet the ancient burghal life of

Kirkcudbright would be a blank without them". See the electronic version, selected by James Bell, 2003 and published on the Kirkcudbright Community Websites.

[84] See the request for information on "Local Characters, Buskers, Street Entertainers'" at www.knowhere.co.uk, and the various local responses across Britain.

[85] B. Lancaster, *Northern Review,* 3 (summer 1996) 5.

[86] B. Deacon and P. Payton, "Re-inventing Cornwall: Culture Change on the European Periphery", in P. Payton (ed.), *Cornish Studies 1* (Exeter: University of Exeter Press, 1993) 72. Area-defined collections include A.L. Humphreys, *Eccentric Characters of Berkshire* (Reading, 1926), J. Houghton, *Eccentrics and Villains of Northamptonshire, Bedfordshire, Buckinghamshire and Hertfordshire* (Dunstable: Book Castle, 1994), A. Barnes, *Essex Eccentrics* (Ipswich: Boydell Press, 1975). A modernized version of H.P. Parker's painting of Newcastle 'Eccentrics' covers F. Graham's *Northumberland and Durham. A Social and Political Miscellany* (Newcastle: F.Graham, 1979); see also D. Bell and E. Patterson, *Characters of Old Tyneside* (Newcastle: Oriel Press, 1969)

GENTLEMANLY CAPITALISTS, MERCHANT PRINCES AND ANGLO-INDIAN BUSINESS CULTURE IN THE EARLY NINETEENTH CENTURY: JOHN PALMER'S MULTIPLE CONSTRUCTIONS OF IDENTITY

TONY WEBSTER

Between 1757 and 1840, the English East India Company conquered most of the Indian sub-continent, transforming itself from a commercial organisation into an organ of government. While the Company continued with mercantile activities such as the opium trade with China, much of British commercial life in India passed to private, non-EIC organisations, known as agency houses. Between 1780 and 1833, these came to dominate banking, commodity finance and production, shipping, currency exchange and the "Country Trade" between India, China and south east Asia. Their connections became global, with contacts with Britain, mainland Europe, the USA and even South America. These international networks involved personal and commercial relationships with individuals from different cultures, including Indian merchants and producers. Inevitably this meant that an appropriate image and reputation were central to the business. This article will explore the creation of a multi-faceted identity by the most prominent of the agency house merchants, John Palmer (1767-1836).

A considerable literature exists on the importance of reputation, trust and identity in the operation of commercial relationships. Sociological research has identified the importance of repeated exchange relations between individuals and firms in developing mutual trust, and in reducing the likelihood of malfeasance.[1] In the difficult conditions of international trade in the late eighteenth and early nineteenth centuries, there were few effective external constraints to curb dishonesty and protect participants. Poor communications, endemic official corruption, war and ineffective systems for monitoring business practices placed at a premium the ability to trust the reputation of distant trading partners in unfamiliar places. Even in modern times, where external checks on behaviour exist, they remain notoriously unreliable.[2] In the context under study, individual reputation and identity were virtually the only basis for trust, and were central to the development of global networks of commerce. But inevitably, acquisition of an attractive image depends upon conformity to the social norms and values of the time. In the period in question, these were shaped by expectations related to kinship ties, patronage, paternalism and Christian morality. In this respect, the notion of "rational economic man" applying principles, logic and behaviours which are disconnected from the existing social context has been challenged. Rather, the rationality which guides economic behaviour is "embedded" in the socio-cultural context of the time.[3] The analysis of reputation as identity formation offered here provides insights into both the commercial behaviour of European merchants in early colonial India, and the commercial disaster which befell British India between 1830 and 1834.

The nature of the agency houses and their business to a large extent determined the construction of an appropriate commercial identity. The first agency houses were established by European private traders not in the service of the East India Company (EIC) during the 1780s. They engaged in commercial activities which did not infringe the EIC's monopoly of trade between Britain and India. Most houses were owned and managed by between three and six European partners. An Indian merchant (*banian*) usually conducted commercial relations with Indian entrepreneurs, helped by a team of European and Indian clerks. Besides engagement in the country trade and the export of opium to China, the houses also invested in shipping, cotton, coffee and indigo production. Crucially, the houses also provided banking facilities. Following financial crises in the 1770s and 1780s the EIC sought help from the British government. Aid was made conditional on major reforms in the EIC's system of administration, particularly the elimination of corrupt private commercial ventures by Company servants. Under Lord Cornwallis, Governor General during the late 1780s, most EIC servants were barred from commerce on their own account, and were compensated by substantial increases in salary.[4] Many EIC employees now earned substantial sums which needed to be safely invested, or repatriated to Britain. By providing banking facilities for Company servants, the houses secured a vast reservoir of capital for loans and investment in commercial activities all over the east. Relationships between agency house partners and their depositors were therefore close, based upon the provision of financial services to meet specific personal circumstances. Indian merchants also took advantage of the opportunities they offered. Agency house partners became closely acquainted with their clients and advised them on more than just financial matters. Similar relationships also developed with agency house debtors, whose domestic circumstances often dictated their ability to service their debts.

An important line of business was the repatriation of the funds of clients. Some needed to send money home to support relatives or finance their own retirement and business deals. Partners in the agency houses also needed to transfer their earnings. These were effected by the agency houses exporting to Britain commodities such as indigo, coffee or EIC bills of exchange payable in London, on their own or their clients' account. Even before the EIC monopoly of trade with India was abolished in 1813, this was possible through the so called "privilege trade", the limited cargo space allowed aboard EIC ships for the Captain and other senior officers to export goods home for sale on their own account. Agency houses bought such space from the officers for their own exports. The sale of commodities in London was not left to chance. Each Calcutta agency house dealt with one or more "corresponding" agency houses in London, firms usually set up by retiring partners from the Calcutta firm. The London East India agency houses sold the goods imported from their Indian sister firms, and for a commission, managed the British financial interests of both partners and clients of the Indian house. Indian agency house partners frequently retired to join the London corresponding firms, repatriating their share of the Indian firm's profits to buy a stake in the London firm. The London houses emerged in the early nineteenth centuries as major stock holders in the East India Company itself, and some of their leading figures emerged as directors of the Company, and powerful figures in their own right.[5]

But the Indian agency houses were not only important for the EIC servants, soldiers, private entrepreneurs and Indian merchants who invested in or borrowed from them. The fortunes of the EIC itself became bound up with the houses. Between 1780 and 1830 to pay for wars with Mysore, the Marathas, Nepal and Burma, the Company in India had to sell government securities (government "bills" or" paper") to its own servants and to the Indian mercantile community. This required the co-operation of the agency houses, not only as purchasers of government paper in their own right, but also in recommending it to their clients. This was problematic since money invested by their clients in government paper often had to be withdrawn by depositors from their agency house accounts. However, co-operation with the Bengal government brought political influence, which compensated for financial loss. In the 1820s, when the agency houses experienced hardship, the Bengal Council sanctioned loans to enable them to stave off crisis. Close relations with the Bengal Council ensured policies amenable to agency house interests, and brought the custom of senior, wealthy EIC officials. The agency houses exported Indian opium to China, vital to the EIC since it furnished profitable return cargoes to Europe in Chinese tea, silks and ceramics. The agency houses smuggled EIC produced opium into China in defiance of the imperial prohibition on import of the commodity. This protected the EIC from accusations of smuggling by the Chinese authorities. The agency house representatives then paid the receipts of opium sales into the EIC treasury at Canton, in return for EIC bills of exchange payable in either London or Calcutta. The arrangement provided the EIC with currency to purchase Chinese produce which it shipped to London on its own ships. In return, the agency houses acquired a secure medium (EIC bills) for the transmission of profits back to Calcutta or London. The China trade epitomised the symbiotic relationship which emerged between the EIC and the agency houses. Consequently for the agency houses, the EIC was one of several important constituencies which had to be placated. The agency houses needed to be seen as trustworthy, not only by the EIC, but also its servants, soldiers and directors in London. Indian merchants, producers, the London corresponding agency houses, and even the representatives of foreign empires, such as the Dutch in south east Asia, were also key groups who had to be satisfied that the agency houses were virtuous, responsible, and competent. The creation of an identity which met the expectations of all of these separate communities was essential for the agency houses. Sometimes the conflicting interests of different stakeholders required that the houses be different things to different clients. It will be seen how one agency house, John Palmer and Co., and its leading partner, created an identity which achieved an unsurpassed degree of success.

John Palmer rose to prominence in the 1790s, first as a partner in the agency house of Barber, Palmer and Co., and from 1800 in the firm of Cockerell, Trail and Co. By April 1809, the latter had become John Palmer and Company, a title it kept until failure in January 1830.[6] The firm became the most celebrated of the agency houses, and Palmer's reputation was legendary in India and Britain. Besides involvement in shipping, indigo production and the opium trade, Palmer and Co. developed extensive commercial relations with the Dutch East Indies, the USA and south east Asia. Following difficulties in the 1820s, the failure of the house so destabilised the Calcutta commercial community that by 1834 all of the other agency houses had suffered the same fate. Palmer's methods of business therefore offer important insights into the calamity of the early 1830s.

Palmer's background both helped and hindered his commercial career. His father, William Palmer rose to Lieutenant-General in the EIC's army, and John exploited his father's senior connections in the army. John's own experience as a midshipman in the navy also smoothed relations with military men.[7] The inter-racial composition of Palmer's family offered other opportunities. John was a child of William's first marriage, but the latter's second marriage to Fyze Baksh, a *begum* (Muslim noblewoman) produced Anglo-Indian siblings.[8] One of these, William Palmer, was an EIC soldier in Hyderabad, but in 1808 set up his own agency house, with the local ruler, the *Nizam* as his principal client.[9] John supplied his brother with advice and capital. He also defended William Palmer and Co. when it was accused of usury in 1820 by Charles Metcalfe, the British Resident at Hyderabad.[10] The cross racial composition of John Palmer's extended family opened access to the Indian community, enabling John to acquire a favourable reputation with Indian merchants and clients.

Palmer cultivated a personal image which could maximise these advantages of birth and circumstance. Two historians have noted his tendency to tell his audience what he thought it wanted to hear, and his reluctance to espouse controversial opinions.[11] Such traits are unsurprising in entrepreneurs at any time, but they were developed by Palmer to an extraordinary degree. His correspondence demonstrates a deliberate strategy of projecting at least four overlapping images of himself which would attract and entice business, and which together formed a very powerful and distinct identity. These "personas" were: "the public and charitable face of British commerce", "the avuncular family man and personal friend", "the defender of the Indian", and "the political sophisticate". Together these constituted Palmer's identity as a "merchant prince" who combined business acumen, wealth, high moral principle and social conscience in all of his dealings, projecting an impression of aristocratic virtue. How did Palmer develop these images of himself? How did they benefit the business, and what problems did they cause?

Francis Rawdon, the Marquis of Hastings and Governor General from 1814 until 1823, was so impressed by John Palmer's wealth and benevolence that he dubbed him the "prince of merchants".[12] It was a title which implied many things. William Prinsep, a partner in Palmer and Co. in its latter years felt it encompassed Palmer's kindness and generosity, as well as his high social status and wealth.[13] However, the full implications of Hastings' tribute are only clear in its historical context. At the time, a global war was being fought to defend the traditional European social order against the threats of revolution and republicanism. In spite of the advances made by those social classes associated with capitalism and industry, Britain remained firmly under the political control of the aristocratic elite. In this context, Hastings was referring to more than Palmer's wealth or "noble" personal characteristics. Palmer was as trustworthy and as interested in the existing order as an aristocrat, and as such was to be regarded as one of the ruling elite. This was not an unusual phenomenon in Hanoverian England and its colonies. Cain and Hopkins have identified the emergence of a class of "gentlemanly capitalists" who developed close links with the aristocracy and adopted their social etiquette and value system.[14] They were bankers and merchants based in the City of London, who from the late seventeenth century supported the British state by funding the National Debt. Increasingly, aristocratic landowners turned to them for finance, and a close affinity evolved between the two groups. Successful gentlemanly capitalists took advantage of the "open" nature of the British aristocracy, and bought their way into its ranks. For example, City families such as the Rothschilds and the Barings were absorbed into the aristocracy during the nineteenth century, regardless of their modest social and foreign origins. Many "gentlemanly capitalists" built their fortunes through colonial commerce, some through the EIC. In this respect, John Palmer was following a familiar path: the creation of a fortune overseas and the cultivation of social superiors well placed to promote one's further advancement after retirement to Britain. Many had followed Robert Clive in using colonial wealth for upward social mobility at home. In this way, Bowen argues that the empire created a trans-continental, imperial "international order of gentlemen", rather than one confined to Britain and the City of London.[15]

Indeed, the partner whose place Palmer took in 1801, Sir Charles Cockerell, was the epitome of a gentleman capitalist created in India. Cockerell rose from the lowly rank of EIC writer in 1775 to become a Senior Merchant, leaving the Company in the early 1790s to join the agency house of Paxton Cockerell and Trail.[16] The financial assistance he gave for Governor-General Richard Wellesley's campaigns against the Sultan of Mysore in 1798-99 were rewarded with a Baronetcy in 1809. After returning to Britain to join the London corresponding house of his former Calcutta firm, he became MP for a succession of parliamentary seats. Marriage in 1808 to the daughter of John Rushout, Baron of Northwick, and the acquisition of Sezincote House near Evesham established Cockerell as a member of the nobility. Cockerell continued to handle the personal finances of the Wellesley family (including the Duke of Wellington), and became a Commissioner on the Board of Control in 1835, the government department responsible for overseeing the affairs of the EIC.[17] Contemporaries anticipated that Palmer would achieve even greater success. How did Palmer construct the component aspects of his "princely" status, and how did they assist the business?

Integral to Palmer's quasi-aristocratic image was a high public profile, which portrayed the virtues associated with the nobility. This included the lavish display of wealth associated with high birth. As early as 1801, Palmer had acquired a house intended to herald his arrival as a man of substance. He employed the master builder, Richard Blechynden to renovate a house at Ishera, just north of Calcutta, creating a home designed to impress the highest ranks of Calcutta society.[18] Several years later, he acquired a mansion in the Lal Bazaar, near the Writer's building, a palace so imposing that it became the subject of a coloured aquatint by James Baillie Fraser.[19] The house was the scene of dinners and other entertainments, intended to bolster Palmer's reputation.[20] An auction inventory for another property owned later by Palmer demonstrates his opulent lifestyle.[21] Besides an enormous quantity of fine plate, thirteen chandeliers, "three of the largest and finest pier glasses in India", there was also a Stoddart grand piano, a collection of ornamental Malay swords and an "extensive and valuable library". There was also a sizeable house on Penang to be sold off.[22] Such ostentation was common among Calcutta's mercantile elite. William Huggins, a commentator on the indigo trade, castigated the Calcutta agency house merchants as a class for their "princely style", "stateliness" and selfishness.[23] Palmer also coveted high office to enhance his reputation. In March 1799 he was elected Commissioner of the Public Lottery in Calcutta.[24] It was the beginning of public life which embraced many roles. Palmer became the head of numerous commercial organisations. In February 1816, Palmer chaired a committee which represented the insurance companies of Calcutta.[25] In 1823 a London based pressure group campaigning for the British retention of

Singapore in defiance of Dutch claims to the island, charged Palmer with the task of rallying his fellow Calcutta agency house merchants to the cause.[26] Two years later, Palmer's office saw the first attempt to establish what would have been a Calcutta chamber of commerce.[27] In September 1818, Palmer had even established his own newspaper, *The Calcutta Journal*, to promote both himself and his friend the Governor-General, Lord Hastings.[28] Unsurprisingly the paper extolled its owner's charitable virtues to the public. In March 1819 it reported a toast to Palmer made at a dinner of the "Sons of Erin" on St Patrick's Day, which described him as "a man whose generosity is bounded only by the distress which surrounds him".[29] Palmer displayed a mastery of what would today be called "Public Relations". This carefully cultivated public image of a fabulously wealthy, politically influential, yet socially responsible and caring man, was very good for business. It created an impression of financial solidity, an enticing prospect for the Company servant or soldier seeking a safe and profitable refuge for his savings. His engagement in mercantile organisations promoted Palmer as a man of impeccable judgement, chosen for leadership by his peers in the business community. If they respected his word, so also should the lowly Company employee. Charitable works further emphasised Palmer's reputation for trustworthiness, suggesting motivation by higher moral considerations.

In his personal dealings, Palmer sought to reinforce this public image of the caring yet competent entrepreneur. Palmer presented himself as a loyal friend who took a deep interest in the well being of his clients. This was particularly apparent in his relations with new arrivals from Britain, usually young army officers or EIC writers. Palmer offered advice, care and occasionally even accommodation in his own home. In January 1811, Palmer reassured Henry Trail, senior partner in Palmer's sister London East India agency house Paxton, Cockerell and Trail, that the young son of Mr Kennedy, a mutual acquaintance, would be given all assistance in establishing a successful Indian military career.[30] Wayward youngsters were chastised and guided to better behaviour. When Thomas Arrow became inebriated at Palmer's table in June 1813, the merchant prince admonished the young man, warning him of the dangers of drink. He also wrote to Captain James Arrow, Thomas's older brother, advising him of disturbing reports about the younger brother's drunkenness.[31] Palmer also kept anxious relatives informed about the progress of their children in India, especially when the relative enjoyed high status. In 1823, Palmer wrote to Major-General Stuart about his nephew in the Indian army, explaining that the young man was using his credit with Palmer and Co. wisely, though he was not popular with his officers.[32] Palmer was seen as a barometer of career opportunities for the young. In September 1823 he advised a Lieutenant Colonel Morrell against a legal career for his son in India, suggesting instead that Morrell purchase an indigo factory for him.[33] Where the enquiring parent, relative or patron enjoyed a senior position in the Company hierarchy,

Palmer was most indulgent. When in 1818 Colonel S. Toone, an EIC director, asked Palmer to help place his son in a position in India, Palmer promised to try to get him into the Guards, on the understanding that Toone would help the son of one of Palmer's friends obtain a Company cadetship in Bengal.[34]

Palmer's large family of twelve children and his comfortable domestic circumstances helped to project an image of an empathic and socially sensitive businessman. Letters to associates and clients frequently digressed into accounts of the progress, problems and failings of Palmer's children, promoting strong feelings of personal intimacy with the merchant prince. Clients were frequently taken under the wing of the family. As a favour to Sir Charles Cockerell, a Miss Ford stayed with the Palmers for several years in the early 1820s while she sought a suitable marriage partner.[35] When in 1809 one Major Weguilin was arranging to send his children home to England from Dinapore, Palmer offered to accommodate them in Calcutta.[36] In the same year Palmer took in a young Mr Standley, brought to Palmer by Dr Glas of Baugulpore, to nurse back to health following a serious illness.[37] This reputation as a generous family man, able to empathise with families separated by the necessities of employment in India, brought business flocking to Palmer's door. Palmer and Co. developed a thriving business in managing wills, estates and trusts for the families of EIC servants and other Europeans, the importance of which is hard to overestimate. When Palmer and Co. failed in 1830, monies held by the firm in trust for dependants amounted to Rs1,816,492, or 10.9 per cent of the firm's total creditors by value. The total number of trusts managed at the time of the firm's failure was 116, and it also controlled the estates of 48 families. Monies held under will arrangements (estates) amounted to Rs1,213,387 (7.3 per cent of total creditors by value).[38] This demonstrates the importance of "family" business as a source of working capital for the firm. The insolvency papers in Calcutta throw light on some individual trust arrangements. For example, in 1818, one Lt Colonel Thomas Hawkins of the EIC died in England, and named Palmer and Co. as joint executors to manage his estate, worth Rs10,000. The principal beneficiary was Mrs Harriet Hunter, and when her husband died in 1819, she and her five children depended solely upon Hawkins' legacy. Palmer emerged as the senior executor, taking responsibility for managing the fund, thereby ensuring that the Hunters' family life, education and prospects could be sustained.[39] Palmer's reputation as a compassionate family man was crucial in winning such business. This was one reason why the failure of the firm, caused so much ruin and bitterness. The vestry at St John's Church was left to pick up some of the pieces. Ann Mayer, widow of George Henry Mayer, a senior official in the Secret and Political department of the EIC administration, was left penniless and "reduced to the greatest distress", together with her five young children, by the loss of the family's savings in the failure of Palmer and Co.[40] Mary Craig, the Irish widow of a non-commissioned officer was left to tend her four children in a small room near the Calcutta military barracks, and was thrown upon the vestry for relief.[41] Ironically, such misery was testimony to the success of Palmer's "family friendly" business strategy. The firm even employed the services of the lawyer Augustus Frederick Hamilton, attorney at the Calcutta Supreme Court. Hamilton provided legal advice to the firm's clients on trusts, wills and other matters of personal or property law.[42] Palmer's image as the personal friend of his clients, did more than secure funds for the firm. It helped create of a global network of trusted contacts which were used for many purposes. These included patronage and assistance for valued clients, which further reinforced Palmer's reputation for generosity and influence. It also ensured that Palmer could be informed of any dangerous developments, and recruited allies to defend his interests. For example, when in 1813 rumours were circulating on the island of Java that Palmer and Co. was in serious financial trouble, the firm's reputation was stalwartly defended on Palmer's request by two clients in the EIC's service.[43]

But Palmer's efforts to secure a reputation for friendship were most assiduously pursued in relations with Indians. The success of the agency houses depended upon the cultivation of close ties with the Indian commercial community. Palmer enjoyed high esteem among Indians as shown poignantly at the time of the failure of Palmer and Co. Within a month, numerous wealthy Indian merchants had devised a scheme for advancing Rs20 lakhs to the firm, under which five years would be allowed for it to honour its debts.[44] Only the monumental scale of Palmer and Co.'s debts thwarted the plan. The response of the Indian community was the result of a lifetime of careful cultivation of Indian merchants by John Palmer. Patronage exercised on behalf of Europeans was extended to Palmer's Indian friends and clients. In September 1818, Palmer sought a lucrative post in the Customs office at Murshidabad for a friend of the merchant Roy Ramsoonder Mitter.[45] Early in 1824, Palmer recommended the young Janoky Doolet Tagore for employment, commending the young man's "honesty and diligence".[46] Even the lowliest of Indians were known to attract Palmer's sympathy. In April 1822, Palmer petitioned James Harington, Acting Judge and Magistrate of Jessore, Bengal, on behalf of one Din Mahommed, the coach driver of W.E. Phillips, Governor of Penang. In 1802, at the age of eight Din Mahommed had been convicted of a robbery in Jessore and transported to Penang, where he met Palmer on a visit to Governor Phillips.[47] Palmer sought a pardon for the young man, but the Jessore court could not find the records of the case.[48] Indian employees of the firm were accorded great respect, and Palmer reacted swiftly when he discovered in November 1826 that one of his junior clerks, Thomas Munshaw had struck a Bengali servant. Munshaw was dismissed, and though Palmer relented and re-admitted him to the firm, the message was clear that physical abuse of Indians was unacceptable.[49] At a time when such humane considerations were rare, Palmer even extended it to the poorest Indian labourer. When Luckeen Sirdar, a Mullingee salt worker at the firm's salt works at Gunga Saugor (Saugor Island, south of Calcutta) complained that he had been beaten by Mr Rees, the salt works supervisor, Palmer expressly forbade any further use of violence, and instructed Rees to allow the salt workers greater freedom to organise their work.[50] In 1829, shortly before the failure of the firm, Palmer described himself as a defender of Indians in the face of deteriorating European attitudes towards them, though he received little sympathy in official circles for this stance.[51] Palmer also associated with prominent Indians of the day. Ram Mohun Roy, the emerging Indian intellectual and political leader was feted by Palmer. In 1818 Palmer sent him a flattering review of Roy's career, published in an American newspaper.[52] Four years later, Palmer donated money for the establishment of a Unitarian Church in Calcutta; one of Roy's most cherished projects.[53] Palmer was so confident that his firm's reputation within the Indian community was unrivalled, that in 1827 he openly boasted of it when petitioning the Bengal Government for financial aid.[54]

There is also compelling evidence that Palmer's high standing in Indian opinion was deliberately cultivated, and that it probably did not reflect Palmer's private view of Indians and their culture. In his communications with fellow Europeans, Palmer was frequently scathing about Indians, employing the negative racist stereotypes which were becoming common currency during the period. Discussing the problems in securing reliable supplies of cotton from Indians in August 1809, Palmer grumbled that he could:

"scarcely remember one single instance of good faith in Blackey since I have been in business – as they never deliver the goods they sell anything like the musters they produce, and one is always sure to be the worse off both for the bargain and the dispute"[55]

The alleged avarice of Indian merchants was a constant complaint by Palmer. Indian indigo planters were tempted into reckless speculations by their "greediness of gain".[56] European clients and friends were warned against borrowing from Indian moneylenders (*shroffs*) because of their rapacious terms.[57] Indians involved in the collection of opium were accused of adulterating the quality of the crop.[58] In spite of Palmer's claims to be a defender of Indian rights, and a supporter of educational initiatives to help them, he believed that there were racial boundaries which should not be crossed. When in 1813 a protégé of Palmer's, the nephew of Sir Charles Mallet, wanted to marry the Eurasian daughter of one Mr Du Plessis, Palmer tried to persuade the Governor General, Lord Minto to forbid the marriage on the grounds that the woman was "as black as coal and utterly uneducated".[59] Although Palmer recommended his friend Bundeh Ali Khan for employment to a Mr Macleod at Patna, he was critical of the Indian's efforts to adopt western manners and customs. Palmer saw employment with Macleod as necessary for the young Indian's "redemption".[60] Even in his dealings with his Anglo-Indian half brother, John Palmer bluntly referred to colour as a determinant of how people should be treated. He advised William Palmer to send his daughter for education in Europe only if she was of fair complexion.[61] If dark skinned, he recommended the United States as a more suitable location. Ultimately, Palmer supported the subordination of the Indian people to the benefits of British rule.[62] In expressing such opinions to a selected European audience, Palmer aimed to be all things to all men; a friend to the Indian in dealings with Indians, and the contemptuous member of the "master race" to most fellow Europeans. Palmer thus offered contrasting identities to different but equally coveted sections of colonial society.

Palmer realised early in his career the importance of powerful political friends, and acquiring a reputation for political sophistication and influence. He therefore sought clients in the highest ranks of the Bengal administration. In 1798, when Palmer was a senior partner in Barber, Palmer and Co., he shipped Madeira and Chinese goods to Britain belonging to Sir John Shore, the Governor General.[63] In May 1801, the firm shipped madeira to Britain for Shore's successor, the Marquis of Wellesley.[64] Nearly a decade later, Palmer blamed the loss of Lord Cornwallis's business on the machinations of rivals in London.[65] But although attempts to win the accounts of Lord Minto and the Marquis of Hastings failed, Palmer established a close relationship with the latter which lasted until Hastings' departure from India in 1822.[66] This friendship promoted Palmer as someone whose political influence made him immune to the hazards of a turbulent commercial world, making it easier to attract and keep the deposits of investors. It also helped secure government contracts and official positions. By 1813, Palmer and Co. were the government commercial agents for Penang, Ceylon and were expecting shortly to secure the same positions for Mauritius, New South Wales and Java. Henry St George Tucker, a former business partner and the Accountant General in the Bengal administration, helped in the campaign to secure the Mauritius agency.[67] Political influence in the East India Company also brought international opportunities, as demonstrated in Palmer's relations with the Dutch colonial administration of Java, re-established at the end of the war in 1815. Palmer and Co.'s reputation for political influence won it the agency in India of the Dutch East Indies Colonial government.[68] The Dutch resented the British acquisition of Singapore in 1819, and made strenuous but unsuccessful efforts to persuade the British to abandon it during the negotiations leading to the Treaty of London of 1824. They regarded John Palmer as someone who could provide intelligence on British intentions. In December 1821 Palmer offered his opinions on British intentions to his Dutch correspondents, aiming to promote more harmonious relations between the two powers.[69] From Palmer and Co.'s point of view, this political relationship with the Dutch opened potentially lucrative commercial opportunities. Tarling shows how during the early 1820s, the Dutch colonial government asked Palmer to raise loans, a requirement which the firm was unable to meet because of current economic difficulties in India.[70] Knight shows that the firm also pursued ventures in coffee plantations on Java.[71] This amply demonstrates that Palmer's name as a political operator brought tangible international commercial opportunities.

Thus, Palmer's identity as a merchant prince, with its component qualities of wealth, nobility, civic and political leadership, combined with charitable compassion, social grace and a kind of *noblesse oblige* in dealing with social inferiors, was ideally suited to the nature of the business. It ensured a supply of capital in the form of funds entrusted with the firm by a wide spectrum of Europeans and Indians impressed by Palmer's reputation for solidity and kindliness towards his clients. It also opened commercial opportunities with governments and other institutions at home and abroad. Unquestionably a great deal of Palmer's success rested on the identity he fashioned. The reverse side of the coin was that it also contributed significantly to the firm's downfall in 1830. Palmer's financial generosity and lavish expenditure were powerful commercial assets when the Indian economy was buoyant, and when competition was restricted to the handful of agency houses who dominated commerce before the end of the Company's India monopoly. After 1813, however, new waves of British entrepreneurs flocked to India, creating a much more competitive climate, in which financial discipline and shrewd calculations of risk were essential for survival. In addition, post monopoly Indian economy proved far more unpredictable than expected. Sudden economic downturns could now trigger widespread commercial failure and default on debt. In 1824 the outbreak of war with Burma forced the EIC to borrow vast amounts in order to fight a campaign lasting over two years.[72] To attract funds, the EIC paid higher rates on its borrowings, threatening to drain the agency houses of capital as depositors withdrew their funds to take advantage of the higher return on Company paper. Consequently the houses themselves had to pay higher rates of interest, which quickly plunged most of the houses into severe financial difficulties. In this harsher environment, it was imperative that the houses adopt a much more rigorous attitude to their financial affairs. The margin for generosity was very thin indeed, and Palmer's strategy of liberality proved woefully inappropriate in a number of ways.

The first problem was Palmer's attitude to those who owed money to him and the firm. Palmer and Co. advanced substantial amounts of money to indigo producers to generate supplies of the commodity for export to Britain and Europe. The supplies themselves formed all or part of the servicing and repayment of the producer's debt, but all too frequently they failed to meet obligations. The market for indigo was notoriously unstable due to climate and the dual function of the crop as a medium of remittance and a source of commercial profit. Indigo producers frequently borrowed from local shroffs as well as the agency houses, increasing the danger that defalcation and bankruptcy would have devastating consequences for the wider commercial community. Consequently Palmer, like other agency house merchants, took a tolerant view of debt, allowing frequent rescheduling of payments. However, Palmer's need to maintain a reputation for "humane liberality" pushed him to greater displays of tolerance than most of his contemporaries. As early as 1809, two thirds of the firm's indigo debtors were on the verge of default.[73] The problem worsened as the commercial environment of the eastern trade became more volatile due to war, monsoon and the ending of the EIC's monopoly in 1813. By 1820, some Rs 100 lakhs (about £1.25 million) had been written off by the firm.[74] Palmer and Co.'s London correspondents, Paxton, Cockerell and Trail, were always alarmed at Palmer's leniency towards debtors, fearing that the burden might ultimately fall on them. But Palmer stoutly defended his liberal policy.[75] By the 1820s, a new generation of partners in the firm were pressing for a more disciplined policy towards debt, which would involve defaulting debtors forfeiting their property. Reluctantly Palmer complied, and by the time of its bankruptcy the firm owned twenty one indigo factories, and were part owners of twenty two others.[76] But although he made some concessions to his partners and colleagues in Calcutta and London, Palmer yielded these grudgingly. He continued to surrender to impulsive gestures of imprudent generosity. For example, when in the summer of 1823 a close friend of his, one Captain Hunter, was dismissed from the EIC's service following allegations of fraud, Palmer purchased an indigo factory for him, on a loose arrangement under which Hunter would repay Palmer once the factory had been established as a going concern.[77]

Additional problems further exasperated partners in Britain and India. Palmer's insistence upon maintaining an ostentatiously lavish lifestyle met with severe criticism, and although he agreed to personal economics, the other partners believed it had severely compromised the financial health of the business.[78] Other practices which reflected Palmer's generosity also came to be seen as a problem. Between 1810 and the early 1820s Palmer built up a substantial fleet of ships, which totalled some twenty four vessels by 1822.[79] Most of the vessels were jointly owned by the firm and the captains of the ships. It seemed at first an ideal arrangement, sharing as it did the costs of trading ventures as well as the profits. But as William Prinsep reflected many years later, Palmer extended his liberality to the captains, applying minimum scrutiny of their affairs. The ships' captains took advantage mercilessly, to the extent that Prinsep claimed that very few of the shipping ventures of the firm made a profit, as the ships' captains brazenly cheated Palmer and Co.[80] Indeed Palmer's preoccupation with the firm's external relations contributed to a woeful lack of internal scrutiny of the firms affairs. A few months after Palmer and Co. failed it emerged that several Indian employees had been systematically pilfering cash from the firm since 1807, to the tune of some Rs 20 lakhs (c£200,000).[81] Astonishingly, Palmer confessed to harbouring suspicions as early as 1816, but failed to act upon them, lest, one suspects, such action might undermine his reputation with the Indian community.[82]

Such naivety drove his partners to distraction. In the end, it and the weight of bad debt proved instrumental in the downfall of the firm. During the 1820s, several partners, despairing of Palmer's cavalier attitude to the management of the business, took advantage of the shortcomings in internal financial security and siphoned off funds to Britain, to relaunch their careers at home.83 The most prominent of these, John Studholme Brownrigg, joined the London sister house of Cockerell and Trail, who were then fully apprised of the organisational deficiencies of Palmer and Co. Unsurprisingly, it was they who precipitated the bankruptcy of the firm at the end of 1829 by demanding that Palmer and Co. instantly repay a substantial portion of the huge debt it had run up to the London house. It was this demand, which Palmer simply could not meet, which prompted the firm to close its doors for the last time in early January 1830.

John Palmer's efforts to base the fortunes of his firm upon a consciously devised identity, based upon the predominantly aristocratic mores of his day, thus contributed to the downfall as well as the rise of the firm. His was not an untypical approach to business. Most of the successful agency houses to some extent employed Palmer's strategy of cultivating a reputation for high standards of morality and congenial support for their clients. As Granovetter would have it, this was a system of commercial rationality which was embedded in the social and cultural norms of the time and cultural context.[84] On return to London, many either joined the ranks of the gentry, or continued to apply their "gentlemanly" business practices in London. In this respect, as Bowen argues, the factors which promoted gentlemanly capitalism stemmed from circumstances at the periphery of empire, as well as from within British society itself.[85] Yet Palmer's reputation was such that he took this business philosophy to the extreme, a factor which contributed greatly to the failure of 1830. Palmer's failure served as a warning for commercial entrepreneurs to balance the maintenance of a popular reputation with stringent observation of sound business practice. Embedded commercial rationality had to change to meet the demands of a more competitive and unstable economic context. When Palmer died in 1836, several obituaries referred to Palmer's "softness of heart" and "an excess of generosity" as major roots of his failure as a businessman.[86] It should be remembered however that gentlemanly capitalism survived and flourished despite the crisis of 1830, and other serious ones later in the nineteenth century. But perhaps the greatest symbolic triumph of Palmer's carefully constructed identity was the fact that, in spite of all the misery his bankruptcy caused, his personal reputation survived. A substantial crowd attended his funeral and all of the obituaries celebrated his generosity, charity and nobility of spirit. Such was the enduring identity of the "prince of merchants".

[1] E.J. Lawler, "Commitment in Exchange Relations: Test of a Theory of Relational Cohesion" *American Sociological Review* 61 (1996) 89-108; 89.

[2] S.P. Shapiro, "The Social Control of Impersonal Trust" *American Journal of Sociology* 93:3 (1987) 623-658; 652-653.

[3] M. Granovetter, "Economic Action and Social Structure: The Problem of Embeddedness" *American Journal of Sociology* 91:3 (1985) 481-510.

[4] A. Tripathi, *Trade and Finance in the Bengal Presidency 1793-1833* (Calcutta: OUP, 1979) 8-9.

[5] See for example the career of David Scott, the Bombay agency house merchant, who returned to Britain to found David Scott and Co. and become a most influential Company director and Member of Parliament in the 1790s and early 1800s, ibid., 21-23.

[6] John Palmer to J. Baker, Madras 3 April 1809 Mss Eng Lett c70 155, Papers of John Palmer, Bodleian Library, Oxford.

[7] Palmer to his mother, 16 December 1782 Mss Eng Lett d105, 1.

[8] W. Dalrymple, *White Mughals: Love and Betrayal in Eighteenth Century India* (London: Harper Collins, 2002) 277.

[9] M.H. Fisher, *Indirect Rule in India: Residents and the Residency System 1764-1858* (Delhi: OUP, 1998) 389-90.

[10] Z. Yazdani, *Hyderabad during the Residency of Henry Russell 1811-1820: A Case Study of the Subsidiary Alliance system* (Oxford: OUP, 1976) 49-50, 60-70.

[11] C.E. Wurtzburg, *Raffles of the Eastern Isles* (London: Hodder and Stoughton, 1954) 525; C.A. Gibson-Hill, "Raffles, Acheh and the Order of the Golden Sword" *Journal of the Malaysian Branch of the Royal Asiatic Society* 29:1 (1956) 1-20; 2.

[12] Obituary of John Palmer in the Calcutta Courier 22 January 1836; cited in the papers of John Palmer, Mss Eng lett d.107, 210.

[13] Memoirs of William Prinsep Eur Mss D1160/1, 252, British Library (BL), London.

[14] See P.J. Cain and A.G. Hopkins, *British Imperialism 1688-2000* (London: Pearson, 2001).

[15] H.V. Bowen, "Gentlemanly Capitalism and the Making of a Global British Empire: Some Connections and Contexts, 1688-1815" in S. Akita (ed.), *Gentlemanly Capitalism, Imperialism and Global History* (Basingstoke: Palgrave Macmillan, 2002) 19-42; 36.

[16] R.G. Thorne, *The House of Commons 1790-1820s III: Members A-F* (London: Secker and Warburg, 1986) 469.

[17] Mr Lightfoot to Sir Charles Cockerell 23 February 1818, Cockerell and Grieve Papers, Dep c.860, 14, Bodliean Library, Oxford. This provides important insights into Cockerell's role as financial adviser to the Duke of Wellington.

[18] The episode is recorded in Blechynden's diary, almost on a daily basis between August 1801 and December 1802. See the diary of Richard Blechynden, Add Mss45618-45623, British Library, London.

[19] See J.P. Losty, *Calcutta: City of Palaces* (London: The British Library, 1990) 88-9.

[20] Prinsep Memoirs Eur Mss D1160/1, 252-254.

[21] Advertisement by Leyburn and Co., *Bengal Hurkaru*, Monday 15 February 1830.

[22] *Bengal Hurkaru,* Wednesday 17 February 1830.

[23] W. Huggins, *Sketches in India, Treating on subjects connected with the government, civil and military establishments, characters of the European and customs of the native inhabitants* (London: John Letts, 1824) 75.

[24] *Calcutta Gazette* 28 March 1799.

[25] *Asiatic Journal* September 1816 (Volume 2) 624.

[26] *Bengal Hurkaru* 29 April 1823.

[27] J.S. Gladstone, *History of Gillanders, Arbuthnot and Co., and Ogilvy, Gillanders and Co.* (1910) Glynne-Gladstone Mss2749, Flintshire Record Office, Hawarden, North Wales.

[28] James Silk Buckingham, *Improved Syllabus of Mr Buckingham's Lectures on the Oriental World, preceded by a Sketch of his Life, Travels and Writings and of the Proceedings of the East India Monopoly during the Past Year* (London: Hurst, Chance and Co, 1830) 7-8.

[29] *Calcutta Journal* 19 March 1819.

[30] Palmer to Trail, 1 January 1811 Mss Eng Lett, c78 274.

[31] Palmer to Thomas Arrow, 7 June 1813; Palmer to Cpt James Arrow, 15 June 1813 Mss Eng Lett c82, 286-299.

[32] Palmer to Major-General Stuart, 10 August 1823 Mss Eng Lett c98, 47-48.

[33] Palmer to Lt. Col. Morrell, 15 September 1823 Mss Eng Lett, c98 201.

[34] Palmer to Col. S. Toone 20 September 1818, and 8 December 1818 Mss Eng Lett c87, 117-118 and 153.

[35] Palmer to Sir Charles Cockerell, 16 January 1822 Mss Eng Lett c92, 103-104; Palmer to Captain T.Ashton of London, 16 April 1822 Ms Eng Lett c93, 128-129.

[36] Palmer to Major Weguilin, 6 October 1809 Mss Eng Lett c73, 79-80.

[37] Palmer to Captain Thomas Stephenson of Huntingdon, 8 February 1809; Palmer to J. Glas, 10 February 1809, Mss Eng Lett c70, 44-46 and 49-51.

[38] These figures are complied from two schedules of creditors found in the Insolvency papers of the firm, dated 1831 and 1873 respectively. The papers are uncatalogued and are held in the records of the Calcutta High Court, West Bengal, India.

[39] Affidavit filed in the Calcutta Insolvent Court, 29 September 1832, uncatalogued records of the Calcutta High Court.

[40] St John's Vestry Meeting 3 February 1830, Minutes of St John's Church, the vestry, St John's, Calcutta.

[41] Ibid., 8 December 1830.

[42] Petition to the Insolvent Court of William Prinsep 30 July 1830, uncatalogued records of the Calcutta High Court.

[43] Palmer to Lt Col. James Dewar at Samarang, Java, 31 May 1813, and Palmer to Lt J. Eckford, Java, 23 June 1813, Mss Eng Lett c82, 257-259; 314-318.

[44] Palmer to Mrs Wilford, 30 January 1830 Mss Eng Lett c112, 115-117.

[45] Palmer to Roy Ramsoonder Mitter of Patna, 6 September 1818 Mss Eng Lett c87, 106.

[46] Palmer to Henry Lane 18 January 1824 Mss Eng Lett c100, 89-90.

[47] Palmer to J. Harington, 18 April 1822 Mss Eng Lett c93,145-146.

[48] Palmer to Din Mahomed, 13 December 1823 Mss Eng Lett c99, 259.

[49] Palmer to Mrs Munshaw in London, 26 November 1826, Mss Eng Lett c104, 231.

[50] Palmer to Mr Rees at Gunga Saugor, 4 March 1826, Mss Eng Lett c103, 83.

[51] Palmer to M. Law at Dacca, 20 April 1829 Mss Eng Lett c109, 296-297.

[52] Palmer to Major General Sir John Malcolm, 14 October 1818 Mss Eng Lett c87, 181-184.

[53] Palmer to Ram Mohun Roy, 12 April 1822 Mss Eng Lett c93, 115.

[54] Palmer to Henry Wood, James Barwell, Charles Morley and H.T. Prinsep 25April 1827, Mss Eng Lett c105, 348.

[55] Palmer to Robert Grant at Cawnpore, 2 August 1809 Mss Eng Lett c71, 117.

[56] Palmer to Henry Trail 6 January 1810 Mss Eng Lett c75, 130.

[57] Palmer to W. E. Bird in Bombay, 30 November 1808 Mss Eng Lett c69, 22-23; Palmer to W. Droz, 30 December 1812 Mss Eng Lett c81, 24-25.

[58] Palmer to Thomas Macquoid, 26 December 1821 Mss Eng Lett c92, 27.

[59] Palmer to G. Forbes at Chinsurah, 21 May 1813 Mss Eng Lett c82, 223-226.

[60] Palmer to N. Macleod at Patna, 24 July 1818 Mss Eng Lett c87, 40.

[61] Palmer to William Palmer 4 September 1809 Mss Eng Lett c72, 144-145.

[62] Palmer to Major S. Stanhope at Madras, 10 January 1817 Mss Eng Lett c85, 128-130.

[63] See Board of Trade (Commercial) Index Vol 24 1798, 95-98, West Bengal Archives, Calcutta.

[64] Board of Trade (Commercial) Index Vol 27 1801. 178, West Bengal Archives.

[65] Palmer to Sir Charles Cockerell, 4 April 1810 Mss Eng Lett c77, 75-78.

[66] Z. Yazdani, *Hyderabad during the Residency of Henry Russell 1811-1820: A Case Study of the Subsidiary Alliance System* (Oxford: OUP, 1976) 60-61.

[67] Palmer to Lt Colonel Nesbitt on Mauritius, 11 October 1813 Mss Eng Lett c83, 146.

[68] See N. Tarling, "The Palmer Loans" *Bijdragen* 119:2 (1963) 161-187; 162.

[69] Palmer to Baron Van Der Capellen, Dutch Governor General of the East Indies, 25 December 1821 Mss Eng Lett c92, 11-15; see also N. Tarling, "The Prince of Merchants and the Lions City" *Journal of the Malaysian Branch of the Royal Asiatic Society* 37:1 (1964) 20-40.

[70] Tarling, "The Palmer Loans".

[71] G.R. Knight, "John Palmer and Plantation Development in Western Java during the Earlier Nineteenth Century" *Bijdragen* 131:2 (1975) 308-337.

[72] Tripathi, *Trade and Finance in the Bengal Presidency* 160-164.

[73] Palmer to C. Todd, 11 August 1809 Mss Eng Lett c71, 171.

[74] Palmer to Trail, 21 May 1820 Mss Eng Lett c90, 50.

[75] Palmer to Trail, 6 January 1810 Mss Eng Lett c75, 129-130; Palmer to Trail, 16 March 1810 Mss Eng Lett c76, 162-163.

[76] Affidavit of Sir Charles Metcalfe and others to the Insolvent Court 20 January 1830. Also petition to the Insolvent Court 25 May 1830 by the assignees of Palmer and Co. Uncatalogued records of the Calcutta High Court.

[77] Palmer to Hunter at Koorootchdee, 9 August 1823 Mss Eng Lett c98, 40-42; Palmer to Hunter, 2 September 1823 Mss Eng Lett c98, 151-152; Palmer to Hunter, 24 September 1823 Mss Eng Lett c.98, 232-235; Palmer to Hunter, 11 November 1823 Mss Eng Lett c99, 102-105.

[78] Brownrigg to Palmer, 8 July 1821 Mss Eng Lett d105, 63; Hobhouse to Palmer, 15 June 1824 Mss Eng Lett d105, 118; Palmer to Brownrigg, 17 October 1824 Mss Eng Lett d105, 147.

[79] J.Phipps, *A Guide to the Commerce of Bengal* (Calcutta, Master Attendant's Office 1823) 91-95.

[80] Memoirs of William Prinsep Mss Eur D 1160/1, 319.

[81] Palmer to Lt. Col. Caulfield on Mauritius, 4 August 1830 Mss Eng Lett c115, 242.

[82] Palmer to Colin Shakepear at Gonateeah, 16 August 1830 Mss Eng Lett c113, 296.

[83] Report of a meeting of the creditors of Palmer and Co., 22 February 1832 *Alexanders East India Magazine* 4:24 (1832) 497.

[84] Granovetter, "Economic Action and Social Structure: The Problem of Embeddedness", 482-483.

[85] H.V. Bowen, "Gentlemanly Capitalism and the Making of a Global British Empire: Some Connections and Contexts, 1688-1815" in S. Akita (ed.), *Gentlemanly Capitalism, Imperialism and Global History.*

[86] Extracts from the Englishman and another, un-named newspaper, Mss Eng Lett d107, 207a and 207b.

CONSTRUCTING IDENTITY: THE STAYMAKER FORMS THE LADY IN EIGHTEENTH-CENTURY BRITAIN

LYNN SORGE-ENGLISH

Thursday. Jan y 12 .... *Employ* .... went to Hauptmans, took measure of her for a pair of Stays & stayd with her and Miss Clagget till near 6. Return'd and began to cut out Mr   Hutching's Childs coat and Hauptmans Stays.[1]

This entry from the diary of Richard Viney, Staymaker, is one of many in which he mentions the physicality of staymaking in the same breath with sociability with his clients. It is small wonder that he inadvertently links the two given the importance of stays to fashion in general and to the eighteenth-century woman in particular. It is commonly accepted that eighteenth-century females of most social strata and of all ages from infancy to adulthood wore stays as a foundation garment.[2] Created from as many as five layers of linen and/or wool, heavily boned with baleen or wood or stiffened with packthread, and lacing up the back and/or front, stays encompassed the torso and moulded the body into an unnatural cone-like shape. The silhouette of the outer layers of clothing was determined, in turn, by the shape of the stays, with the bodice of the gown or jacket fitting snugly on top of the stays and duplicating the shape lying beneath. As an article of clothing, then, stays played a vital role in establishing the visual aesthetic of eighteenth-century female clothing and the female body, something which Viney subconsciously understood.

Richard Viney lived in Pudsey and Birstall in the West Riding of Yorkshire, in 1744, the year in which he meticulously kept the diary. A member of the Moravian Brethren, Viney left a diary which is highly valued as a primary document "... of the religious revival of the eighteenth century,"[3] with parts of it having been selectively transcribed and published in the *Proceedings* of the Wesley Historical Society.[4] While, in and of itself, this is of historical significance, the diary's usefulness as a source for trades history has been overlooked. Annotated bibliographies never mention that Viney was a tradesman, let alone a Staymaker.[5] Yet his diary is as rich in detail of the life and work of a regional Staymaker as it is of the inner workings of the Moravian Brethren. Containing an entry for almost every day for the entire year, Viney carefully penned his narratives under the headings "Employ," "Mind," "Health," "Weather," and "Occurrencies," and in so doing left a document which not only provides fascinating detail of the work of designing and creating stays – the only primary source of its kind known to this author, but more importantly for the purposes of this paper, he also amply provided the kind of personal detail which most social historians hope to find, but which often proves to be elusory.[6]

While economic, social and dress historians have written about the work of tailors in eighteenth-century Britain, and while much has been said about various aspects of the lives of women of the upper and middling sorts, little has been written about the relationship between bespoke tradesmen in general or tailors in particular, and the group to which they are thought to have been subservient.[7] Amanda Vickery's *The Gentleman's Daughter: Women's Lives in Georgian England*, is probably the work in social history which comes closest to divulging something of the relationship between tradesman and client, and although Vickery does mention staymakers, she does not discuss their relationship with their female clients.[8] Acquiring an understanding of the character and personality of tradesmen in the eighteenth century is not an easy undertaking, but the work done by Eric Hobsbawm, Joan Scott and Alfred Young on shoemakers is exemplary. All have gone some way to accounting for shoemakers' reputations as political radicals, identifying lifestyle and character traits which might have contributed to their personae as intellectuals.[9] Although parts of their analyses might be applied to tailors, none address specifically the concerns raised in this paper. The question remains, then, what was the relationship between client and tradesman, how and why was it formed, what degree of familiarity did relationship participants enjoy, were gender differences relevant, how much influence did the tradesman have over his clients, and to what extent did this influence affect both clients' and tradesman's lives? This paper, part of a larger work on tailoring and body transformation in eighteenth-century Britain,[10] is a micro-study of a Staymaker and his clients, and although its findings are limited by the fact that Richard Viney was only one Staymaker who had one set of clients in one regional area of England, it discusses a source so rich in historical detail that some preliminary conclusions can be drawn. It will argue that bespoke tradesmen moved across clearly-defined boundaries of class and gender to play a significant role in the lives of their clients, in the subsequent formation of their identities, and those of the communities in which they lived.

There is much discussion about the "meaning of things" in current scholarship – consumption theory as it pertains to material culture is a case in point,[11] but there is also something to be said of "meaning" in human, everyday social interactions, as well. Erving Goffman's *The Presentation of Self in Everyday Life* provides a useful framework for this paper.[12] Using a dramaturgical approach, Goffman thoughtfully draws analogies between theatre and life, reducing each to its component parts and analyzing the tensions and anxieties, both real and perceived, within the relationships among them. Goffman, characterizing those participating in social interactions as the actors and the interactions themselves as the performances, attempts to show how people develop identity as a function of interaction with others. Thus, to place the subject of this paper inside this framework, within the interactions among the players involved in designing and producing stays–in this case, Richard Viney-and in consuming and wearing them - his clients - the stage is set, the actors and audience take their places, the production is directed, and the performance is played out. Yet within the complex world of producer and consumer, tradesmen and client, the roles played by each are not static, but are formed, blended and shifted in various ways by and for the individuals, depending upon which players occupy front stage at any given time. The minute workings of the interchanging roles of tradesman and client are important contributors to construction of individual identities, but are also elements of larger social systems which functioned importantly in the formation of the identity of the community in which they all lived, as will be seen.

In imparting a sense of the man, personal details of Viney's life, such as his age and birthplace, are unknown to date,[13] but his diary clearly captures his strong sense of self and multi-layered, personal identity. Viney's diary reveals him to have led a full life, and divulges his paid occupation to have been that of a Staymaker. Living and working in a small rural community, Viney travelled extensively to visit clients in their homes, where on the first visit, he took their orders and measured them for stays; he visited a second time to fit them before the stays were completed, and a final time to deliver the finished product, try the stays on and collect payment. But his diary also shows his role within his community to have been much broader than that of simply a tradesman: he was also a scholar and bookbinder, an amateur medical practitioner, a sometime preacher and religious zealot, an employer, traveller, husband, father and friend. Viney was well-read, and his wide-ranging reading interests included works on anatomy, physick, and law. In his words:

> Friday. Feb. y 24 …. London …. About 3 o clock I went from Wildstreet to Paternoster Row and Bought Sydenham & Shaws works on Physick, ….
> August ye 16 …. Took measure of Stockill's daughter of Castlehouse hill (who came here for that purpose) and Cut them out basted & ruled fit for stitching, read some of Laws Appeal.[14]

He was constantly teaching himself new things, utilizing the written word as his primary teaching tool. His interest in healing was known throughout his community, and his abilities as a medical practitioner were highly sought after, as evidenced by the following passage:

July ye 7 .... While I was out a child was brought for me to act as a Surgeon on, whose face is terribly torn by a kick of one of John Hutchisons Horses, but I not being at home, after waiting 4 or 5 hours they carry'd it to Bradford.[15]

His intellect was also highly regarded, so much so that during the year in which he kept the diary John Wesley proposed that Viney accompany him to Newcastle, a 76-mile journey which took him 4 days on foot.[16] Once he had arrived, Wesley asked him to catalogue his library, which appears to have been extensive, and to pack it up for shipment to London. Viney took on the task with obvious great relish, spending the better part of 12 days carrying it out:

May ye 28 .... I ... finish'd what has busy'd me for some days, (viz) putting all ye Books in such order and making a Catalogue of them that any one might presently find any they wanted ....[17]

On his return journey, also on foot, he decided to call into Durham, a distance of 12 miles on his first day. After dining at 'ye Boot & Shoe', he visited the town Library, describing it in minute detail, including the 'curious' order of cataloguing. Had he had more time, he would have been quite contented to sit and read. As he put it:

June ye 4 .... I met here with a book which I could have been glad to read if time and opperutunity admitted: it was The Anatomy of Melancholy, wrote by Democritus Jun. 6th Edit, London, Printed 1652.[18]

His scholarly pursuits also carried over into bookbinding, and early in 1744 he built a book press. In his words:

Tusday. Jan y 10th .... Went to the Carpenter and got a piece of Oke to make a book press, and after Breakfast went to Br Horns Room at Hillas's and made y Press.... Try'd y Press in cutting some writing books I had by me.[19]

The remainder of his diary is rife with references to his binding personal journals for friends and colleagues; his book press was in heavy use throughout the year.

Viney's role as an employer is also well defined in the diary. For much of the year, he had so much staymaking work that he was forced to take on an employee, James Stansfield, to help him complete his orders.[20] Stansfield worked with Viney closely, and almost daily, for the better part of 1744, until, much to Viney's chagrin, he went into business for himself as a Staymaker, a situation which Viney viewed both as a betrayal and a breach of trust. In Viney's words:

November ye 25 .... James Stansfield I find is setting up Master Staymaker, and for that end has sent for tools from London which are already come to Pudsey. He also brought a pair of stays to Stitch to Rachel Gott last ye 18. He has for some time past behaved haughtily and very selfconceited, and has never hinted any thing to me of his Intentions.[21]

Viney's sense of betrayal appears to have been acute, particularly since he taught Stansfield the craft of staymaking, and at various times throughout the year, Stansfield even lived with Viney and his wife. Furthermore, Rachel Gott was the person whom Viney employed to stitch the bone casings when he was too busy to do the stitching himself. Stansfield using the same seamstress with whom Viney had worked diligently to impart his exacting standards must have been perceived as an additional disloyalty. Yet, only a short time later, Stansfield as Master Staymaker was unable to procure enough work, and Viney's comments are telling, "Dec ye 9 .... James Stansfield was here Dec ye 4 and having nothing to do seems much alter'd for ye best, Humble, and mean in his own Eyes."[22] Viney prided himself on his honesty and integrity; to sense otherwise in a work colleague must have been unsettling at best.

Viney's character comes through loud and clear in the diary, character which lent itself well to exerting an influence over those with whom he had dealings, particularly those of the opposite gender. For one thing, he had exacting standards of himself and of others, standards which included self-discipline, and a love of exactitude and order:

June ye 3 .... A Man is never safe from Confusion when he has every day to consider what he shall do. Therefore some fix'd rules for Employing his time is necessary, & ye want of them is ye occasion of so many changes of mind & weak resolutions ....[23]

The identity he presented to the world was one of independence, strong-mindedness, competence, confidence and ambition, and nothing in his diary indicates that he believed himself to be any less than equal among men. All of his dealings with others, many of whom appear in his diary on numerous occasions, illustrate these qualities in one way or another. The relationship he had with Ann Carter is a case in point, and shows his independent nature and strong mindedness. Although he does not mention making stays for her, she was a family friend, and at one point she even proposed that she share lodgings with Viney and his family. The two appear to have had a particularly familiar relationship:

Octo. Ye 18 .... Ann Carter took upon her this Morning to rebuke me pritty harshly for not contriving my business better. Having observ'd long that the troubling herself about other peoples business was her greatest hindrance I took an opportunity in ye Evening when she came of speaking plainly to her about it. She seem'd convinced of ye Truth of what I said.[24]

Viney similarly spoke his mind on other occasions, as well, showing little propensity for tactfulness, and revealing himself to have somewhat of a judgemental nature:

Wensday. Jan. y 11th .... Ann Banks came to us this Evening complaining of her Sinfulness, but did not seem to have any sence of it. I spoke a little sharply to her. She has not been here since christmass till now and has not behaved well towards her husband as I am told, and now when I put it to her she acknowledg'd it.[25]

Viney's exacting standards and upwardly mobile nature led him to consistently strive to better his situation and employment status. The diary does not indicate the length of time during which he had been a Staymaker, but his entries regarding his design and creation of stays indicate that he was a fully qualified and extremely competent Staymaker. He seemed dissatisfied with his chosen vocation, however, and his ambitions led him in other directions. His diary is filled with reflections similar to the following:

April ye 14 .... *Mind.* Varied almost with ye Hours, sometimes thought of beginning a school in Yorkshire. But ... as soon as my Wife is up again to remove to Islington or some place near London and follow my business ....[26]

The very fact that he considered moving to Islington just outside London and carrying out his business as a Staymaker–to a community where competition with other Staymakers undoubtedly would have been keen, is testament to his belief in his abilities, and in his confidence as an able tradesman.

Viney's role as Staymaker is one of great interest for the purposes of this chapter. On the one hand, he was a professional Staymaker providing a service for his clients, while on the other hand, he was a member of a small community who operated on a sophisticated social level. What he actually did as a Staymaker is enlightening in and of itself–and his diary is filled with references to the material creation of stays, but his work as a Staymaker was also bound up with an active social life with his clients. For one thing, he carried out his work purely on a bespoke or made-to-measure basis, and while this involved receiving the order, measuring and fitting the clients in their homes, and delivering the finished stays, it also centred around him "having discourse" with his clients on various subjects. For this he often stayed to tea or for a meal, and several times he spent the night at his clients' homes. On Saturday, February 4, 1744, for example, he prepared work for Stansfield, and then at 2pm set out for Lady Margaret's with her completed stays in hand.[27] In recounting his journey, he explains, ".... got to Lady Margarets at Aberforth just at 7. Supd, sit a while with her and Sis Holland .... Tryd on Lady Margarets Stays & went to bed." He adds that on the following day, Sunday, Lady Margaret proposd to me to stay till Wensday night to keep y Society but I excusd myself on account of getting my Business done that I might go to London.[28]

Viney's social interactions were not limited to those with the upper sorts only, however. Class seemed to make little or no difference in his dealings with his clients. Even those who could ill afford stays approached him about having them made on a bespoke basis. On one occasion he spent the night in Chindley with a friend, Tom Bennett, where he records that, Octo. ye 4 .... One Ann Gee ... who lives 1 mile from hence was here & staid all night. She spoke to [me] about Stays but wanted them cheap.[29] Viney obviously declined, for there is no mention of Ann Gee among his clients in his diary. The interesting thing is, though, that even though she could not afford to have bespoke stays, she wanted them anyway, she must have felt she had a right to them, and she unselfconsciously approached him with her request. Orders for stays from the middling sorts are also well represented in his diary. On April 6, for example, he set out to spend the day measuring and delivering stays to clients, after having borrowed Gussenbauer's boots, and John Hutchison's horse. At Field-Head, he:

> April ye 6 .... Took measure of Fernlys daughter for Stays, had some discourse with Dame Fernly .... Then went to Little Gummersal, took measure of John Rhode's Wife, staid and din'd there, and past one oclock set away for Smithouse, got thither by 3. lcft ye Horse there and Walk'd to Suffhomes with Howarths both Stays. Drank Tea with Mrs Howorth and daughters ....[30]

Not only did Viney design and make stays for clients, then, but he also developed a close personal relationship with many of them, which in turn, would have encouraged them to place their trust in him as a Staymaker. And trust him they did, recommending his skills widely. As Viney wrote with uncustomary pride:

> July ye 7 ...Went to Beeston Hall, found Mrs Moor & Mrs Loyd with her. She profest much regard for me as a good Staymaker, promis'd me to do all she could to help me to Business, ...[31]

Sentiments such as this would not have been expressed had Viney's clients not placed their trust in him as a staymaker. Furthermore, separation of Viney's work from his social life was nonexistent:

> Thursday March y 22 .... and from thence to Mrs Moors at Beeston at 5, drank tea with her, took measure of her for a pair of stays, visited her husband who is like to die. Then went home to Pudsey whither I got before 6. Eat, and then cut out Moors stays.[32]

He finished and delivered the stays to Mrs. Moors, but later that year he had to
alter them. In his words, "May ye 11 .... Began to work on Mrs Moors (which I
have to make wider.) & staid at home all day."[33]

It is entirely possible that Mrs. Moors had gained weight and her stays had to
be made larger. Yet nowhere in the diary does Viney make any comment on the
shape of his clients' bodies, nowhere does he mention that a particular body was
difficult to fit, and in all cases, he writes of creating stays for his clients and fitting
their bodies in a matter-of-fact tone, therein denoting his respect for the female
form. One of the reasons for this might have been that he was comfortable with
bodies. As mentioned earlier, Viney read and studied anatomy and "physick," and
although not well enough off to purchase books in any quantity, he records having
borrowed them often. In July of 1744 he borrowed a book, *Drakes Anatomy*, from
his friend, Dr. Brooks, and read it from cover to cover.[34] He was so comfortable
with his knowledge of women's bodies, in fact, that he took it upon himself to
lance his wife's breast and nurse her back to health when she had a medical
problem following the birth of her sixth child, possibly a blocked milk duct, a boil
or some kind of skin infection. He considered calling in a medical doctor but never
did so, clearly feeling competent to deal with the problem himself.[35] His level of
comfort with women's bodies would have contributed to the trust they placed in
him as a Staymaker, and in turn, would have made them comfortable with him
measuring and fitting them for stays. Additionally, it is also possible that women
felt a degree of ease with Viney as a Staymaker because he was known within the
community as being a deeply religious man. His convictions were strong, and at
various times during the writing of his diary he acted as lay preacher and gospel
reader at informal gatherings. However, he held uncompromising beliefs about the
manner in which religious leaders should conduct themselves, and it was these
beliefs which "... led to his excommunication from the Moravian Church," and to
his ongoing search for inclusion in another religious society.[36] The fact that Viney
was clearly seen as having a strong faith might further have predisposed females to
place their trust in him as a Staymaker, and to have felt comfortable having him
acquire a degree of familiarity with their bodies.[37]

Viney also crossed class lines and penetrated barriers. He was poor, and of this
there can be little doubt. He did not own a horse, and went everywhere on foot. At
one point, he journeyed to London, walking most of the way, and recorded in detail
his trip which took him many days.[38] Whenever he borrowed a horse, he also had
to borrow a pair of boots. The Moravian brethren wanted to make him a suit of
clothes, but he declined their offer several times.[39] He and his wife lived in 2
different lodgings during the year in which he kept the diary, and in each case, they
had only one room in a house with another family. After they moved to the second

accommodation, Viney's wife had a baby. Here they lived in particularly cramped quarters:

> June ye 13 .... ye abiding here is very Inconvenient: to live, work, write, Read, have ye Cries of ye Child, my Wife often ill & people coming to see her or about business, Nellys wanting to be gone and we having no conveniency for lodging another (for my wife cannot do with out somebody with her) ....[40]

Viney had 5 older children, all of whom lived with and were cared for by the Moravian brethren in another community. Following his falling out with the brethren, he worried a great deal about the future of his children. He considered having them return to live with him and his wife, but his recounting of the conversation he had with one of the brethren makes it clear that Viney believed this to be financially nearly impossible:

> June ye 15 .... [I told him that] I thought it unreasonable for me to let them 'bide, but as I could not pay for their being there, so neither could I pay for their bringing hither. .... I had not great prospect of maintaining them here, ...[41]

However, although Viney must have made little more than a meagre living as a Staymaker, and although he appears to have been poor in almost every sense of the word, he did not consider himself to be so. In fact, during his trip to Newcastle, he passed through Richmond which he described as follows:

> May ye 21 .... It is no great town for Trade, it lying out of any great Road and chiefly depends on ye Papist Gentlemen who live around about there. The poor people knit much.[42]

This passage is as much a comment on Viney's perception of his own state of wealth as it is on that of the knitters of Richmond. The fact that he mentioned it at all indicates that his view of himself did not include poverty, something which undoubtedly helped him to cross class boundaries–he thought of himself as an equal.

Thus, we see here Richard Viney to have had a clearly defined, highly developed, multi-layered identity, one which he carefully nourished, sometimes consciously and sometimes subconsciously. At the same time, and perhaps even unknowingly, he also helped to construct his clients' identities. Although they came from all classes, as we have seen, Viney's clients had much in common. For one thing, they all must have had a desire to be fashionable, for they all commissioned Viney to design and create stays for them. Since it was the stays which laid the foundation for the eighteenth-century visual aesthetic, and which set the tone for fashion, Viney as Staymaker was well placed to become a formative influence in his clients' lives. Élite women's writings abound with comments on fashion, and although those used here come from complementary sources, there is no reason to suppose that Viney's clients would have felt differently. The letters of Lady Sarah Lennox, for example, are rich with references to fashion overall, but even more importantly, they speak volumes of the crucial role played by stays. Keeping up a correspondence with her childhood friend, Lady Susan Fox Strangeways, for nearly 60 years, in a letter dated August 6, 1761, Lady Sarah wrote: "If anything should put off your coming (which I hope it won't), pray send a pair of stays for a measure, as the embroidery is to be measured upon them, & that is the longest piece of work."[43] It is likely that Sarah was intending to embroider, or have embroidered by someone else, robings for the bodice of a gown for Susan, and requested that she send her stays so that the correct length of fabric needing embellishment could be calculated.[44] The stays came first, then, with the gown to follow, underlining the primary importance of stays to fashion. Given Viney's comfortable mix of business with sociability with his clients, it is no surprise that he was able to influence the construction of their identities.

Additionally, Viney's clients must have had an awareness of the clothed, female shape which was deemed to be aesthetically pleasing, and they all must have felt that Viney could achieve this on their bodies. Again turning to complementary sources, we can see that women had definite ideas about female physical form, and possessed strong opinions about what was aesthetically pleasing. Being thin, for example, was highly desirable. In a letter written to Lady Anne Campbell between 1735-40, Jane Cockburn noted: "Mrs. Cronte ... is grown thin and looks very well ...."[45] and in Mary Coke's letter to her sister, Lady Strafford, c.1745, she commented on a group of people calling on Lord Harington in Richmond Hill:

> ... I was mightly disappointed when I saw come oute of the Coach a Woman little less than a house; & a man as big as her, it seems all this Bulky company was come to see the house; how they gott in at the doers god knows for I did not stay to see; ...[46]

Neither did body shape which was viewed in a positive light escape comment, as evidenced in the observations of Lady Sarah on the physical form of the Princess of Monaco: "... her figure [is] the most perfect made of any woman in the world, I believe."[47] The point is, women were acutely aware of body shape, and it is extremely unlikely that they would not also have been cognizant of the possibilities for enhancement and refinement of body shape open to them via the talent and skills of the Staymaker. It is not difficult to understand why Viney was so much in demand as a Staymaker.

Yet it was not only those from polite society who aspired to fashionability through the wearing of stays; women from all walks of life used and cherished them. Steven King has noted several instances of stays being provided to "...'the poor' who came within the remit of the Old Poor Law."[48] Neither were novelists immune to the desirability of stays to women. In *Memoirs of a Woman of Pleasure*, written in 1748, John Cleland portrayed his protagonist Fanny Hill coming from a poor family in rural Lancashire, and orphaned at the age of fifteen. By her own admission, one of the lures for going to London to seek her fortune was "... the prospect of exchanging my country-cloaths for London finery," which included stays. She was enticed into a life of prostitution prior to marrying into a higher social class, but many of Cleland's references to clothing during her years as a "woman of pleasure" feature stays prominently: "... where his impatience would not suffer him to undress me more than just unpinning my handkerchief, and gown, and unlacing my stays," is a case in point.[49]

Furthermore, each and every one of Viney's clients had him make stays for them on a completely bespoke, one-of-a-kind basis, and this includes women of *all* classes. No two pairs of stays were alike in any way other than in fabrics and boning. Each size and shape was completely different, since each pair was made for a specific individual. Thus, each woman would have had a strong sense of her own uniqueness, which in turn would have contributed to the construction of her individual identity. Viney was instrumental in helping her to form the identity of the person she presented to the public, but it all began in her very private world where, to return to Goffman's framework, the multi-faceted interactions between Viney and his clients enabled him to play the role of director of the production for which he also wrote the script. The performers or actors were Viney's clients, and in his design and creation of stays for them, he was preparing them for the first time they would wear his stays, which, in essence, would be their 'opening night.' The interaction between Staymaker and client is, in this case, the performance of which Goffman speaks. Until the stays were completed, in his relationship with his clients Viney was closely allied to the concept of "front," which Goffman describes as "... that part of the individual's performance which regularly functions in a general and fixed fashion to define the situation for those who observe the performance."[50] Viney behaved with his clients in expected ways which came to be seen by them as the norm. Acting as front stage, he projected accepted character and personality traits which had normative meanings for his performers, which gave them a degree of comfort, and which enabled his clients to rely upon him to shape their bodies for fashion in the first instance, but which also played a crucial role in the construction of their identities. However, once the execution of the stays had been realized, the roles played by tradesman and client changed swiftly, as shall be seen.

Additionally, because women from all walks of life in Viney's community wore his stays, he inadvertently helped to bestow a collective indentity upon them, an identity where class played little or no role. Whether his clients were poor, of the middling or the upper sorts, they shared the wearing of his stays in common with each other. This collective identity was further enhanced later in the year when Viney somewhat abruptly changed his design concept. From January to September 1744 he made stays from what are now thought of as 'common' fabrics–linen or wool, using traditional stays construction techniques. However, in September this changed dramatically when Viney began to cover the stays with a coloured outer fabric, sometimes even silk, ceasing at the same time to stitch the bone lines through to the outside. The remainder of the diary reveals that he never did revert back to old method. From that time forward a typical entry reads:

> Octo ye 30 .... Then clos'd Priestlys Stay. Got ready and went and tryd it in ye Afternoon. Return'd. went to Turners and Carters to see for some Covering for it.[51]

Furthermore, not only was it the method he used for stays he was designing new for his clients, but he also used it for those which he had made earlier and which his clients later asked him to cover. In his words:

> Octo. ye 16 .... we got Mitchels for trying and at 10 I tryd them. Cut em fitt for Stansfield & at 11 set out for Smithouse, got there by one, dined. Discours'd with Mrs Holms, got Eliz. Ridings Stays to cover & Melia Stephensons Stay to cover and at 4 set homeward ....[52]

This is perhaps the most interesting thing: It must have been so important to his clients that they appear in the newest fashion that they asked Viney to cover stays which he had completed some time ago, and which were well-worn and already broken in.[53] They obviously wanted to join a collective of those wearing covered stays, they wanted to 'belong' to the world of the fashionable. Their collective identity thus shows itself to have been every bit as important as was their individual identity, and Viney's assistance with its construction was a determining factor in its development.

We see Viney, then, to have had a strong and independent nature, and a love and appreciation of rule and order. He was a caring person, but he had high expectations of himself and others. He had exacting standards of conduct, and held definite views on virtue, honesty and treatment of others. But he also was an incredibly sociable person who regularly visited his neighbours, fellow tradesmen and clients when it was a usual occurrence for him to sit and visit, stay to tea or for a meal, and often spend the night. The relationship he developed with many of his clients became one of familiarity and comfort where he was treated more as a friend, advisor and confidant than as a mere tradesman. While his paid work was as a Staymaker, and while he was commissioned by his clients to design and make them stays, his close bond with them enabled him to have a great deal of sway over their lives. For while he was controlling and shaping their bodies for fashion, and providing them with a sense of belonging, he was also helping to mould their identities, both individually and collectively. Furthermore, the fact that he made stays for all classes indiscriminately, and on a bespoke basis, must have helped to break down class barriers by enabling the lower sorts to take on the community collective identity. To apply Goffman's analogy here, Viney appears to have been very much in demand as the director of the production, with his clients acting as his players during the interactive process. Although they were being prepared and directed for *their* front stage performance, paradoxically the garments which were being designed and created for them, and which would enable them to confidently play leading roles for a live audience, were garments which would be relegated only backstage status, playing support roles to the more visible, front stage floating mantuas and gowns. Once his players were dressed, Viney, the Staymaker and director, took his place in the audience, making way for his clients to present themselves to their public. They, in turn, became the directors of their own performance. As Goffman says of the interchangeable nature of roles such as these, "... those who help present a team-performance differ in the degree of dramatic dominance given each of them and ... one team-routine differs from another in the extent to which differentials in dominance are given its members." Thus, while Viney was carrying out his tradesman's work, he enjoyed the position of dramatic dominance in the relationship with his clients, but once the stays had been completed and delivered, the balance of power shifted to his clients who became the dramatically dominant force. Moreover, Goffman also makes it clear "... that dramatic and directive dominance are dramaturgical terms and that performers who enjoy such dominance may not have other types of power and authority."[54] Viney's lead role as a Staymaker in the small communities of Pudsey and Birstall would almost certainly have been one of power and authority, and although he was clearly respected as a citizen, whether he enjoyed the same influence in his everyday life is questionable. One thing is clear, though, Viney's interactive role with his clients must have gone some way toward assisting him with the formation of his own identity. His skills and talents as a Staymaker were needed and in demand by his clients, he occupied a place of importance to them socially, and his opinions on various matters were sought on an individual basis. Furthermore, he was so secure in his position with his clients that he confidently gave them advice on a regular basis. These are not the actions of one who has a weak sense of self; instead, they show Viney to have had a highly-developed sense of his own identity and self-worth. Clearly, then, construction of identity here had dual agency, and Viney's clients were as important to the construction of his identity as he was to theirs.

Crossing boundaries of class, gender and occupation in several ways, Richard Viney, Staymaker, played a much more meaningful and positive role as a tradesman than might have been imagined.

As stated at the outset, this is a micro-study of one Staymaker and his female clients, and of course, it does not purport to be inclusive of all Staymakers specifically or tradesmen in general, nor can a study limited to only one narrative source be conclusive in any way. But it is a study of two groups of people diverse culturally, socioeconomically, and in gender, and does perhaps open the door to a revisitation of perceptions of tradesmen as little more than servants to the upper classes. Peter Earle and Leonard Schwarz have convincingly argued that tailors occupied the lowest position in the hierarchy of wealth among London's manufacturers.[55] Any assumption that economic scale equates with social status is called into question through an analysis of Richard Viney's identity and his relationships with his clients as it is clear that his prestige and influence within his community belied his poverty. The wider questions regarding economics, social structure and relations remain to be answered, but when doing so, the contribution of a mere tradesman to the construction of individual and community identities needs to be carefully considered.

I would like to thank conference participants for their constructive feedback following the presentation of this paper at the *Identities* Conference, Edge Hill, 31 March–1 April 2005. I am also grateful to Steven King for his perceptive commentary on an earlier version. The research for this chapter as part of a larger work was funded through a Dalhousie University Travel Grant, Social Sciences and Humanities Research Council of Canada Doctoral Fellowship, an Oxford Brookes University Research Studentship, a Royal Historical Society Grant, a Faculty Small Grant and Richard Newitt Prize, University of Southampton, a KG Ponting Memorial Bursary, and a Social Sciences and Humanities Research Council of Canada Research Grant. I gratefully acknowledge this support.

[1] British Library Add MS 44935, Diary of Richard Viney, Staymaker, 1744, f. 8 v (hereafter referred to as Diary). I am deeply indebted to British Library Manuscripts for enabling me to transcribe large portions of the Diary.

[2] For documentation of stays being worn by the common sorts, see Anne Buck, *Dress in Eighteenth-Century England* (New York: Holmes & Meier Publishers, Inc., 1979) 121, 122, 143, 146, 147, 154, 155. For evidence of stays being worn by the poor, see Peter and Ann Mactaggart, "Some Aspects of the Use of Non-Fashionable Stays," *Strata of Society: Proceedings of the Seventh Annual Conference of the Costume Society April 6-8, 1973* (London: Victoria and Albert Museum, 1973) 20; Steven King, *Poverty and Welfare in England, 1700-1850: A Regional Perspective* (Manchester: Manchester University Press, 2000) 157-158, 162. For discussion of the wearing of stays beginning in infancy, see Gillian Clark, "Infant Clothing in the Eighteenth Century: A New Insight," *Costume* 28 (1994) 47, 53, 57. Also see Anne Buck, *Clothes and the Child: A Handbook of Children's Dress in England 1500-1900* (Carlton, Bedford: Ruth Bean Publishers, 1996) 75, who notes that

Mary Blundell's father '... bought material and whalebone for stays, ... in 1706', before his daughter turned three.

[3] H. J. M. Milne, "A Moravian Brother's Diary," *British Museum Quarterly* XI, 4 (September, 1937) 181-182.

[4] Marmaduke Riggall, ed. "Richard Viney's Momoranda, 1744," *Proceedings of the Wesley Historical Society* 13 (1922) 78-80, 107-113, 149-153, 187-187-190; 14 (1924) 13-21, 25-31, 49-54, 83-89, 97-104, 137-145, 192-201; 15 (1926) 72-78, 122-125, 189-195.

[5] C.S. Handley, *An Annotated Bibliography of Diaries Printed in English*, 4 vols., vol. II, (Aldeburgh: Hanover Press, 1997) 1744.1, for example, has annotated Viney's diary only as a source for religious history, making no mention of his work as a Staymaker.

[6] Diary, ff. 1 + 120. Parts of these first two paragraphs were first published in Lynn Sorge-English, "'29 Doz and 11 Best Cutt Bone': The Trade in Whalebone and Stays in Eighteenth-Century London," *Textile History* 36 (2005) 29, 33.

[7] For guild decline/rise of trade unions with specific reference to the tailoring trade, see, for example, Michael John Walker, "The Extent of the Guild Control of Trades in England, c. 1660-1820; A Study Based on a Sample of Provincial Towns and London Companies" (PhD dissertation, Cambridge University, 1985) 235-238, 337-340; John Rule, *The Experience of Labour in Eighteenth-Century Industry* (London: Croom Helm, 1981) 51, 57, 62, 103-105, 152-156; Rule, *The Labouring Classes in Early Industrial England, 1750-1850* (London: Longman,1986) 255-284. For the role tailoring played in the development of the English middle class and in London's economy, see Peter Earle, *The Making of the English Middle Class: Business, Society and Family Life in London, 1660-1730* (London: Methuen, 1989) 27-29; Leonard Schwarz, *London in the age of industrialisation: Entrepreneurs, labour force and living conditions, 1700-1850* (Cambridge: Cambridge University Press, 1992) 4-5, 58, 67, 103-105, 183-184, 189-194. For tailoring and staymaking within the context of retail distribution, see David Barnett, *London, Hub of the Industrial Revolution: A Revisionary History 1775-1825* (London: Tauris Academic Studies, 1998) 70-75, 152-154. For specifics regarding the infrastructure of the tailoring trade, see Madeleine Ginsburg, "The Tailoring and Dressmaking Trades, 1700-1850," *Costume* 6 (1972) 64-68. For business practices of regional tailors, see Christina Fowler, "Robert Mansbridge, A Rural Tailor and his Customers 1811-1815," *Textile History* 28 (1997) 29-38; Stuart Maxwell, "Two Eighteenth Century Tailors," reprinted from the *Hawick Archaeological Society Transactions* (1972) 23, who mentions one of the tailors he studied in Scotland making and mending stays. For information on ready-made stays, see Beverly Lemire, *Dress, Culture and Commerce: The English Clothing Trade before the Factory, 1660-1800* (Great Britain: Macmillan Press, 1997) 62-63, 166, n.71. For discussion of the material origins of stays, see Janet Arnold, *Patterns of Fashion I: Englishwomen's dresses & their construction c.1660-1860*, 2 vols., vol. I, (London: Macmillan London Ltd., 1972) 3-8; Peter and Ann Mactaggart, "Ease, Convenience and Stays, 1750-1850," *Costume* 13 (1979) 41-51; Lynn Sorge, "Eighteenth-Century Stays: Their Origins and Creators," *Costume* 32 (1998) 18-32. Also generally see Norah Waugh, *Corsets and Crinolines* (New York: Theatre Arts Books, 1954). For an investigation of corsets within their cultural context, albeit mainly those from the nineteenth century, generally see Valerie Steele, *The Corset: A Cultural History* (New

Haven: Yale University Press, 2001); Leigh Summers, *Bound to Please: A History of the Victorian Corset* (Oxford: Berg, 2001).

[8] AmandaVickery, *The Gentleman's Daughter: Women's Lives in Georgian England* (New Haven: Yale University Press, 1998), has painted an invaluable picture of the lives of gentry women in the eighteenth century. She mentions stays, noting her subjects wearing them in two instances, and that tailors were often employed inside Alkincoats itself '… cutting stays and petticoats; …', among other items (ibid., 144, 185, 140).

[9] E. J. Hobsbawm and Joan Wallach Scott, "Political Shoemakers," *Past & Present* 89 (1980) 91, mention that shoemakers had 'an uncommon degree of literacy', positing various reasons for this; also generally see Alfred F. Young, "George Robert Twelves Hewes (1742-1840): A Boston Shoemaker and the Memory of the American Revolution," *William and Mary Quarterly*, 3rd ser., 38 (October 1981) 561-623; Young, *The Shoemaker and the Tea Party: Memory and the American Revolution* (Boston: Beacon Press, 1999). I appreciate Valerie Burton drawing my attention to these references.

[10] Lynn Sorge-English, "The British Tailoring Trade, Stays and Body Transformation: Production, Consumption, Gender, Bodily Aesthetics and Health, 1680-1810" (PhD diss., Oxford Brookes University, forthcoming).

[11] For an overview, see Lorna Weatherill, *Consumer Behaviour and Material Culture in Britain 1660-1770* (London: Routledge, 1988. Second edition, 1996); Weatherill, "The Meaning of Consumer Behaviour in late Seventeenth and Early Eighteenth Century England," in *Consumption and the World of Goods* John Brewer and Roy Porter (eds), (London: Routledge, 1993) 206-227; Weatherill, "Consumer Behaviour, Textiles and Dress in the Late Seventeenth and Early Eighteenth Centuries," *Textile History* 22 (1991) 297-310; Amanda Vickery, "Women and the world of goods: a Lancashire consumer and her possessions, 1751-81," in John Brewer and Roy Porter (eds), *Consumption and the World of Goods*. (London: Routledge, 1993) 274-301.

[12] Erving Goffman, *The Presentation of Self in Everyday Life*, rev. ed. (New York: Doubleday, 1959).

[13] Riggall, *Proceedings*, says he discovered Viney's Diary "…at the Moravian Mission Room in Fetter Lane," and subsequently edited and transcribed portions of it for *Proceedings* [13 (1922): 78]. He summarizes what is known of Viney in the context of his religious life, but makes no mention of personal details [ibid., 14 (1924) 13-14].

[14] Diary, f. 30, 95v.

[15] Diary, f. 81v.

[16] Diary, f. 60v, 62v. Throughout the diary, Viney recorded Wesley's name using the spelling 'Wesley' and 'Westley' interchangeably.

[17] Diary, f. 64v.

[18] Diary, f. 69.

[19] Diary, f. 7v.

[20] Diary, f. 14v. This is the first reference to Viney hiring James Stansfield.

[21] Diary, f. 115v.

[22] Diary, f. 116v.

[23] Diary, f. 68v.

[24] Diary, f. 110.

[25] Diary, f. 8.

[26] Diary, f. 50v.

[27] Riggall, *Proceedings*, 14 (1924) 19, n.1, tells us that "Lady Margaret Hastings was married to Mr. Ingham on Nov. 12, 1741, at the residence of her brother, the Earl of Huntingdon, in London. She was twelve years older than her husband and in 1744 would be in her 45th yar."

[28] Diary, f. 20 v, 21.

[29] Diary, f. 107.

[30] Diary, f. 47v.

[31] Diary, f. 81v.

[32] Diary, f. 42v.

[33] Diary, f. 59v.

[34] Diary, f. 81.

[35] Diary, f. 58v, 60v, 71, 71v, 72, 73, 73v, 74, 76v, 77, 77v, 78.

[36] Riggall, *Proceedings*, 14 (1924) 13-14, used the term "excommunicated," but Viney discusses this happenstance in his life as his "exclusion" from the Church (Diary, f. 2).

[37] I am grateful to Valerie Burton for suggesting this line of thinking in the discussion which ensued following my paper presentation at the *Identities* Conference held at Edge Hill on 31 March–1 April 2005.

[38] Diary, f. 24 – 32v. His journey to London took him 11-18 February 1744, and he did not arrive home again until 3 March 1744. The account of his travels is remarkable in its attention to detail, including distances covered, amounts spent, and his impressions of the communities through which he passed.

[39] Diary, f. 8, is one example of many in the Diary.

[40] Diary, f. 73.

[41] Diary, f. 74v.

[42] Diary, f. 62.

[43] Countess of Ilchester and Lord Stavordale (eds), *The Life and Letters of Lady Sarah Lennox 1745-1826*, 2 vols., vol. I, (London: John Murray, 1901) 111.

[44] The word 'robings' is the eighteenth-century term used to denote the decoration applied lengthwise to the front edges of the bodice, and often to the front edges of the skirt of an open robe, as well.

[45] British Library Add MS 22256 (36), Strafford Papers, letter from Jane Cockburn (London: British Library), f. 20.

[46] British Library Add MS 22229, Strafford Papers, letter from Mary Coke (London: British Library), f. 255.

[47] Ilchester, *Life and Letters*, 172.

[48] Steven King, "Reclothing the English Poor, 1750-1840," *Textile History* 33 (2002) 37, 38, 41. Please see note 2 for additional sources.

[49] Peter Sabor, ed., *Memoirs of a Woman of Pleasure by John Cleland*, 1748-9, (Oxford: Oxford University Press, 1985) 2, 9, 39. For more on stays and consumer attitudes, see Sorge-English, "Trade in Whalebone", 29-35, of which this paragraph forms a part.

[50] Goffman, *Presentation*, 22.

[51] Diary, f. 113v.

[52] Diary, f. 109.

[53] An example of stays which were covered after having been made can be seen in Sorge, "Eighteenth-Century Stays," 26-28.

[54] Goffman, *Presentation*, 105.

[55] Earle, *English Middle Class,* Table 2.1, 32; Schwarz, *London*, 58.

IMAGINED SOLIDARITIES: THE LEFT, CLASS AND PHYSICAL IDENTITY IN THE 1930S

ROGER SPALDING

Back in the dear old thirties' days
When politics was passion
A harmless left-wing bard was I
And so I grew in fashion:
Although I never really *joined*
The Party of the Masses
I was most awfully chummy with
The Proletarian classes[1]

The development of a small, but significant and often socially prominent middle class left meant that "chumminess" with "the Proletarian classes" was something of a vogue in the 1930s. In his 1962 novel, *In the Thirties*, another veteran of the decade, Edward Upward, testified to the existence of this sentiment. At the beginning of this novel Alan Sebrill, a fictionalized Upward, arrives on the Isle of Wight to stay with Richard Marple, a fictionalized Christopher Isherwood. Shortly after his arrival Marple tells Sebrill:

> I'm thoroughly in with the so-called lower classes here...I've realised lately that the time has arrived for me to show definitely that I'm against the plus-foured poshocracy, and for the cockneys and the lower orders.

To which Sebrill responds, "I'm for them too...And I've always wanted to get in with them."[2]

In the event "getting in" with the lower orders proved easier to write about than to effect. To a very large degree this was because the upper middle classes defined themselves in relation to the working class in terms of their physical identities. This process of definition can be divided into two areas: personal hygiene, and notions of beauty. To put it in simple terms: the middle classes believed the working class smelt, and they did not, and also that they were beautiful and the working class was not.[3] A 1932 *Punch* cartoon by Wallis Mills neatly encapsulates both attitudes.[4] In this a tall elegant 'lady' confronts a short, bald and distinctly rumpled plumber saying: "I do hope you'll get the bath done soon. It's really most inconvenient." To which he replies: "We'll do our best, lady. When's yer bath-night?" The humour of the cartoon derives from the total incomprehension that each character displays for the other's lifestyle. This is particularly the case for the woman, who is obviously startled by the assumption that she shares the bathing habits of the working class. It also demonstrates a sharp contrast in the depiction of the social classes, a contrast no doubt in accord with the perceptions of *Punch's* readership. Around the basic factors of perceptions of beauty and body odour were interwoven, as the cartoon partly demonstrates issues like taste, dress, accent and posture. Together these can be seen to have operated as a discourse of class identity.

The middle-class left of the 1930s was acutely aware of these defining perceptions of class identity. George Orwell's claim that the middle class believed the working class smelt so embarrassed Victor Gollancz, publisher of the Left Book Club that he felt moved to write a special Foreword for *The Road to Wigan Pier*.[5] Gollancz adopted a three strand strategy for dealing with Orwell's claims: He stated that he was brought up in a close Jewish community which did not have class divisions of this type, thereby denying that he shared this opinion; he stated this belief may be held by some members of the middle class, but only 'a very small proportion'; and finally he praised the book for exposing the prejudices of the middle class.

> I know, in fact, of no other book in which a member of the middle class exposes with such complete frankness the shameful way in which he was brought up to think of large numbers of his fellow men. This section will be, I think, of the greatest value to middle class and working class members of the Left Book Club alike: to the former because, if they are honest, they will search their own minds; the latter, because it will make them understand what they are "up against".[6]

Clearly this is rather contradictory. If the attitude described by Orwell is confined to a very small proportion of the middle class, why would the book be so illuminating for club members? On one level Gollancz is simultaneously trying to distance the Left Book Club's selectors from *The Road to Wigan Pier*, and sell the merits of the book. On another level Gollancz is trying to salvage the prospect of cross-class solidarity, because Orwell's claim is a re-assertion of a key feature of middle-class self-definition in relation to the working class, even, as he says, for those members of the middle class who call themselves communists.[7] The likely fact of working class body odour must have been apparent to all of the readers of the 'Proletarian' writing of the period;[8] but this was not the issue, it was Orwell's assertion that a belief in this body odour was a part of the middle class world view that was the problem. Indeed, Gollancz never actually addressed the question of whether or not the working class did smell.

Heterosexual relationships across class boundaries, invariably with the man coming from the superior social class, carried an old-established cultural burden. One element of this was the 'wicked squire tradition' seen in such works as *The Hound of the Baskervilles* and *Tess of the d'Ubervilles*.[9] The other element consisted of those who were sexually attracted to 'dirt'; an attraction fed by the feeling that the dirty were less 'pure', or at least more physical than women of their own class, or, in nineteenth century terms, were 'bad' women. As Leonore Davidoff put it:

...the naturalness even "rankness" of working class people, servants in particular, could have a subtle attraction.[10]

Both of these perceptions of cross-class sexual relations were operative in the 1930s. In his 1934 novel, *It's a Battlefield* Graham Greene depicted an ageing, middle-class communist, Mr.Surrogate, picking up a young working class girl, after a Party meeting. The language employed by the young woman, Kay, during their sexual encounter demonstrates both her subordinate position, and her sexual enthusiasm-or 'badness'.

No, Mr.Surrogate, no. Please no," afterwards on the pillow whispering into his ear how bad he was, how strong.[11]

Kay puts up a ritualized resistance, which is, in reality enthusiastic compliance to the requirements of a social superior, addressed throughout as "Mr". Her sensual nature is underscored by Mr. Surrogate's post-coital reflections on his dead wife:

Things would have been different...if Margaret had been less artist, more woman, had been less cold...[12]

Political and social solidarity across class boundaries was therefore fraught with difficulty. The next section of this work is given over to an examination of how two left-wing writers attempted to resolve this issue through the medium of fiction.

Edward Upward's novel, *In the Thirties* explores the political movement of a young middle-class poet towards the Communist Party. Alan Sebrill (Upward) is acutely aware of the class barrier that separates him from his would-be comrades. When he makes his first contact with the Party he chides himself for wearing too "bourgeois" an overcoat.[13] Despite this initial embarrassment Sebrill moves closer to the Party and eventually joins. During the same period he becomes romantically involved with Elsie, an elementary school teacher and Party member. She is very definitely lower middle class, unlike the Public School and Cambridge educated Sebrill. The class differences between them cause him a great deal of unhappiness. He unfavourably contrasts her lack of response to his physical advances with that of an earlier bourgeois lover. He later explains this unresponsiveness in terms of Elsie sensing his lack of sincerity, caused by:

> ...a deeply surviving class snobbery in him, which shrank back from every sign, whether in her speech, or dress or manners, that she was ignorant of upper class customs.[14]

Later, after they decide to marry, Sebrill is so upset by the "mean" little maisonette that Elsie has found for them to view as a prospective marital home that he tells her: "Oh Elsie, you are so ugly."[15] This assertion of her ugliness is produced by the prospect of the loss of the spaciousness and comfort of his parents' bourgeois home. The daunting prospect of a petit bourgeois existence in the tasteless, modern maisonette becomes bound up with her lack of conventional beauty. For Sebrill, clearly, the whole notion of feminine beauty was intimately bound up with a discourse of class definition.

Sebrill eventually reconciles himself to the relationship by re-casting Elsie's 'flaws' in a positive light:

> The very inelegance of her walk increased her attractiveness for him, because it helped to assure him-just as did her avoidance of standardized female allurements like high heels and rouge-that the appeal she had for him might arise from her real worth.[16]

In effect this conceded that feminine beauty was the prerogative of the upper and upper middle classes. It simply re-interprets the absence of the constituent qualities of beauty as something positive. Ultimately, though, Sebrill accepts this relationship because of its political significance. Towards the end of the book, at a Party picnic, Sebrill has this thought:

> ...the increasing grimness of their struggle would be reflected, as from a mirror far up beyond the outer layers of the earth's atmosphere, the light of the future freedom. He could see this reflection now, in the faces and in the characters of the comrades around him. This was what distinguished them from non-Communists, raised them above even those whose abilities were greater than theirs. This in Elsie was what, more than anything else, made him love her.[17]

Sebrill's final affirmation of his relationship with Elsie, does not resolve the question of his perception of her physical presence, it postpones it. She becomes the embodiment of what is to come, of future rather than present delights, and this renders her lovable.[18] It is indicative of the strength of the difficulties of cross-class relationships that this issue should form so large a part of a work written over twenty years after the events it describes. A work written, furthermore, by an author who, unlike so many of his contemporaries remained politically active on the left.[19]

Naomi Mitchison's novel, *We Have Been Warned*, like Upward's *In the Thirties*, is very closely based on her own life.[20] The principal character, Dione Galton (Mitchison) is married to an Oxford don, Tom. Both of them are on the left of the Labour Party, and Tom is the candidate for a fictionalized midlands constituency, Marshbrook Bridge. Tom's candidature provides a central element of the book, which is a contrast between the bourgeois comforts of the Galtons' life in Oxford, London and Scotland (Dione comes from a landed Scottish background) and the proletarian hardships of the constituency. Dione feels "a foreigner" in Marshbrook Bridge, adversely compares the ugliness and dirtiness of the constituency with Oxford, and finds the taste of local Labour Party members difficult to cope with.[21]

Despite all of which Dione yearned to make a real connection with the working class. How this might be effected is suggested by the way that Mitchison deals with the manifestation of social class, which is to link it to physicality and sexuality. Early on in the novel she claimed that lower class men had sweeter breaths than those of other social classes because "they can't afford constant alcohol and tobacco and meat twice a day".[22] Like Upward, Mitchison turned a negative, in this case relative deprivation, into a positive. Conversely, excessive consumption was also deplored. Dione, observing the commercial bourgeoisie of the constituency, decides:

> They were proud; they were ugly; they didn't know they were ugly; they moved badly; they talked about money; they wanted to have things - a step from that, they would be horrible to be made love to by - they wouldn't wait, they'd snatch and grab...[23]

The economic drive of the bourgeoisie was, therefore, directly equated with their sexual manners. What, though, was to be counter-posed to them, the sweet-breathed workers? To which the answer was a qualified yes, qualified because the workers showed a distressing inability to recognise their historic role as defined by the Labour left. Asked whether her Party really represented the people, Dione answered, "I think it does. But the people always rather hate being set free."[24]

This inability to make political progress is linked, in the same passage, with the difficulty of making real human contact with members of the working class. In a later episode Mitchison provides an explanation for the non-porous social solidarity of the working class, in the form of sexual loyalty. A working class woman student tells Tom Galton of her intention to marry her working class boyfriend after she graduates, "I'm glad I'm marrying a working man. I'm glad I wasn't got at here in Oxford so as to despise him."[25]

Unfortunately, this refusal to be "got at" at Oxford also entailed a rejection of the knowledge and enlightenment offered by the like of Tom Galton. "Are you going to chuck-all this?" Galton says, putting his hand on a pile of books. "Yes, I've got to", she replied.[26] The logic of this sexualized view of social class is that meaningful contact with the working class must take place at a sexual level. Before pursuing this idea it would useful to place Mitchison within a specific political context.

She belonged to the Socialist League, which was formed in 1932 by the minority of the Independent Labour Party (ILP) that wished to remain within the Labour Party. This was a small organization, never more than 3,000 strong, that was dominated by the upper middle classes, three barristers, Sir Stafford Cripps, D.N.Pritt and G.R.Mitchison (Naomi's husband), for example, occupied leading positions. The politics of the League were radical, but always electoral in nature.[27] Essentially the League set itself the task of creating the conditions in which Labour would win an electoral victory, in creating what it called: "the Will to Power".[28] How precisely this was to be achieved was not specified, beyond a recognition that it would involve the exertion of "the maximum influence upon the workers of this country" The class composition of the Socialist League made this a difficult objective to achieve. The class gulf between the League and its target audience is clearly apparent in the following extract from Cripps' 1936 work, *The Struggle for Peace*:

> If our imagination can carry us out of our comfortable chairs and away from our well-filled tables to the homes of the unemployed or the lower paid wage-earners, we shall find a truly devastating state of affairs in every capitalist country in the world.[29]

Indeed, shortly before the above passage Cripps referred to:

> Those who have read such books as Walter Greenwood's *Love on the Dole*, or seen the play adapted from it, will have no difficulty in realizing the stark tragedy of life to the younger generation today.[30]

Cripps clearly numbered himself amongst those whose visions of working class deprivation derived from Greenwood's fiction, rather than experience.

The fictional Dione Galton was at one with Cripps on this issue, guilelessly telling her working class host in Marshbook Bridge that she really knew about how most people lived "out of books".[31] However, prior to this experience of working class domesticity, Mitchison had provided her character with a very dramatic opportunity for "contact" with the working class. In the summer of 1932 Dione and

Tom were to visit the Soviet Union. On the eve of her departure Donald Maclean an unemployed Communist, and the estranged son of Dione's Scottish mother's gardener, arrived on her Oxford doorstep. He was "on the run" after having assassinated Daniel Coke-Brown, a newspaper proprietor. Dione decides that she will smuggle him out of the country to the Soviet Union, passing him off as her brother Alex, who agrees to disappear for the duration of the visit.

In the course of the voyage Dione discovers that Donald is a virgin, who has spent long nights reading Engels to sublimate his sexual desires. Donald reveals that he has avoided sexual contact through an aversion to girls who were not "nice", and a fear of producing pregnancies. Dione's response further confirms her book-based knowledge of the working class:

> I thought-oh Donald, I thought a riveter would surely have his girl to match him, a strong jolly girl who wouldn't make a fuss and be intellectual and talk about it the way we do! I thought of men like Lawrence's miners.[32]

Dione decides that it is her duty as a socialist woman to relieve Maclean of the burden of his virginity. "I am here", she tells him, "to untangle you."[33] "How could I leave you all oppressed and bound as you were?"[34] However, despite the commitment she makes *en route* to the Soviet Union, this act of sexual/political solidarity never takes place. This is largely because Mitchison's character clearly experiences acute class unease at the prospect of its realization. After their arrival in the Soviet Union, while out with Maclean, the comments of some passing Russians produces the following reaction:

> As he held her tight in his arms, half-leaning against the parapet, she heard some laughing comment in Russian from a girl passing by. She felt horribly uncomfortable. She felt like a housemaid with her young man. With her out-of-work riveter.[35]

Dione struggles against this response, but it nevertheless reveals that within the thought-world of her class a sexual relationship of this kind is socially debasing. Later, in conversation with Maclean, she reveals the fear that she feels in strange towns, in particular in working class districts. This is clearly a class fear with a strong sexual element.

> I'm frightened of men looking at me, I expect. Yes, I suppose at bottom I'm frightened of rape or at least-of people coming up behind and-kissing me or something. But I'm frightened of women sometimes...women who've been hurt, probably, and who want to hurt back when they see me wearing nicer clothes than theirs.[36]

Maclean responds to this by telling her, "I'm thinking you have as much to be cured of as I have...They're folks like me..."[37]

This neatly sums up the function of this relationship. Sexual intercourse with Maclean is the key to real solidarity with the working class. Dione's continuing ambiguity about this possibilty, is presented as the product of the persistence of her class fear.

On the night that is eventually set aside for their sexual congress Maclean fails to appear. This is because he had fallen in with a group of Russian women workers. One of them, Marfa, an engineer, proves to be just the sort of 'strong jolly girl' that Dione had imagined as a partner for Donald. As they undress she asks him: "You got-rubber goods-comrade?"[38] He hasn't, but it does not matter, in the land of the Soviets Maclean finds political solidarity and sexual fulfillment. Maclean notes that Marfa's hair has a stronger smell than Dione's, and that her breasts are broad and brown, not "white and chickenny" like the breasts he has seen on "dirty postcards". She has the odour and physicality of a worker, and in the context of the Soviet Union these are presented as virtues. Back at the hotel Dione, waiting for Maclean smells one of his dirty shirts, "What did she think of it? Nice, not nice? She didn't know, she couldn't make up her mind...."[39] This inability to decide about the smell is emblematic of her continuing ambivalence towards working class physicality.

Mitchison's treatment of this episode can be partly explained by her membership of the Socialist League. The League sought to galvanize the working class as a means to secure an electoral victory for Labour. The League's point of contact with the working class was on the issue of consumption. The class fear and guilt that Dione displayed in her conversation with Maclean, quoted above, focused on her superior levels of consumption. Indeed, when Mitchison described the motivation for Tom's (Dione's husband) conversion to socialism she explicitly eschews political theory and places all of the emphasis on consumption:

> Tom had joined the Labour Party ten years ago for no elaborate economic reasons, although he was an historian and an economist, but just because he hated other people to be overworked and underfed and not have so much leisure time or such a good time as he had.[40]

In this light it is possible to see her response to Maclean as that which characterized him as an underprivileged consumer of sexual satisfaction. At one point she says to him: "Mustn't we share everything".[41] What she is proposing to share is her sexual knowledge, and her capacity for sexual fulfillment. This is confirmed by her actions in other parts of the novel. When, for example, she discovers that a working class couple in Sallington are leading a celibate life because they cannot afford more children, and are ignorant of birth control, she provides the address of a Clinic, and the way back to conjugal bliss. "But Mrs. Taylor! Mary! My dear idiot, you're very fond of your husband, aren't you?"[42] Sexual satisfaction was a commodity that Dione had in plenty, and was happy to dispense to those deprived of it. It was also a distinguishing feature of her class, or her section of the class, the civilized, professional upper middle classes. It was not to be found, as we have seen in the commercial bourgeoisie. The idea of raising consumption levels for the deprived did not necessarily imply a fundamental redistribution of goods, or a serious change in lifestyle for the likes of Dione. Hence, she was eager for him to become a satisfied sexual consumer, but not keen on becoming the object of consumption, because that would involve a major adjustment in lifestyle.

This dichotomy is well illustrated by the relationship that Tom Galton forms when he joins his wife in the Soviet Union. Shortly after his arrival he and Dione visit the Nikolaevsky family, to whom they have been given an introduction. The family, have a daughter in her early twenties, Oksana. Dione, seeing that there is a mutual attraction between Tom and Oksana, encourages her husband to initiate a sexual relationship with her, expressing, for example pleasure that Tom will see the girl naked when the three go swimming. Oksana is politically committed, weeping for the Galtons because they live in country that has not had its revolution, and sexually advanced.[43] Indeed Mitchison's vision of the Soviet Union is of a society that is inherently free in its sexual morality. In this she was completely at odds with contemporary trends in Soviet society,[44] but completely at one with the tendency of contemporary left-wingers in Britain to project on to the Soviet Union the fulfillment of their particular aspirations.[45] Oksana, whose father was an academic, and whose mother was a doctor, was also from the same section of society as the Galtons. Mitchison famously claimed that she and her husband had an "open" marriage.[46] Her depiction of the *menage* with Oksana, conducted with the complicity of her parents, is of a society where such attitudes are the norm. In Mitchison's presentation the Soviet Union was a society that embodied the advanced sexual notions that in England were, according to her, the preserve of the educated upper middle class. This is strongly confirmed when Dione asks Tom what his would-be constituents in Marshbrook Bridge would make of the arrangement, "In fifty years-no, in twenty perhaps-they'll see and approve. In the meantime they don't know.[47]

The Soviet Union, and the Galtons are, then, at least twenty years in advance of the British proletariat. Although, even in the Soviet Union such advanced practices are best played out with people of one's own background. For Mitchison post-revolutionary Russia appeared to be a society governed by the sexual morality of advanced thinkers from Hampstead and North Oxford. Oksana as an educated practitioner of this morality thus became an ideal extra-marital partner; whereas

Maclean, the puritanical British Communist who described D. H. Lawrence as a
"parcel of filth", was not.[48]

This perception of the Soviet Union must have been very comforting for
"advanced" thinkers like Mitchison and her circle. It did not though resolve the
question of close fraternal/political contact with the British working class, either
within the novel, or in Mitchison's life. E.M.Forster rubbed salt into this open
wound by remarking after a party at the Mitchison's large Hammersmith house:

> I enjoyed it myself but couldn't help reflecting that the left wing either knows no
> working class people or else doesn't regard them as suitable guests.[49]

The fugitive, Donald Maclean, had described Dione's fear of rape in working
class districts, as "class consciousness", by which he meant it was a class-based
fear. Mitchison, the novelist resolved the question of cross-class solidarity by using
the act of rape. During a stay in the constituency Dione visits the new ice-rink.
There she meets Idris Pritchard, one of the instructors, and a member of the
Communist Party. Pritchard introduces himself with a 'Would you care to dance,
comrade?'.[50] A greeting that, especially when combined with Pritchard's good
looks, virtually compels Dione to respond in a fraternal manner. She arranges to
meet him later, and pays for a meal in a restaurant. After the meal she goes back to
Pritchard's flat, where he rapes her. The prelude to the assault is shaped entirely in
terms of consumption:

> "I do hate you as one of your class." He laid a hand on her knee. "But I am not
> hating you yourself." She was reminded of Donald. She stroked the hand on her
> knee. "You shall have them, you shall have them!" she said; "I do want you to have
> them!" "You do?" he said. "Truly? Dione fach, you want us workers to have
> everything you've had, everything of yours?" "Yes," she said, "yes," wanting so
> much to dispel the hate and envy in his mind...[51]

Whereupon, Pritchard forcibly consumes Dione sexually, enjoying the privileges
and good things of her existence are equated with the sexual act. For Dione, after a
very brief period of self-recrimination, the rape acts as a Road to Damascus
experience, opening her mind to the true degradation of working class experience.
This revelation first comes to her, significantly, in Pritchard's bathroom as she
attempted to clean herself up. There, where people literally bare themselves and
tend their bodies she rationalized Pritchard's behaviour by relating it to the
condition of the room:

> ...suddenly she was overwhelmed by the nastiness, the inadequacy, the pity of this
> dreadfully private little room where the people in this house were used to strip
> themselves, see their bodies in the twelve-inch cracked mirror backed by the grimy

bath and the tooth brushes. No wonder Idris Pritchard was like he had shown himself to be. No wonder. Poor Idris. Poor people in this house. In the other houses like it. Oh, poor dears, poor dears, how could one blame them for anything![52]

The behaviour of Idris Pritchard is presented as indicative of the conditions of the entire working class. Thus, the rape was Dione's rite of passage admitting her to the core of working class experience. Janet Montefiore notes that the Dione character survived the experience of this assault "without much trauma".[53] Indeed, Dione herself wakes the next morning feeling "virtually unshaken". However, at the same moment she wonders whether she will be able to approach "the revolution" with the same *sang froid*.[54] The two are of course linked, political solidarity with the working class was a necessary pre-condition for "the revolution". This combination of thoughts strongly suggests that in the immediate aftermath of the rape Mitchison's character believed that she had achieved that pre-condition. After this point in the novel Dione's new contact with the working class works out in what at first sight would appear to be rather unexpected directions. This becomes apparent when she meets Pritchard again a few weeks later at the Hyde Park rally of the 1932 Hunger March. He had lost his job at the ice rink and believed that Dione was to blame. Once that was cleared up Dione thinks "...oh...I mustn't be so nasty to him, poor little man." She then offers to use her influence to find him a job at the Oxford ice rink, and to pay his fare for him to move to Oxford to take it up. In the event Pritchard refuses this offer because of his commitment to Party work, but the significance of the moment is that she deals with her rapist by deploying upper middle class patronage; however when they separate she expresses admiration for his commitment to the Party. This encounter, in other words is characterized by the inter-play of two very different forms of political/social discourse upper middle class paternalism and proletarian solidarity.

This combination of discourses characterizes the whole of Dione's day at this particular rally. At one point she saves herself from being run down by a mounted policeman by crying out: "Look out, my good man!". A form of address which immediately tells the constable that he dealing with a "lady", and he moves off telling her: "You clear out, ma,am!".[55] Later, she has a fierce encounter with a bourgeois couple walking by the park. Their hostility towards her is presented as the product of their hatred for a class traitor, the man tells her: "you, madam, you have the voice of a lady, but you behave like one of the criminal classes".[56] The encounter ends with the man boxing Dione's ears, an action which is presented as a substitute for a sexual assault.

The things they'd said were a good deal worse than the immediate pain. You haven't time to teach her now, said the words; you haven't time to rape her now said the tone.[57]

Later, when rescued by sympathetic Communists, including Pritchard, Dione describes the episode as "Good practice for the revolution..."[58] Dione followed up practicing for the revolution with attendance at a distinctly bourgeois, if bohemian, studio party where, this being the 1930s, she indulged in a mild sexual flirtation with a young poet. The non-proletarian character of this event being underscored by her musings on what Sallington Labour party members would make of it.

At this stage it is necessary to consider what we can make of the highly sexualized view of politics and social class that Mitchison presents in this novel. A key difference between Mitchison's work and that of Upward is that Mitchison's leading character has no desire to permanently become one with the working class. The future has to be secured by the construction of solidarity with the working class, but the values of the future will be those of the Galton's. Hence the liberal attitudes they express, and the sexual advice they dispense throughout the novel find their post-revolutionary counter-parts in the Soviet Union in the attitudes of the Nikolaevskys, Oksana's family. Unlike the enlightened, attractive and cultured intelligentsia the workers, even within the Communist Party are sexually inept and unfulfilled. In return for their political support, the intelligentsia will bestow the gift of sexual enlightenment, and civilization upon their working class allies. The limits to this cross-class sexual/political solidarity are clearly demonstrated by the relationship between Dione's brother Alex and his working class lover, Nellie. This relationship began when Alex picked up Nellie as a prostitute in South Shields, where he was hiding while Donald Maclean took his place on the trip to the Soviet Union. When Nellie becomes pregnant Alex writes as follows to Dione:

> My fool of a girl, Nellie, has gone and started a baby...it looks like my having to support a little bastard now. I don't much mind, for I don't feel like marrying. I thought of marrying Nellie, but she'd obviously be uncomfortable and I don't think there's much point. I shall see the kid's all right and gets decently educated and all that....[59]

In this instance cross-class sexual relations are sanctioned, but the working class woman is not be admitted to Alex's social/family circle, she will remain socially and geographically distinct from the rest of his life-to save her social discomfort. Dione makes no comment whatsoever on the arrangement proposed by Alex, which is thereby sanctioned by her, and through her by Mitchison.

The enemy against whom this cross-class physical/political alliance was directed might be described as the philistine bourgeoisie. The principal representatives of this group in the novel are the Coke-Browns, to whom the Galtons are related by the marriage of Tom's sister. The philistine quality of the Coke-Browns is indicated by a number of apparently trivial, but significant episodes. In the immediate wake of Daniel Coke-Brown's murder Dione is telephoned with the news by a young sympathetic Coke-Brown who tells her:

> "I say, I thought you'd be pleased!" the girl's voice said, "he was an awful old man. He gave us the most rotten set of fish-knives for a wedding present!" [60]

Many rationalizations have been advanced for political assassinations, but only the upper middle class British left of the 1930s could have used bad taste as a justification. For both the Galtons the ultimate demonstration of the dangerous and uncivilized nature of the commercial bourgeoisie exists within their sexual manners. Tom Galton's dislike of his industrialist brother-in-law, Reginald Coke-Brown is expressed in terms of his horror at the thought that for the last twenty years Coke-Brown has been sleeping with Tom's sister.[61] Dione Galton, as we have already seen characterized the commercial bourgeoisie as sexually predatory and prone to rape. Towards the end of the book in a supernatural passage Dione is allowed a vision of what the future might hold. She is shown the counter-revolutionary overthrow of an elected Labour Government.[62] One consequence of this is the rape of her daughter by members of a counter-revolutionary militia, one of whom the daughter recognizes as the local sweet-shop owner, a classic petit-bourgeois figure.[63]

Mitchison's novel, presents a sexualized vision of the Socialist League's social location and political orientation. The professional, middle class socialists of the League are distinguished from their commercial and industrial peers by their civilization, in particularly their civilized sexuality. This view seems to be compounded of a mixture of traditional patrician contempt for those "in trade", and an endorsement of the works of D.H. Lawrence and Sigmund Freud. The sexuality of the commercial bourgeoisie is, for Mitchison, a metaphor for its acquisitiveness and violence; the embrace of the bourgeoisie is, literally deadly.

The sexual mores of the working class are also flawed, but this was the product of their deprivation; a state which is susceptible to the remedial action of the civilized middle classes. This sexualized version of the class struggle gave, therefore, a privileged role to those like Mitchison and to the largely middle class Socialist League, because their morality represented the morality of the future. However, political progress was dependent on the achievement of solidarity with the working class, this was a difficult and, in some respects unpalatable necessity. Mitchison's character, Dione, only achieves the level of contact required through the experience of rape. This erased her perceived failure (i.e. non-coitus) with Donald Maclean. The effect of the rape, and the understanding that it brings of the proletarian condition has the effect of validating Dione's existing lifestyle as it simultaneously confirms her at-oneness with the workers and the superior values of her civilization. This is demonstrated by the pregnancy that she discovers at the end of the book. At the very beginning of the book Dione states, to herself, that a further pregnancy (like Mitchison she already had four children) was out of the question because it would not be fair to benefit from her comfortable situation, that was so different from that of the constituents of Marshbrook Bridge.[64] After considering the possibility of an abortion, Dione eventually positively embraced the pregnancy. Indeed, in a euphoric passage Mitchison presents this pregnancy as symbolic of the new dawn of the revolutionary future.[65] It is as if the experience of the rape confirmed Dione's role, and the role of her comrades in the Socialist League as the embodiment of civilization and, therefore, the hope of the working class. Or, to put it another way, Dione's class identity and the struggle for socialism were not incompatible.

The development of left-wing sympathies among a section of the upper middle classes opens a window on the processes of class definition during the 1930s. Clearly, although this is not a comprehensive survey, it does demonstrate that the adoption of new political affiliations was a rather more complex issue than one of simply taking out a membership card. It involved, for the middle classes a re-appraisal of their entire social identity. The difficulties caused by this process were compounded by a number of developments, which were calling into question the status and identity of the professional middle classes. Graduate unemployment was relatively low, but it was high enough to cause concern.[66] Many young graduates felt themselves compelled to take jobs that were somehow beneath them. For others the whole crisis-ridden experience of the post-First World War period called into question established values and institutions. John Strachey, a scion of Britain's intellectual establishment, and Britain's foremost Marxist publicist, declared:

> That whole unparalleled structure of repressions and taboos which the theorists and theologians of the Anglo-Saxon bourgeoisie had managed to build up had been smashed by the war, and for good or ill would not be repaired.[67]

Although, establishment values were not as secure as they once were Strachey was perhaps rather premature in claiming that they had been destroyed. This is apparent in the responses of many of his peers to the onset of mass culture and mass education. The expansion of mass education stimulated the development of popular fiction directed at a new mass market and mass circulation newspapers like the *Daily Mail* and the *Daily Express*. The thirties also saw the development of cinema and wireless. The former brought both the voice and image of the United States to a mass British audience. The latter projected a public voice into the private space of the home. For many intellectuals these developments spelt cultural debasement. The Leavises, for example, loathed cinema, and set about creating the "Great Tradition" as a cultural barrier to this process.[68] Mitchison railed against the cheap souvenirs that were the by-product of mass tourism to the Highlands.[69]

Orwell wrote a number of positively splenetic passages attacking the new consumerism in his novel, *Coming Up for Air*. A novel in which, significantly, the principal character looks back to his children in the Golden World before the First World War.[70] The new mass culture of the 1930s changed the face of the world in which the middle class left had grown up, and in which they assumed they had a secure place. It even blurred, to some degree, the distinctions between the classes at a physical level. The new mass culture created a world in which, as J.B.Priestley put it, there were "factory girls looking like actresses..."[71]

Within this rapidly changing world the newly radicalized middle class did not step forward as blank sheets cleansed of all of their previous attitudes, rather they were like the survivors of an explosion who emerged with their clothing in varying degrees of disintegration. Some of them, depending on age, background and other factors, retained rather more or less of their previous outlooks. All were convinced of the need for change, but the nature of that change, and the nature of their involvement in it was less certain. In the case of Mitchison this involved the re-casting of social class and political progress in such a way as to give her own social grouping a leading role and identity. For Upward it ultimately appeared to involve a mystical experience in which he submerged himself not so much in the working class, as in the historical process. In the passage quoted earlier, in which Upward talks about the "light of future freedom" shining down from space, he comes very close to describing a Pentecostal event. In both of these examples, however, the key to the resolution of their political problems is presented as the ability to reconcile themselves to the working class body.

---

[1] J.Heath Stubbs, "The Poet of Bray" in Kingsley Amis (ed.), *The New Oxford Book of Light Verse* (Oxford: OUP. 1978) 294.

[2] E.Upward, *In the Thirties* (London: Quartlet, 1978) 5.

[3] In her 1979 memoir Naomi Mitchison reflected on the smell of inter-war crowds, made up of people unable to regularly wash their underwear. N.Mitchison, *You May Well Ask* (London: Victor Gollancz, 1979) 45; See, also Upward's account of Sebrill's first encounter with the Communist Party. E.Upward, *In the Thirties*, 51-2.

[4] *Punch* 1932. Reproduced in *The Punch Cartoon History of Modern Britain* Part 3 (London: Punch, n.d).

[5] G.Orwell, *The Road to Wigan Pier* (London: LCB, 1937) 159-160.

[6] V.Gollanz, Forward to G.Orwell, *Road to Wigan Pier*, xv-xvi.

[7] G.Orwell, *Road to Wigan Pier*, 159.

[8] See W.Brierley, *Means Test Man*, first pub. 1935 (Nottingham: Spokesman, 1983).

[9] Upward's character, Sebrill says of his working class lover: "He had committed himself to her now. To try to go back on what he had done would be treachery not very different...from the treachery of an eighteenth century gentleman abandoning the cottager's young and only daughter whom he's seduced." E.Upward, *In the Thirties*, 183.

[10] L.Davidoff, "Class and Gender in Victorian England" in J.L.Newton; M.P.Ryan, J.R.Walkowitz (eds), *Sex and Class in Women's History* (London: RKP, 1983) 25-6.

[11] G.Greene, *It's a Battlefield*, first pub. 1934 (London: Penguin, 1971) 132.

[12] *Ibid*, 132.

[13] E.Upward, *In the Thirties*, 44.

[14] *Ibid*, 180.

[15] *Ibid*, 214.

[16] *Ibid*, 165.

[17] *Ibid*, 282.

[18] N.Annan, *Our Age* (London: Weidenfeld and Nicholson, 1990) 242.

[19] See E.Upward, *No Home But the Struggle* (London: Quartlet, 1979).

[20] N.Mitchison, *You May Well Ask*, 184-187.

[21] N.Mitchison, *We Have Been Warned* (London: Constable, 1935) 62, 119, 400-1 respectively.

[22] *Ibid*, 26.

[23] *Ibid*, 54.

[24] *Ibid*, 103.

[25] *Ibid*, 153.

[26] *Ibid*, 152.

[27] S.Cripps: 296 H.C.Deb.5s, columns 1260-1, 19th December 1934.

[28] "The Fight Goes On" *The Socialist Leaguer* No.5 Oct/Nov 1934.

[29] S.Cripps, *The Struggle for Peace* (London: Gollanz, 1936) 40-1.

[30] *Ibid*, 40.

[31] N.Mitchison, *We have Been Warned*, 386.

[32] *Ibid*, 229.

[33] *Ibid*, 239.

[34] *Ibid*, 241.

[35] *Ibid*, 252.

[36] *Ibid*, 254.

[37] *Ibid*, 255.

[38] *Ibid*, 275.

[39] *Ibid*, 261.

[40] *Ibid*, 21.

[41] *Ibid*, 241.

[42] *Ibid*, 505.

[43] *Ibid*, 292.

[44] C.Wood, *Stalin's Russia* (London: Arnold, 1993) 198.

[45] See H.Johnson, *The Socialist Sixth of Humanity* (London: Gollanz, 1939) 366.

[46] N.Mitchison, *You May Well Ask*, 70-1.

[47] N.Mitchison, *We Have Been Warned*, 317.

[48] *Ibid*, 128.

[49] Quoted in N.Mitchson, *You May Well Ask*, 105.

[50] N.Mitchson, *We Have Been Warned*, 402.

[51] *Ibid*, 412-3.

[52] *Ibid*, 415.

[53] J.Montefiore, *Men and Women Writers of the 1930s* (London: Routledge, 1996) 60.

[54] N.Mitchison, *We Have Been Warned*, 423.

[55] *Ibid*, 453.

[56] *Ibid*, 455.

[57] *Ibid*, 456.

[58] *Ibid*, 457.

[59] *Ibid*, 519.

[60] *Ibid*, 207.

[61] *Ibid*, 194.

[62] J.T.Murphy, *Preparing for Power*, first pub. 1934 (London: Pluto, 1972).

[63] N.Mitchison, *We Have Been Warned*, 544.

[64] *Ibid*, 3.

[65] *Ibid*, 516.

[66] N.Wood, *Communism and British Intellectuals* (London: Gollancz, 1959) 37-8.

[67] J.Strachey, "The Education of a Communist" in *New Left Review* No.3 1934.

[68] Q.D.Leavis, *Fiction and the Reading Public* (London: Chatto and Windus, 1932) 16-17.

[69] N.Mitchison, *We Have Been Warned*, 45.

[70] G.Orwell, *Coming Up for Air,* first pub. 1939 (London: Penguin, 1962) 25-6.

[71] J.B.Priestly, *English Journey* (London: William Heinemann Ltd, 1934) 401.

'THE ORDINARY GOOD MOTHER': WOMEN'S CONSTRUCTION OF THEIR IDENTITY AS MOTHERS, OXFORDSHIRE C. 1945-1970

ANGELA DAVIS

In the years after World War Two post-Freudian psychology, most notably espoused by the child-psychologists John Bowlby and Donald Winnicott, provided new rationales for the idealisation and enforcement of women's maternal role.[1] Winnicott and Bowlby stressed the importance of the mother-child relationship and the need for mothers to remain at home with their children, although they approached the subject from different angles. Winnicott praised mothers, emphasising the positive benefits to both the individual and society which, "the ordinary good mother" made, through being devoted to her infant.[2] Bowlby highlighted the dangers if women reneged on this role. He discussed the problem of maternal deprivation and the damaging effects upon the mental health of children when the mother-child relationship was broken.[3] The conclusion they reached was the same: a woman's place was at home with her children. The view that maternal care in infancy was crucial for the physical development of the child had long roots, stretching back to the late nineteenth century. What was new was the idea that mere physical separation from the mother could be a pathogenic factor in its own right. Bowlby had concluded that, "What is believed to be essential for mental health is that the infant and young child should experience a warm, intimate, and continuous relationship with his mother."[4] Lee Comer argues that Bowlby's theory of maternal deprivation was exactly what the world had been waiting for. He provided a "scientific" basis for what was, by then, the status quo.[5] This chapter will investigate how and to what extent these ideas became incorporated in women's conception of motherhood at this time in light of the feminist critique of these theories that developed from the late 1960s.

The chapter is based on an analysis of twenty oral history interviews conducted by the author with women who lived in the Oxfordshire villages of Benson and Ewelme when they were bringing up their children.[6] The women range in age from their late-fifties to mid-eighties and their first child was born between 1938 and 1975. They enjoyed varying levels of education, from minimum age school leavers to graduates. By interviewing women from diverse backgrounds it is possible to see how locality, education and class influenced women's experiences. A number of social surveys, community studies and medical studies were conducted between 1945 and 1970. These studies do shed light on attitudes towards motherhood, but the information they can provide is limited because the questions asked reflect the interviewers' preoccupations rather than the concerns of the women they are talking to. There were studies looking at class, housing, employment patterns and social mobility, but not how these factors could determine women's experiences of motherhood. The British authors of social surveys and community studies were conventional in their desire for the stability of marriage and the nuclear family, taking the different roles for men and women for granted. Oral history has played a significant role in historical enquiry into domestic life and can add to understanding women's experiences of motherhood.

The birth of a first child was a life-altering event for most women in the years between 1945 and 1970 and there was intense debate surrounding the role of women at this time. Many questions were being asked: How did women become a mother, was it innate, or learnt? If it was learnt where should this education take place? What happened if women were educated to be workers rather than mothers? How significant a factor was class? This chapter will address these questions, and will also investigate the ways in which locality intersected with ideas of gender and class to affect how women saw themselves as mothers at this time. In addition, it will examine how oral history can be used to augment existing knowledge and challenge some of the assumptions made about women's experiences at the time.

Benson and Ewelme

Benson and Ewelme are neighbouring villages in South Oxfordshire. They lie twelve, fifteen and forty miles from Oxford, Reading and London respectively. Wallingford, the nearest town, is three miles away. Oxfordshire was principally a rural county, but during the course of the century agriculture was in decline. Many of the men who had previously worked in farming moved into developing industries such as the Northern Aluminium Company which opened in Banbury in 1931, or the car works in Oxford that grew rapidly in the years after the First World War.[7] The Barnett House Survey[8] estimated that there were around 3,000 ex-agricultural workers in the Cowley motor industry by 1936 with twenty-four Benson men and five Ewelme men employed in Morris Motor Works and Pressed Steel.[9] There were clear incentives for these men to switch jobs: wages in agriculture were notoriously low and this was exacerbated by the depression of the 1920s with farmers keen to dispense with labour.[10] After World War Two English agriculture again went through a long period of depression and many Oxfordshire farmers went of business. At the same time, the industrial areas of Oxford and

Banbury continued to expand. Oxfordshire experienced both a decline in agriculture and a rapid industrial development during the twentieth century, particularly resulting from the rise of the motor industry. By the postwar period most men and women worked outside of Benson and Ewelme changing the character of the villages and its consequences were keenly felt.

Living conditions in the villages were also transformed during the postwar years. While mains-water and electricity were supplied by the 1920s they were not universal until after World War Two and sewerage did not come until the mid-1950s.[11] Despite these improvements the housing shortage after the war meant many of the women lived in very basic conditions such as a caravan and a wooden shack. None of the women interviewed had their own car and without transport women heavily relied on services provided within their village. Benson was fortunate in having a range of services throughout the period. In 1939 there was a boot mender, postmaster and newsagent, three dairies, two butchers, three general shopkeepers, a hairdresser and a shop selling coffee, tea, cocoa and salt products. Although there was no shoe repairer by 1970, there was still a newsagent, a supermarket and two smaller grocers, two hairdressers and a weekly barber, a bookmaker, greengrocer, two butchers, a drug-store and a hardware and home decorating store. There was a reproduction furniture store, two antique shops, a dry-cleaner and launderette and a sub-branch of Barclay's Bank. Many tradesmen delivered and there was a milk round, bread round, calling greengrocer and a Library van.[12] During the twentieth century Benson changed from a declined and static agricultural community to a diverse village, four times its previous size with a range of services, facilities and people, the majority of whom were employed outside the village. Ewelme has not been so fortunate. Before World War Two there had been several shops including a draper, general store, dairy, bakery and two or three sweet shops. By the mid-1970s the closure of Greenway stores had left Ewelme without a permanent village shop.[13] In contrast to Benson's rapid expansion Ewelme has grown by less than half, its population was just under 500 in 1881 and 870 in 1991.[14] While some of the old villagers do remain, Ewelme has principally become a commuter village and tourist attraction.

Village life: neighbours, housing and class

Benson and Ewelme faced an influx of new people in the second half of the twentieth century. In Benson's case the village itself expanded with large areas of new housing built. At the time of the First World War Benson's population was 985.[15] Even in the 1950s the village itself only had a few new houses with some council houses at Sunnyside built during the late 1940s and early 1950s. In the late 1950s Benson was designated as an expanding village. Houses were built on farmland, open spaces and derelict yards. In the 1960s, the plan for Benson envisaged an eventual population of 4300. This number was not quite reached but by the 1970s there was new building in the Westfield Road and Blacklands Road estates, Sands Way, and areas between Mill Lane, St Helen's Avenue and Old London Road.[16] As a far smaller village than Benson, Ewelme saw less development, but a private housing estate was developed in the early 1960s at Chaucer Court on the site of an old barn and had a significant effect on village life. Many of the women who were newcomers to the villages moved into these recently built estates. Nina Newsom moved into Chaucer Court in 1969. She remembers the strong sense of community that developed there, with constant socialising amongst the residents.[17] Deborah Denning always lived on estates and describes the feeling of community that could develop on them. She remembers first moving onto the estate where she lived in Brighton. "[When I] looked at the house I saw this nice lady smiling at us over the fence, and I though ah, that looks good. And you know we just helped each other out, and we got to know each other quite quickly, and well everybody round about was quite friendly. There were lots and lots of young families in pretty much the same situation really."[18] Their experience of life on the estate in Brighton was so good that she and her husband deliberately chose to live on an estate again when they moved to Benson. Most of her close friends came from the estate she lived on and she liked life on the estates because they were full of people in a similar situation.

Class cleavages were felt in the villages and they determined where people lived and worked. New private estates were popular with middle-class commuters and the strong sense of community that developed on these estates was encouraged by the uneasy relationship their residents enjoyed with the native working-class villagers. In Ewelme's smaller community this discord was particularly acutely felt. There were also sharp class divisions in employment. Based on their husbands' employment half the women interviewed would be classified as working class and half as middle class. Most of the working-class husbands had worked at some point in the Cowley works, and some of the women's fathers had also worked there. The car factories, reached by bicycle and later by works bus, began attracting village men from the 1930s. The wages were better than those available locally in agriculture and the factories remained a major employer of Benson people until the 1980s. Mary Matthews describes how her husband worked, "down the car factory at Oxford, I think everyone worked down there."[19] There were jobs for professionals such as the vicar or doctor, but by the postwar period increasing numbers of middle-class residents also lived in the villages and travelled elsewhere to work. The villages became popular with those working for the Atomic Energy Research Authority at Harwell, Aldermaston and Culham.[20] Employment outside the village had become the norm for both classes by the postwar years.

Indicators of class were under modification. Mary and Maud Matthews, two sisters-in-law, described how they thought that class distinctions had weakened.

Mary Matthews explains, "I've heard Keith and I've heard Jack say it, "We're working class and proud of it", and I sort of say "I'm not working-class I'm working upwards mate", and it's sort of more that, and I don't think there is a class distinction as such. They don't say you're rich, you're poor, you're on a different level. It's moulded in a lot more. But there's always going to be obviously where you're born and who you're born to."[21] For Mary Matthews class was as much about self-identification as employment. In addition, there was an overlap between divisions of class and divisions between old and new villagers. Betty Brown's class identity and local identity were intertwined. It was the working-class residents who shared a common status and lifestyle.[22] Women recalled going wooding or their husbands going poaching as part of traditional rural life,[23] but these were working-class customs and not shared by the middle-class residents; neither were they shared by the new immigrants. The nature of village life could reduce class divisions though, as well sharpen them. Mothers of both classes met at Church, the baby clinic, or in the shops. While working-class women were employed as cleaners by their middle-class counterparts, unlike in towns and cities they also met regularly outside of this employer-employee role. The difficulties in assigning women to a class based on their husband's occupation were also demonstrated in the villages. Fran Farley's mother was a shop assistant and she felt that she and her middle-class husband were from very different backgrounds.[24] Isobel Innes was married to a dentist and was herself university educated. She was however the daughter of a cooper from a family of Irish immigrants. She later worked as a receptionist at her husband's practice.[25] If her class was to be determined by her father's occupation, her husband's occupation and her own occupation each would have a different outcome.

Many sociologists believed they were discovering a decline in neighbourliness during the period. The relocation of families from traditional working-class areas to new suburban estates coincided with an emphasis on the nuclear family, encouraging debate about privatisation of the family. For example, comparing Oxford's suburb of Barton with the city-centre region of St. Ebbe's, John Mogey found that the neighbourhood-centred society of St. Ebbe's had been replaced by a family-centred society at Barton.[26] Josephine Klein argued the findings of studies such as Mogey's could be applied to other areas using the theory of transition, which assumed social change took place at variable rates in different localities; the implication being that all groups would reach the same level of progress at some point.[27] The findings from Benson and Ewelme challenge this hypothesis, though. Neighbours continued to form the principal source of support for the women interviewed and this was true both for natives and immigrants, for those who lived in the older parts or new peripheral estates, and remained the case throughout the period. Helen Harris's husband was in the RAF so her friends took on an even more important role. When she went into hospital to have her second child her husband was away and she had to leave her daughter with her neighbour. In her road there were five women who all had children around the same age so they organised a childcare rota. Each neighbour would have the children one morning of the week so the others were free to go shopping to Wallingford or such like.[28] Providing childcare for one another was mentioned by several of the women. Despite being a native villager with all her family living nearby Betty Brown still remembers her closest companion as being her next-door neighbour.[29] For the vast majority of the women it was friends and neighbours who provided support, advice, and companionship. Jenny James lived with her mother but still found friends to be hugely important.[30] For those women whose family lived far away friends were remembered as their principal means of support. The interviews demonstrate the key role that neighbours continued to play for mothers of young children, whatever other social changes were taking place.

About half of the women interviewed were born and brought up in the villages or the surrounding area and the other half moved there as adults. For the women born in the villages, it was more than somewhere to live and was part of their heritage. Benson and its transformations were important subjects for Betty Brown. She explained what it is like to have been born and bred there saying, "I do feel sorry sometimes for people who sort of flit from one place to another and never really getting to know somebody properly, and really, really knowing them, and knowing their history. Cause you see living in a village and if you know what their mum was like and what their mum's mum was like they can't put on any airs and graces because you know exactly what stock they've come from and they know that about us, so there's no pretence, there's no putting on airs and graces, so you know all about them, so you're relaxed with them."[31] She remembered a feeling of community and co-dependence that she felt characterised working-class village life that had been lost as the population expanded and became more transitory. Even the women who moved to the villages as adults had now lived there for about forty years, a long time in contrast to many current villagers. Georgia Green, a resident of Ewelme, felt she had come to experience some of the things Betty Brown had mentioned. She explained that, "I lived in towns before I moved out here, and when I first moved here I though oh, oh dear, the middle of the country, away from anything, what have I let myself in for. But in fact it's a much more friendly community here than I've ever been in before."[32] While there was a difference in the way natives and immigrants to the villages articulated a sense of belonging, because these immigrants were now some of its longest inhabitants this contrast was probably less marked now than it had been when they first moved there. All the women talked about the villages and village life with great affection, stressing how important the community had been to them when their children were young.

Becoming a mother: learnt or innate?

The idea that motherhood should come naturally to women existed long before the postwar period. In her critical history of the maternal instinct Elisabeth Badinter argues the belief that women possessed the impulse to love and care for children gained momentum from the eighteenth century.[33] By the nineteenth century it was expected that all women whether biological mothers or not had a maternal instinct. Psychoanalysis reaffirmed that motherliness was a normal characteristic of a woman's femininity. Difficulties in adjusting to marriage and motherhood indicated a failure in their psychic growth. John Bowlby argued a mother's motivation to look after her young derived from the intense bond between mother and offspring and that, "the child's tie to his mother is the human version of behaviour seen commonly in many other species of animal seems now indisputable."[34] These theories entered into popular culture, but to what extent did women support these views? Some of the women interviewed did say they felt that caring for their babies came naturally to them and there was such a thing as a maternal instinct. Helen Harris's father was a farm worker. She believed that being brought up in a rural locality helped her to adapt to motherhood, "I saw the animals with their babes and whatnot and they took to it naturally, so perhaps it's part and parcel of that."[35] Interestingly Patricia Parker thought there was a maternal instinct but that she did not possess it. It was not something she considered innate to all women.[36] The women who believed there was a maternal instinct were very accepting of what happened to them, which might be why they thought motherhood came naturally. They did not question they would have children or be full-time mothers. In contrast Patricia Parker had an unplanned baby and had not wanted to be a mother, which may have led to her difficulties in adjusting to motherhood, and encouraged her to feel she had no maternal instinct.

Psychoanalysis also stressed the importance of the mother-daughter relationship. Freud asserted that a woman's relationship with her mother was the, "original one" with all other relationships based upon it.[37] Women relived their experience of being mothered with their children. The relationship with a first child was therefore a special and intense one, like the relationship a woman had or wished to have had with her mother. This belief that women learnt mothering from their mothers was one element of a wider interest in the mother-daughter relationship, notably celebrated by Willmott and Young in their study of Bethnal Green.[38] The women echoed the view that they learnt their mothering technique by remembering how their mothers behaved towards them and felt women who did not have a mother around when they were young had difficulty adjusting to motherhood. Mary Matthews was brought up in care and thought it, "caused a lot of trouble", when her own children were born.[39] As well as this psychoanalytic view of women re-enacting their fantasies of being mothered, commentators felt girls learnt from their mothers in a more practical way. Housewifery was a shared profession among women, passed down from mother to daughter, and which strengthened the bond between them. Many women believed they learnt more in the home in subjects such as cooking and needlework than they did in school. Experts at the time maintained that if women did feel unready for caring for their children, it was the result of demographic changes, with increased mobility and smaller families meaning girls did not have younger siblings, cousins or nieces and nephews to care for.

Several of the women interviewed did come from large, extended families and had experience of looking after younger brothers and sisters. Isobel Innes was the eldest in a family of five, the daughter of Irish immigrants. She was fourteen when her youngest sister was born and very involved in caring for her siblings. While this should have been the perfect preparation she explains that, "when I got home from the hospital, and I needed to change this baby and I suddenly realised I didn't know what to do...even having seen my mother looking after her own babies...[You have] this overwhelming feeling, you suddenly realise that you're responsible for this little person."[40] Looking after younger brothers and sisters did not match the reality of having your own child. Women could experience the practical side of childcare, but could not prepare emotionally. Neither was coming from a large family a guarantee that women would have experience of running a home. Maud Matthews had a younger brother and her mother also fostered other children, but she had not been expected to help in the home in any way, "Mum done everything. And I mean everything, she was marvellous you know."[41] Moreover, women described the silence that surrounded pregnancy and childbirth within the family. As children, they often did not know when their mothers were pregnant and were kept out of the way if babies were born at home. Kathy Knight's mother was Benson's district nurse from the 1940s and she remembers pregnant women coming to her mother for their antenatal care, yet her mother never told her anything about pregnancy or childbirth.[42] In this climate of secrecy it is questionable how much women really did pick up from being around family members.

At the end of the war there was a renewed focus on what form girls' education should take. The Norwood Report (1943) argued that domestic science was valuable to girls because it would ready them for their future career as housewives. Girls were all potential homemakers, whereas boys were expected to find paid employment.[43] The Oxfordshire school system followed this belief in a gendered schooling and was fairly typical of the educational opportunities open to girls throughout the country. Domestic science was not taught in the village schools but girls went to Dorchester to learn cooking while the boys learnt woodwork and gardening. At eleven, the most promising pupils from both schools sat the examination for scholarships for Wallingford Grammar School. As there were only four places for South Oxfordshire, competition was intense. Most children remained at their village school until they left at fourteen to find work. Following the 1944 Education Act the schools became Church of England (Controlled) Primary Schools. There was no secondary school in either village. Children attended Wallingford Grammar School or Dorchester Secondary School until the late 1950s when the Abbey School, Berinsfield and Peers School, Littlemore opened.[44] The women had a gendered education learning subjects designed to prepare them for their future roles as housewives, although this was less marked at the grammar schools. Despite this concern with educating girls to be wives and mothers, throughout the period women left school without receiving any education pertinent to childbirth. Patricia Parker who had her first child in 1947, said, "You know it's terrible I didn't really know, you know, what happened, what to expect."[45] Even in the mid-1960s Deborah Denning described a similar situation:

What about when you were at school, had you ever had any lessons?

What about sex education?

Yes and about childbirth.

Oh no, no. First time I ever saw a picture of childbirth was when I was about to have one myself [laughing]. And it was all a bit of a shock to us all.[46]

Apart from home and school the other principal means of preparing women for childbirth was supposed to be antenatal care. In the 1940s there was no single provider of care, midwives, doctor, health visitors and local authority clinics could all be involved. When the National Health Service came into operation in 1948 GPs became increasingly important figures for women. Until 1953, however, when Dr Andrew Millar moved to the village, Benson did not have a resident doctor. It was part of the Dorchester practice with daily surgeries held in a private house in the village.[47] Ewelme never had a resident doctor and most patients from Ewelme went to the practice in Benson. The most notable fact about medical care in the villages during the period was the presence of a female doctor. Dr Anne Millar originally came to Benson solely in the role of doctor's wife, but she gradually became more involved in the practice. Having a female doctor who was a mother and an approachable figure was a constantly mentioned and obviously important fact for the women. She was well-known around the village and established a good rapport with her patients. Isobel Innes explained how, "if I'd ever had any doubts about it, there was Dr Anne here in the village and she was absolutely fantastic. She gave you a lot of confidence in how you were doing. She ran a clinic and you could take your child along and have it checked to make sure everything was ok. And she was incredibly reassuring and encouraging and you just felt that if things weren't right she'd tell you, and it gave you a lot of confidence so yeah, we were lucky."[48] Georgia Green specifically mentions the fact she was a mother as being why she valued her advice: "She'd got older children, but you got the feeling she knew what she was talking about. She's been through the same sort of thing."[49] The women held her knowledge as a mother in as high regard as much as they did her professional knowledge as a doctor, indeed they felt they could consult her on subjects they could not discuss with their own mothers.[50]

The number of women receiving antenatal care was undoubtedly rising during the period. Several of the women interviewed did not receive any specific antenatal education in the form of classes, however, even in the 1960s. There were no antenatal classes in Oxfordshire until 1961, and even then these only occurred in two locations.[51] For Deborah Denning who had her first child in Brighton there were not any classes because the consultant at the hospital, herself a mother of four, did not agree with them.[52] Where there were classes they were mostly slanted towards the theoretical and practical preparation for labour so could not provide much help for women who did not have normal deliveries. It was the opportunity to talk with women in the same position rather than the taught aspect of antenatal classes that appealed to many women. Clare Caswell found this to be the highlight of attending National Childbirth Trust classes in the early 1970s. "If you went to an NCT class, you were then into a social network. And if you were new to the area it was fantastic really."[53] The classes continued to be important after the women had their children as well. Jenny James's antenatal group continued to meet for a couple of years after their babies were born.[54] While the women did not remember the educational aspect of the classes as being particularly beneficial they did remember the opportunity to meet other mothers as a great asset. In sum, the women held equivocal attitudes towards education for motherhood. They did not believe women could be prepared for childbirth. They felt they suffered from a lack of preparation, but also that women today knew too much which could lead to even more anxiety.[55] Having their first child was a nervous time for the women, but they thought this was a normal, or at least unavoidable, situation rather than something that could be solved.

During the period there was debate about the extent to which ambivalence towards motherhood was principally a problem for university-educated women.[56] Did educated mothers face more conflict in their construction of identity? A quarter of the women interviewed had been to university. Although they all left work when their first child was born they did not express regret at this or indicate they felt that their education had been wasted, rather they believed it helped them in their role as mother. For example Isobel Innes thought, "just having had that higher education, it makes you understand how exciting knowledge is...Therefore you can impart more knowledge to your children I think, if you've had the education yourself."[57] Nevertheless, women who had their children at the end of the period seemed more apologetic that they had not fulfilled the potential their education gave them and were keener to demonstrate that they did do something for intellectual stimulation. Georgia Green, who had done a Masters degree, explains how she became an Open University tutor after her third child was born. She says, "After I'd had Helen which was 1978, a friend said to me, 'you ought to be an Open University tutor', she said 'stop you getting intellectually stale while you're at home with your children'."[58] However it does seem to be time period rather than education alone that encouraged this need for justification. Fran Farley, who left school at sixteen, expressed similar feelings. She stressed getting involved in playgroups meant she was more than simply a stay-at-home mother.[59] The women also felt the need to justify why they had not returned to their jobs after their children were born. In today's climate where it is common for women to return to full-time work shortly after their children are born the women needed to explain why they did not, both to their audience and to themselves.

Increasing numbers of married women entered into paid employment in the postwar years. Maud Matthews thought women's participation in the labour market had grown. She explained that her mother's generation did not work, "you just had to rely on the man's wage didn't you, and then our generation went out to work sort of part time, but now they've got to work full time most of them."[60] The women remembered their mothers as being full-time housewives, however in the course of the interviews it became clear the mothers of the working-class women did work, usually on a casual basis, cleaning, or in other domestic services. While the women thought the 1950s and 1960s were a time when women did not participate in the labour force, in fact many of them were working outside the home. Women who married middle-class men frequently undertook unpaid voluntary work. In some cases this work eventually led back to employment. Working-class mothers were more likely to take on some form of paid work because they needed the money. Nonetheless these were jobs that could be fitted around childcare, and were often domestic work. While all of the women did some sort of paid work after their children were born they constructed their identities as mothers rather than as workers and described themselves as having been full-time mothers. Women who had their children at the end of the period were more concerned with identifying themselves with work outside the home, but they all regarded being a mother as their primary identity and this was the same regardless of their education.

Conclusions

While few of the women referred to John Bowlby's theory of maternal deprivation or Donald Winnicott's idea of the "good enough mother" specifically, they were very much influenced by the idea that it was important for mothers to be at home with their children when they were young. In fact the belief that young children need the care of their mother was supported across age, class and level of education. Women expected to leave work when they had children; it was the norm of the time. Even women whose employers were happy for them to continue working and enjoyed their jobs still supported this view. Reiterating the pronouncements of Bowlby the women thought that it was important for their children's wellbeing and growth that they should provide continuous care. For example Helen Harris believed that it was essential for mothers to be at home with their children before the age of five because, "I was always brought up to understand that the first five years of a child's life are their actual development years."[61] Elaine Edwards, a former paediatric nurse, echoed Bowlby's theory that separating children from their parents in hospital resulted in behavioural difficulties.[62] The arguments of Winnicott and Bowlby were highly pervasive and many of the women repeated their theories without knowing their source. None of the women seemed to question the validity of these arguments and were highly supportive of them; they were part of the mother identity at this time. What is perhaps most interesting is that the women maintained these views despite the re-evaluation of Bowlby and Winnicott initiated by feminists from the late 1960s onwards.

In contrast to the generally optimistic view of family life authors of the earlier studies had taken, Hannah Gavron and Ann Oakley discovered the frustration and disappointment women could feel in the home and the ambivalence present in their attitude towards motherhood.[63] The women interviewed in Benson and Ewelme also expressed regret at the time they spent doing housework; unlike childcare it was not something they said they enjoyed. Nonetheless, they did not describe the levels of loneliness and isolation Gavron and Oakley reported. The passage of time is probably a factor in explaining this difference. The women were reviewing their lives and therefore they had a different relationship to the events they were talking about. Locality is, however, also important. The experiences of women in villages like Benson and Ewelme were different from those living in London. It is noticeable that unlike in London the women felt they had a strong social network around them, which was mainly provided by neighbours. They referred to mixing with other mothers and their children as one of the most enjoyable things about raising children. The village community provided women with friendship, support and advice. This role locality plays in shaping women's attitudes towards and experiences of motherhood was largely overlooked by the authors of the studies conducted between the 1945 and 1970; the discourses of class and later gender dominate their analyses. Using oral history has helped to understand the complex web of factors that influenced how the women of Benson and Ewelme constructed their identities as mothers at this time. Class and gender are undoubtedly

significant in determining how women viewed themselves but, as the women of
Benson and Ewelme articulated, locality conditioned their effects.

---

[1] Nancy J. Chodorow, *The Reproduction of Mothering: Psychoanalysis and the Sociology of
Gender* (Berkley: University of California Press, 1978) 5-6. John Bowlby was a child
psychiatrist who trained at the British Psychoanalytic Institute. His training analyst was Joan
Riviere a close associate of Melanie Klein, and Melanie Klein herself eventually supervised
him. D.W. Winnicott was a paediatrician and worked at Paddington Green Children's
Hospital for forty years. Winnicott was also analysed by Joan Riviere. The work of Melanie
Klein was a great influence on both Bowlby and Winnicott.
[2] D.W. Winnicott, *The Child and the Family: First Relationships* (London: Tavistock, 1957)
83, 142.
[3] John Bowlby, *Maternal Care and Mental Health* (Geneva: World Health Organization,
1951) 11, 57.
[4] Bowlby, *Maternal Care and Mental Health*, 67
[5] Lee Comer, *Wedlocked Women* (Leeds: Feminist Books, 1974) 142-143.
[6] Pseudonyms have been used.
[7] The factories in Oxford linked to the car industry were Osberton Radiators in North
Oxford, and Pressed Steel and Morris Motors in Cowley.
[8] The implications of rapid population growth for the social, economic, and administrative
development of Oxford and its neighbourhood was the subject of a two-volume study
undertaken in the late 1930s for Barnett House, the Social Studies Department of the
University. A.F.C. Bourdillon (ed.), *A Survey of the Social Services in the Oxford District, I,
Economics and Government of a Changing Area* (Oxford: Oxford University Press, 1938).
[9] Ibid., 290, 310.
[10] R.C. Whiting, *The View from Cowley: The Impact of Industrialization upon Oxford 1918-
1939* (Oxford: Clarendon Press, 1983) 39-40.
[11] Ibid., 137. Anne Chisholm (ed.), *Glimpses of an Oxfordshire Village. Ewelme 1900-2000*
(Ewelme: The Ewelme Society, 2000) 14-15.
[12] Alison Reid, "Twentieth-Century Benson", in Kate Tiller (ed.), *Benson: A Village
Through its History* (Wallingford: Pie Powder Press, 1999) 137-139.
[13] Chisholm, *Glimpses of an Oxfordshire Village*, 18.
[14] Ibid., 9, 101.
[15] Reid, 'Twentieth-Century Benson', 129.
[16] Ibid., 157-158.
[17] Nina Newham, interviewed by author, 8 December 2004.
[18] Deborah Denning, interviewed by author, 27 July 2004.
[19] Mary Matthews, interviewed by author, 26 June 2004.
[20] Janet Burtt and Peter Clarke, *Benson, A Century of Change: 1900-2000* (Wallingford: Pie
Powder Press, 2004) 67.
[21] Mary Matthews, interviewed by author, 26 June 2004.
[22] Betty Brown, interviewed by author, 15 June 2004.
[23] Raphael Samuel demonstrated how wooding and poaching were part of the rural economy
and social life in Headington Quarry, Oxfordshire, in the late-nineteenth and early-twentieth
centuries. Raphael Samuel, "Quarry roughs': life and labour in Headington Quarry, 1860-

1920. An essay in oral history", in Raphael Samuel (ed.), *Village Life and Labour* (London: Routledge & Kegan Paul, 1975) 207-227.

[24] Fran Farley, interviewed by author, 13 June 2004.

[25] Isobel Innes, interviewed by author, 7 June 2004.

[26] J.M. Mogey, *Family and Neighbourhood: Two Studies in Oxford* (Oxford: Oxford University Press, 1956) 152-153.

[27] Josephine Klein, *Samples from English Cultures* (London: Routledge and Kegan Paul, 1965) 176-177

[28] Helen Harris, interviewed by author, 15 June 2004.

[29] Betty Brown, interviewed by author, 15 June 2004.

[30] Jenny James, interviewed by author, 7 July 2004.

[31] Betty Brown, interviewed by author, 15 June 2004.

[32] Georgia Green, interviewed by author, 24 June 2004.

[33] Elizabeth Badinter, *The Myth of Motherhood: An Historical View of the Maternal Instinct* (London: Souvenir Press, 1981) 117.

[34] John Bowlby, *Attachment and Loss: Volume I: Attachment* (London: Penguin, 1984) 183.

[35] Helen Harris, interviewed by author, 14 June 2004.

[36] Patricia Parker, interviewed by author, 30 July 2004.

[37] Sigmund Freud, "Female Sexuality", in *S.E.*, vol. XXI, 227-231

[38] They found the mother-daughter relationship underpinned the continued role the extended family played in Bethnal Green. Michael Young and Peter Willmott, *Family and Kinship in East London* (London: Routledge and Kegan Paul, 1957).

[39] Mary Matthews, interviewed by author, 26 June 2004.

[40] Isobel Innes, interviewed by author, 7 June 2004.

[41] Maud Matthews, interviewed by author, 26 June 2004.

[42] Kathy Knight, interviewed by author, 13 October 2004.

[43] Board of Education, *Curriculum and Examinations in Secondary Schools* (Norwood Report) (London: HMSO, 1943).

[44] Reid, "Twentieth-Century Benson", 146.

[45] Patricia Parker, interviewed by author, 30 July 2004.

[46] Deborah Denning, interviewed by author, 27 July 2004.

[47] Oxfordshire Federation of Women's Institutes, *Oxfordshire Within Living Memory* (Newbury: Countryside Books, 1994) 15.

[48] Isobel Innes, interviewed by author, 7 June 2004.

[49] Georgia Green, interviewed by author, 24 June 2004.

[50] Isobel Innes, interviewed by author, 7 June 2004. Georgia Green, interviewed by author, 24 June 2004. Mary Matthews, interviewed by author, 26 June 2004. Deborah Denning. interviewed by author, 27 July 2004.

[51] Centre for Oxfordshire Studies, 1961, Annual Report of the Medical Officer of Health MOH 1961, 9.

[52] Deborah Denning, interviewed by author, 27 July 2004.

[53] Clare Caswell, interviewed by author, 30 July 2004.

[54] Jenny James, interviewed by author, 7 July 2004.

[55] Helen Harris, interviewed by author, 14 June 2004. Annie Armstrong, interviewed by author, 29 June 2004. Deborah Denning, interviewed by author, 27 July 2004. Mary Matthews, interviewed by author, 26 June 2004. Rachel Roberts, interviewed by author, 20 October 2004.

[56] The woman's page of *The Guardian* was noted for running letters from dissatisfied housewives at this time.

[57] Isobel Innes, interviewed by author, 7 June 2004.

[58] Georgia Green, interviewed by author, 24 June 2004.

[59] Fran Farley, interviewed by author, 13 June 2004.

[60] Maud Matthews, interviewed by author, 26 June 2004.

[61] Helen Harris, interviewed by author, 14 June 2004.

[62] Elaine Edwards, interviewed by author, 29 July 2004. John Bowlby's colleague James Robertson made the film *A two-year-old goes to hospital* (Robertson and Bowlby 1952) about children he had been observing in hospital who were separated from their mothers. The visiting of children in hospital by their parents was severely restricted at this time and the film demonstrated that the children, too young to understand their mothers' absence, became afraid and upset by the separation.

[63] Hannah Gavron was testing the findings of studies such as *Family and Kinship in East London* on young married couples in the light of changes in the role of young women within the family. She interviewed forty-eight working-class women and forty-eight middle-class women from North London in the early 1960s. Hannah Gavron, *The Captive Wife: Conflicts of Housebound Mothers* (Harmondsworth: Penguin Books, 1968). Ann Oakley's books on women's attitudes to housework were provoked by Hannah Gavron's work and were a feminist challenge to the concealment of women in sociology. They were based on interviews with forty London housewives, half working class and half middle class, selected on the base of their husband's occupation, and were conducted in 1971. Ann Oakley, *Housewife* (London: Allen Lane, 1974), Ann Oakley, *The Sociology of Housework* (London: Martin Robertson, 1974).

DEAF BY CHOICE: ISSUES OF IDENTITY IN THE BRITISH DEAF COMMUNITY

MARTIN ATHERTON

Most external conceptions of deafness refer to deaf people in medical or pathological terms, that is as people who have a loss or an impairment which needs to be cured or overcome, and this negative perception has profound impacts on the way deaf people are dealt with by the hearing world.[1] This perception has a very long history, Aristotle declaring "those who are deaf are also dumb".[2] Whilst it is believed that he used "dumb" in its original definition of "being without speech", this came to be interpreted as "stupid" or "incapable".[3] This perception has largely held sway ever since, gaining strength from its adaptation by religious groups and passing into various legal systems. The Jewish Talmud, although acknowledging that deaf people had certain rights (such as the right to have a marriage ceremony conducted in sign language), denied them others, and this situation was echoed by both Greek and Roman law. This perspective of deaf people in turn passed into the canons of the Christian Church, even finding expression in the Bible, and thus took hold in the perception of the wider population. This negative image of deafness is regularly encountered by deaf people on a daily basis even today, with the predominant perspective of hearing people being "a view that the principal characteristic of deafness is the *lack* of something, i.e. hearing and/or communication ability".[4] The response of the hearing majority to this perceived lack has been to try and cure deafness by making the deaf person as "normal" as possible. This process of normalisation was pursued during the post World War Two period through a policy of education based largely on the development of clear speech and lip reading ability, and the use of technology such as hearing aids to achieve this goal. Only those deaf people who managed to communicate effectively in English were regarded as academically successful; the use of sign language was only appropriate for those who were considered to be educational failures through their inability to develop good speech and reading skills.[5]

Many people who are deaf share these negative perceptions of their deafness, particularly those who have become deafened after having lived as a hearing person. In such cases, deafness can indeed represent a profound loss, and many of those who become deafened consider deafness to be a disability that has left them impaired or handicapped.[6] In 1998, research by Young, Ackerman and Kyle suggested that around 8.5 million people in Great Britain had some form of hearing loss-a ratio of deafened people within the overall population of around one in seven.[7] Padden argued that those who are deafened prefer labels such as "hard of hearing", which are seen more positively than "deaf". [8] For such deaf people, who form the majority of the deaf element within the broader population, deafness does not contribute positively to their cultural identity. There are, however, a significant number of deaf people for whom spoken language is inappropriate as a communication method and this has important consequences for their sense of self and collective identity. From data collected in 1989, the British Deaf Association (BDA) estimated that there were approximately 62,500 people in England, Wales and Northern Ireland, and a further 7,000 in Scotland, who were deaf and whose first or preferred language was British Sign Language (BSL) (British Deaf Association). These figures confirmed earlier statistics quoted by Ballantyne and Martin which showed a roughly similar distribution, and Young, Ackerman and Kyle's more recent figures.[9] These deaf people view themselves not in medical terms, but as members of a distinct cultural and linguistic minority. The central identifier for culturally deaf people is the use of sign language as their first or preferred method of communication, and sign language is acknowledged as the most appropriate form of communication for profoundly deaf people. For this group of people, deafness *per se* is not seen as the disabling factor in their lives, and the notion of deafness as a disability is rejected, although they accept that they may be disabled as a result of widely held perceptions of deafness based solely on medical perspectives. [10] What is rejected is the notion that this disability arises from deaf people themselves; instead, culturally deaf people echo Devas in considering that it is the attitude of the hearing majority towards deaf people that is the disabling factor. [11]

A convention was adopted in the early 1970s to distinguish between the two supposedly distinct groups of deaf people, which involves the use of upper and lower case "D" when writing the word "deaf".[12] "Deaf" is used when referring to those people who regard their deafness as a culturally defining factor in their identity–the group generally referred to as "the deaf community". This group includes those deaf people whose first or preferred language is sign language and the capital D is a major factor in expressing a positive deaf identity. "deaf" is used for those people whose deafness means merely being unable to hear, rather than having any linguistic or cultural connotations. This group includes those people who refer to themselves as "deafened", "hard of hearing", "hearing impaired" and similar labels, and so the use of a lower case "d" has strong links to the concept of deafness as a disability. Indeed, the "big D/little d" debate has taken on increasingly political overtones in recent years as certain members of the deaf community began to use the lower case "deaf" in pejorative terms. At times, there have been echoes of Orwell in the way 'Big D good, little d bad' has almost become an unacknowledged consequence of the struggle to assert a separate deaf cultural identity.

The non-recognition of British Sign Language as a native language of Britain, coupled with the continuing dominance of medical perceptions of deafness, is at the heart of the deafness as disability debate for many deaf people. Whilst the British Government finally recognised BSL as a true language in 2003, sign language– regarded by deaf people as one of the central cultural identifiers of their community-still has no official status as a native language in Britain. For many sign language users, this only serves to underline their belief that their deafness classifies them as second class citizens, as the cultural foundation of the deaf community, expressed as it is through sign language, is not fully acknowledged. However, in circumstances where being considered "disabled" can bring advantages, there is a marked ambivalence in the attitudes of some deaf people who otherwise reject the label. In Britain, deaf people are officially classified as disabled and are therefore entitled to specific State benefits. These include Disabled Living Allowance and Disabled Students Allowance. Many deaf people are happy enough to claim these benefits, and indeed fiercely defend their rights to do so, whilst at the same time rejecting any notion of deafness being a disability. Whether this attitude towards the material benefits of being considered disabled represents hypocrisy or pragmatism on the part of those deaf people claiming these benefits is not a matter for discussion here. Nevertheless, it does demonstrate the often complex nature of the debates concerning deaf identity, both internally and externally to the deaf community.

The major difference between the deaf community and other minority communities is that deaf people do not have an obvious geographical focus; there is no area of a town or country where deaf people group together to live in the way that other communities do. Deaf people generally live in isolation from each other in their daily lives, except for members of their family who may also be deaf. One reason for this is that the vast majority of deaf people are born into hearing families with two hearing parents; nor do deaf parents necessarily have deaf children, particularly if one or both parents have become deafened through illness or injury rather than for any genetic reason.[13] It might be considered then that the deaf community does not constitute a locational community. However, location has been an important factor in the development and continuing existence of notions of community based on shared deafness. Instead of living together in geographical communities, deaf people have found alternative ways of coming together, with residential deaf schools and the extensive network of deaf social clubs around Britain playing a vital role in bringing deaf people together and introducing younger deaf people to the life and culture of the community. Deaf children were artificially brought together in the residential deaf schools, which inadvertently provided them with access to others with whom they naturally formed a community based on common characteristics and shared residence. For many deaf people, the deaf schools provided their first experience of regular contact with other deaf people and their first opportunity to engage in effective and meaningful communication. Despite the large scale failings of deaf education recorded by Conrad and others, deaf schools are often fondly remembered by deaf people because of the sense of identity and belonging they found there.[14] Once schooldays were over, this gathering together of people from similar audiological and experiential backgrounds continued via the network of deaf clubs which grew up in virtually every large town and city in Britain during the nineteenth and twentieth centuries. As Kyle and Woll assert, "the central environments for deaf interaction are the social clubs which exist throughout the UK".[15] Even when coming together as a community of likeminded people with similar outlooks and life experiences, deaf people as a community remained largely isolated, but in this case by choice.

The issue of choice is an important one, as it served as a motivating factor for deaf people to become involved in the activities of the deaf clubs. Hill, in attempting to define leisure, differentiates between the lack of choice involved in working life and the exercise of choice during free time:

"Leisure ... represents freedom, time in which individuals can 'be themselves', when they can reveal their authentic nature as autonomous human beings".[16]

As Padden states:

"Deaf people consider social activities an important way of maintaining contact with other Deaf people ... One reason is certainly that Deaf people enjoy the company of other like-minded Deaf people. They feel they gain support and trusting companionship from other deaf people who share the same cultural beliefs and attitudes". [17]

This support and companionship was gained in the deaf clubs, and these clubs can be regarded as the geographical centres for the deaf community in lieu of any centralised home environment. In exercising choice through joining a deaf club, members thus found the opportunity to "reveal their authentic nature". It was through involvement with the network of deaf clubs and their associated social activities that many deaf people came to accept their deafness as an important part of their identity. [18]

So what activities did membership provide access to? Using reports from twenty-eight deaf clubs across north-west England published in *British Deaf News* during the period 1945 to 1995, a variety of social events were found being enjoyed by their members. Not only were the types of activity found those which one would expect to see in other types of voluntary association across the region, such as Working Men's Clubs or political clubs, but deaf club members also had a more extensive shared social life in terms of the number of events organised for and by them. Many of the twenty-eight deaf clubs were holding events on a monthly basis, in addition to the regular club nights when members gathered once or twice a week for general socialising and to play bingo, darts or cards. The sheer volume of deaf club events helps to illustrate the important role these played in bringing deaf people together and the value members placed on opportunities to escape into the sanctuary from the hearing world provided by the deaf clubs. In terms of general leisure, these included trips and holidays, dinner dances in the clubs, educational events, various societies and interest groups, specific events for children and pensioners, fundraising ventures and religious events amongst others. An entry under "trips and holidays"–by far the most popular activity, accounting for 25% of all reported events–encompassed a wide range of outings. At one end of the scale, a deaf club outing might involve a short trip to a neighbouring deaf club for a game of cards, darts or bingo; on the other hand, a trip could encompass 120 members sharing a Mediterranean cruise, as reported by Preston Deaf Club in 1975. These trips were important not just as holidays or days out, but also because they allowed members of a geographically dispersed community to meet other community members. In the days before the introduction of technology such as textphones (which enable deaf people to use the telephone network) and email, deaf club events were virtually the only means of contact sign language users had with other deaf people outside their immediate vicinity. Anecdotal evidence suggests that many people attended events they had no real interest in for the sole purpose of meeting other deaf people, even extending this to seeking out potential husbands and wives. An integral part of virtually every trip was the inclusion of a visit to a deaf club in the vicinity or on the way home. These visits thus helped to maintain involvement in a wider deaf community, and in doing so strengthened feelings of identity which stretched beyond the confines of a particular deaf club.

Trips and holidays were only one element of this community building process. Virtually every important event in the lives of deaf people was celebrated with other members, including births, christenings, marriages, anniversaries and even deaths. Through the clubs, deaf people were kept informed of major events in the world, such as elections, changes in available benefits and the introduction of decimal coinage, through invited guests giving presentations in deaf clubs. Involvement in several sports was also a regular part of the social life that revolved around–but necessarily solely in–the deaf clubs. Nor were these isolated events; many clubs were very active, holding many events each year. The data collected shows that clubs averaged between four and eleven such "special" events annually, and that these were in addition to the more commonplace activities club members took part in every week. The evidence indicates a rich and varied diet of leisure activities being provided for deaf club members, and this played an important part in the development and maintenance of a distinct deaf identity, both as individuals and as members of a community of people with similar outlooks and interests. Deaf club members chose to share their leisure time with each other because of these shared life experiences, not because of any limitations based on notions of disability. In addition to these social events, sport also played a vital role in maintaining notions of belonging to a deaf community. Contests between individual clubs took place throughout the year, and clubs would often travel great lengths to play football matches against other deaf teams in the national competition. Deaf identity was also strongly reinforced amongst deaf teams who joined leagues of hearing opponents, as happened in virtually every sport deaf people took part in. Here, issues of deafness as a disability were often a subconscious motivational factor for both deaf and hearing competitors.[19] Sporting contests between deaf clubs also served a broader bonding process, as virtually every such event was accompanied by a dance or other social event in the evening. The extent and variety of deaf social life, which has only very briefly been touched on here, showed that deafness was not a barrier to involvement in a fulfilling and rewarding social life.

It can be argued that deaf clubs did not provide the escape *from* normality that is a motivating factor in all leisure activity; instead, the clubs provided an escape *into* a world of normality that could not be found in the outside world. In their everyday lives, deaf people were defined on the basis of their exclusion from the 'normal' world, and treated accordingly. They lived in a world in which their deafness marked them out as "different". As deaf people, they were seen by the majority of the hearing world as abnormal, deficient, handicapped or disabled and subjected to any number of similarly negative perceptions. Profoundly deaf people were seen to be worthy of pity or charity, rather than being accepted and acknowledged as a distinct social and cultural group. However, in their social lives, deaf people countered this perception by their actions. They came together to share leisure time with others with whom they shared similar life experiences, culture and language. The social life provided through the deaf club was as much to do with cultural cohesion as it was with "passing the time". Deaf club members were not dependent on 'able-bodied' others for this social life (in the context of deafness, hearing people), beyond using sign language interpreters for some events. As for being disabled through an inability to do 'ordinary things', the evidence of leisure activity shows that deaf people were perfectly capable of taking part in exactly the same leisure activities as anyone else. Not only did they choose the same types of leisure activities as their hearing neighbours, but also the way they engaged in these activities was essentially ordinary in that their participation was almost always exactly the same as that of hearing people. The only difference in the way deaf people took part in certain leisure activities was the language of interaction.

As a final illustration of the lengths to which deaf people would go to be a part of this social life, the following report of a trip made to Liverpool by deaf people from London serves as a useful and by no means untypical example.

"The Federation of London Deaf Clubs came for the return match at football on April 16. Travelling from Euston they arrived in Liverpool at 4.30 a.m. and were met by the Chairman of the M.A. Social Club. Coaches took the party first to Speke Aerodrome, then after breakfast to the Cathedral and to Chester, where lunch was enjoyed at the Stafford Hotel. Then the teams met on the Belvidere Football Club Ground at Jericho Lane, Aigburth. Major G.H. Verburgh kicked off and a stirring game was played resulting in a win for the visitors by 2 to 1. Tea was prepared at the Institute in Princess Avenue, and an entertainment was given in the evening, consisting of a short Cinema Show, a Shadowgraphy item, and a play, 'Paddy's Mistake'. The visitors returned to London by the 12.00 midnight train from Lime Street."[20]

The number of events planned around a mere football match, and no doubt involving many people with no direct interest in the game, shows how sharing leisure time with other deaf people was important no matter what the context. The variety of events also shows that deafness was no barrier to enjoying precisely the same types of social activities as hearing people. Through communal leisure time, the positive group and self-identity that resulted from shared deafness and sign language use provided an important counterpoint to commonly held perceptions of deafness as disability. Without deaf clubs, deaf people would not have had the opportunity to see themselves in a more positive light and developed a more meaningful identity. Deaf people were not required to join a deaf club; they did so of their own free will and in doing so were (whether consciously or subconsciously) choosing to be deaf. This choice was not based on notions of shared disability or handicapped, but instead resulted from a desire to share their leisure time with those of a similar background and shared life experiences. The communication barriers that arose from living in a predominantly hearing world were not a factor in deaf clubs, and the stereotypical perceptions of deaf people needing help and assistance to live a "normal" life could be left once inside the club or engaged in its social activities. The variety and extent of leisure activities enjoyed by deaf people shows that they were in no way inhibited from engaging in the same types of social intercourse as their hearing neighbours. In doing so, they were not only choosing the type of social life they wanted but were also making a positive statement about their identity as deaf people.

[1] H. Lane, R. Hofmeister and B. Bahan, *A journey into the DEAF-WORLD* (San Diego, DawnSignPress, 1996).

[2] P. Higgins, *Outsiders in a Hearing World* (London: Sage, 1980).

[3] M. McLoughlin, *A History of the Education of the Deaf in England* (Gosport: Ashford Colour Press, 1987).

[4] J. Kyle and B. Woll, *Sign Language: The Study of Deaf People and Their Language* (Cambridge: Cambridge University Press, 1985).

[5] R. Conrad, "Towards a definition of oral success" in Raymond Lee (ed.), *Deaf Liberation,* (London: National Union of the Deaf, 1992) 27-32.

[6] D. Wright, *Deafness: A Personal Account* (London: Allen Lane, 1969).

[7] Lane and others, *DEAF-WORLD.*

[8] C. Padden, "The deaf community and deaf culture" in S. Gregory and G. Hartley, *Constructing Deafness* (London: Pinter Publishers, 1991) 40–45.

[9] J. Ballantyne and J. Martin, *Deafness* (Edinburgh: Livingstone, 1984).

[10] M. Corker, *Deaf and Disabled or Deafness Disabled?* (Buckingham: Open University Press, 1998).

[11] M. Devas, "Support and access in sports and leisure provision", *Disability and Society* 18 (2) 231-245.

[12] J. Woodward, "Implications for sociolinguistic research amongst the deaf "*Sign Language Studies* (1972) 1–7.

[13] The incidence of a deaf child having two hearing parents is as high as 90 to 95% according to Bhan et al, 30.

[14] C. Mason, "School experiences" in S. Gregory and G. Hartley, *Constructing deafness* (London: Pinter Publishers, 1991) 84 – 87.

[15] Kyle and Woll, *Sign Language.*

[16] J. Hill, *Sport, Leisure and Culture in Twentieth Century Britain* (Basingstoke: Palgrave, 2002).

[17] Padden "The deaf community and deaf culture".

[18] P. Ladd, "The modern deaf community" in D. Miles, *BSL, a Beginners Guide* (London: BBC Books, 1988) 37-38.

[19] For examples of the underlying tensions in sporting contests between deaf and hearing opponents, see M. Atherton, D. Russell and D, Russell and H. Graham H. "More than a match" *Soccer and Society* Autumn 2001, 22-43.

[20] *British Deaf Times* 1938.

CONFRONTING A LEGACY: THE ATLANTIC SLAVE TRADE AND THE BLACK COMMUNITY OF LIVERPOOL

MURRAY STEELE

The city council acknowledges Liverpool's responsibility for its involvement in three centuries of the slave trade. The untold misery which was caused has left a legacy affecting black people in Liverpool today. The city council expresses its shame and remorse for the city's role in this trade in human misery. But black people are still prevented from playing their part in the life of the city because slavery left white people with a stereotypical view they were only fit for servitude. The slave trade left behind a residue of racism and intolerance which disfigures our city to this day. I call upon the black community never to forget its history of struggle against inequality, but to forgive the past and claim its future.[1]

Adopted symbolically at the final Council meeting of the millennium (9 December 1999) to close off an era of racial oppression, this declaration brought together two closely related issues which, when they had been considered, had been considered separately: how Liverpool should confront its historical identity as a prime participant in the Atlantic slave trade; and how it should address the needs of its black, African and African Caribbean community.[2] This chapter attempts to explore the link further, to demonstrate that the historical airbrushing/minimising of Liverpool's role in the trafficking of slaves had parallels with attitudes to its black community, both phenomena continuing well into the twentieth century when at last attempts were made to remake its identity as a multicultural community. In making this preliminary sketch, it employs a wide variety of sources, including the visual record of the slave trade and its close cousin, imperialism.

Liverpool and the slave trade: initial representation

Britain's outlawing of the slave trade in 1807 created a legacy that Liverpool was for many years reluctant to confront. From a safe distance, mid-Victorian observers outside Liverpool pontificated on a system which had been a "moral blot on the character of the town", and which "painful as it may be, but still it must remain in the records of the town"[3]. In Liverpool, local sensitivities, roused initially by incidents such as actor George Frederick Cooke's notorious outburst at a local theatre that every brick of the town was "cemented with an African's blood",[4] remained a consideration even after abolition had been accomplished. The city was trading in slave-produced commodities from the United States and Brazil up to emancipation there later in the nineteenth century, a circumstance that inclined Liverpool merchants towards the Confederate cause and against American abolitionists such as Harriet Beecher Stowe, who visited the town in the 1850s. Even as late as the 1880s, 'Dicky Sam's' exposé of the Liverpool slave trade appeared under a pseudonym, as his friends had warned "that a great deal of mystery, and more of silence is thrown over the Slavery question as it existed here".[5]

In their survey of the slave trade and Liverpool historians, Cameron and Crooke[6] have suggested that until recently, their response had been to excise it from the city's history altogether and present abolition as a victory for morality over economic vested interests, and a sufficient recompense for past misdeeds. However, a quick survey of school textbooks, general histories and other materials drawn from the nineteenth and early twentieth century demonstrates a more varied response. At one extreme, simple omission: Nelson and Sons' *A Little History of Lancashire* (1899),[7] written for adults, had an admittedly short section on Liverpool, but managed to avoid any mention of slavery or trade in slaves. Sometimes, this omission was clearly shame-faced. John Belchem has referred to the City Council's decision to omit slave trade materials from the official catalogue to the 1907 Historical Exhibition of Liverpool Antiquities, a significant censoring of uncomfortable items from the City's heritage.[8]

Alternatively, the slave trade could be reported without comment, as in Walter Rhodes' *A Short History of Lancashire* (1907). Admittedly Rhodes has included William Roscoe in his list of Lancashire Worthies, but strangely he says nothing about his abolitionist activities.[9] Where expressions of shame and regret were made, they often included some form of qualification. E G Hewlett (*Lancashire: Oxford County History*, 1913), written for schools, referred to "unholy gains", but added that the world was now a better place, thanks to abolitionists like Roscoe.[10] Or the traders were otherwise "good men" who had had the misfortune to have been caught up in a "noxious traffic" (F Hird, *Lancashire Stories*, 1912).[11] A J Berry's more forthcoming *Story of Lancashire*, written for local schools after the Great War, sets out two chapters which, he maintained, could not be read without feelings of shame: its share in the slave trade, and "child slavery" in Lancashire's cotton mills (although Berry does not mention slave production of cotton), the result of "temptation to profit-making" now curbed by the teachings of Wesley and the effects of the French Revolution.[12] More recently, Lamb and Smallpage's *Story of Liverpool* (1946), describing itself as a local history for schools, suggested that some of the slave captains "were remarkably kind-hearted men" who allowed the slaves to dance up on deck.[13] Alternatively it could be interpreted according to the *zeitgeist* of the eighteenth century: as George Chandler almost defiantly puts it in his *Illustrated History of Liverpool* (1972), Liverpool's domination of the slave trade was "not due to any particular moral failing in her merchants but to world economic forces which Liverpool was well fitted to serve".[14]

However, the most pervasive 'excuse' was one that was often implied rather than stated: Britain had atoned for the slave trade by bringing God and good government to the African continent. One aspect of this mission is especially relevant here, the campaign against the so-called Arab slave trade in East Africa; or to put it in another way, the projection of past European sins onto present (and in this case, black Muslim) sinners in Africa. R M Ballantyne's *Black Ivory* (1873) described the trade in all the vivid detail expected by his young readers, but was quite open in its propagandist purpose, to involve them in the cause of the "total abolition of the African slave trade".[15] The less well-known author W H G Kingston developed the evangelising theme further in his novel *The African Trader* (1873), in which the black sailor Paul Balingo shows that he is a better Christian than the (Liverpool-born) white narrator, and once a British warship has delivered him from the clutches of a Spanish slaver, takes up his calling to become a missionary to his people in Nigeria.[16] School text-books in the next century made an explicit link between the anti-slavery campaign and the imperial mission as a whole. Gillian Klein quotes thus from the *Oxford Junior Book on Africa*, in use well beyond the Second World War: "The Europeans in Africa abolished slavery and stopped the endless fighting between tribes".[17]

Slavery and the Imperialist Tide

In seeking to create a new, more comfortable identity, the New Imperialism of the late nineteenth-early twentieth century thus generated a new discourse of imperial responsibility and trusteeship that effectively submerged the issue of the slave trade and its recognition, but in turn creating a further legacy which has had to be addressed.

John MacKenzie's pioneering studies of imperialism and popular culture point to the period after 'the imperial climacteric' of the later 1890s as the heyday of popular imperialism.[18] His works, plus those of other researchers, have reviewed the impact of imperialism on school text-books, noting that they tended to gloss over subjects like the slave trade.[19] Instead, as Joan Blyth has commented, schools opted for the teaching of history as a form of "national propaganda", in which key dates were learnt, and stories about monarchs and great Englishmen (usually) were told.[20] In his autobiography, Norman Bridge notes that the first history class he taught at the Granby High School in the early thirties was on the British Empire.[21] Geography lessons tended to emphasise the differences between "us" and the exotic, though usually savage "other", based on often outdated and stereotypical information that endured into the 1950s, with children being given the impression that all Africans lived in grass huts. A loan collection of lantern slides put together by the Liverpool Education Committee in 1928, for use in elementary schools, no doubt contributed to these stereotypes with depictions of "native life" in East, West and Central Africa: a note asks lenders to return them as soon as possible, "as they are in almost daily use".[22]

From the 1930s, and reflecting new trends in colonial policy, the emphasis in school literature moved to the emergence of a developing Commonwealth, with Britain exercising its responsibility as trustee to improve the welfare of its African subjects. Liverpool schools took full advantage of the Imperial Institute's Empire Lectures Scheme onwards from 1950, while in that year thirteen Liverpool teachers were on secondment overseas, four in sub-Saharan Africa. By 1955, the Royal Africa Society had been added to the lecturing roster, while a Student Christian Mission Conference held in the city heard an address on imperialism, and sixth formers attended a conference on world citizenship.[23] This new moral tone was captured by a war-time text, written for pupils aged 12 and over, on the subject of citizenship that foreshadowed some of the topics covered in the current National Curriculum Citizenship syllabus, and incorporated a section on the 'Empire Overseas', drawing the familiar analogy between dependent territories and children growing up in a family; this was followed by a detailed explanation of the differences between Crown Colonies, Protectorates and Mandates.[24] The ethos of the new imperial morality was such that in the Festival of Britain year (1951), the Liverpool Council could admit the role of the slave trade in the development of the city and, in contrast to 1907, exhibit some of its artefacts, but diminish their significance by setting them against a utopian vision of post-war Liverpool as a "New Jerusalem".[25]

'Hangovers' of slavery and empire

In the meantime, slavery and empire had set their imprint on the public architecture and art of Liverpool, although to what degree and effect has become the subject of debate. Though it has lingered in folk memory, much of the visual evidence of Liverpool's slaving past has disappeared: demolished, superseded or simply destroyed (most notably, the Goree Warehouses, a casualty of the 1941 blitz). Klinkenborg[25] describes modern Liverpool as an essentially Victorian city: the Albert Dock (1845), now housing the Merseyside Maritime Museum and the neo-classical St George's Hall (1855), are representative of Imperial Liverpool. Of its older structures that seem to have associations with slavery, two have attracted the most interest: the Nelson Statue (1813) on the Exchange Flags, and the Town Hall frieze (c 1754). Yarrington has maintained that the chained figures on the Nelson monument, representing the Admiral's four major naval victories, have a "veiled" meaning; veiled because a less ambiguous presentation was prevented by the membership of slave owners, as well as abolitionists, on the fund-raising committee.[26] The association of manacles with slaves is of course a long one, a symbolism employed by the abolitionists in their publicity, but equally chains are associated with prisoners of war. While one can understand how Melville's eponymous hero in his novel *Redburn* picked up a resonance of slavery when he saw the statue in the mid 1850s,[27] the figures shown are clearly not negroid in appearance, they are simply French prisoners. The meaning of the Town Hall frieze is apparently clearer, with many commentators describing the figures as "slaves".[28] But the character of the frieze as a whole, depicting elephants and other tropical fauna, points to a less precise artistic formulation. Many of Liverpool's public buildings and business offices are decorated with similar tropical images, symbolising the city's status as one of the great world ports of the Victorian and Edwardian period. Cavanagh's less contentious description of "exotic foreigners"[29] is perhaps a more objective assessment. Ironically, the one monument that does have associations with slavery, the Albert Stevens statuary that was originally placed on the pediment over the St George's Hall southern portico, and showed a personification of Africa as a woman, her chains broken by Britannia, "in a posture of gratitude and humility with her sons in her arms" was removed after World War II as its decayed condition rendered it unsafe.[30]

The future place of these artefacts in third millennium Liverpool has become a sensitive issue to certain elements of its black community. They are condemned as constant reminders of the humiliation of slavery and imperialism, unacceptable symbols of the past; on the other hand, to the dominant white culture in Liverpool, they remain a vital part of their British and local heritage.

The other principal-this time invisible-hangover of slavery and empire has been the residuum of racist and stereotypical attitudes to black people, and the way such views were handed down to children by parents and supplemented by peer groups, racially biased literature, textbooks and other media, creating a mutually reinforcing cycle of racialist beliefs across several generations. One of the most enduring racial stereotypes in popular culture has been the Golliwog, described by Bob Dixon as belonging to "the patronising and condescending category of racism which includes 'coons' and 'nigger' minstrels".[31] His most notorious appearance in modern Liverpool took place in 1984, when organisers of the Garden Festival ignored protest from the black community and its supporters to make him the symbol for the "Jam Garden".[32]

Calls to remove racist images from children's literature and textbooks had been made from the 1950s onwards, but it was not until the early 70s that a concerted campaign was launched in Liverpool. The Merseyside Community Relations Council (MCRC) instigated a trawl of such materials in four multiracial city schools, mounted an exhibition and published *Sowing the Dragon's Teeth: Racial Bias in the Books We Teach* [1973], with typical examples. MCRC investigators found history and geography books from the 1930s and 40s still in use, perpetuating outdated images of "strange people in strange lands", or listing great twentieth century figures without a single black name.[33] MCRC pressure eventually produced results against an initially resistant general public. In May 1987, Liverpool's post-Militant council introduced regular monitoring of "books, tapes and films etc", within the framework of LEA Code of Practice 173 'to Combat Racist Behaviour'.[34]

Towards an apology: learning about the slave trade

Although there has been a continuing feeling that the History National Curriculum, introduced under the 1986 Education Reform Act, has not addressed the cultural background of minority communities in Britain, it did provide an avenue for introducing the study of the Atlantic slave trade as constituting one of the historical forces that have shaped modern British society. The Black History Resource Working Group, operating within the Liverpool LEA, exploited this opening to produce *Slavery: An Introduction to the African Holocaust*, in 1995, designed for Key Stage 3 pupils. Its achievements were many. It corrected the popular view, endorsed by the History Association as late as 1973,[35] that the abolitionist movement was an entirely white enterprise; it sharpened the visual awareness of pupils about Liverpool's past as they explored its streets; it challenged the racially biased images of older school text books, drawing on earlier MCRC research. But it had shortcomings. It was heavily reliant on Eric Williams' *Capitalism and Slavery*, quoting his opinion that "the abolitionist role has been seriously misunderstood and greatly exaggerated", while nevertheless devoting considerable space to black abolitionists; and, more seriously, ignored the research of Seymour Drescher into the wide-ranging popular, as well as "elite", support for abolition during the anti-slavery campaign. The shadow of "elite history" also fell across the choice of African and American pre-colonial societies to be covered, with an over-emphasis on "empires" that ironically forms a mirror image of traditional British history teaching, while overlooking the many achievements of small-scale, often acephalous pre-colonial societies. Despite these reservations, the study pack makes an important contribution to educating school pupils about the realities of the slave trade.[36] Recently, the Liverpool council has followed this up with a CD ROM, *Liverpool and the Transatlantic Slave Trade* (2003), designed for Key Stage 2 pupils. Further materials of this type have been promised.

Meanwhile, an important stage in the process of public education on the slave trade, and a substantial step towards its recognition, was provided by the opening of a new gallery at the Merseyside Maritime Museum in October 1994, with the title "Transatlantic Slavery: Against Human Dignity". The changing intellectual atmosphere towards African history in British universities formed an important background to this initiative. Africa had emerged from its traditional status as a continent with apparently no history worth recording until white men came to rule it to become the focus for research by a group of young historians from Britain and North America. P E H Hair, based at the University of Liverpool, was one of the pioneers of slave trade studies. The symposium he edited with Roger Anstey, *Liverpool, the Atlantic Slave Trade, and Abolition* (1976), published by the Historic Society of Lancashire and Cheshire was a landmark event. Another trigger was provided by Lord Gifford's report *Loosen the Shackles* (1989), which rebuked the Maritime Museum for glossing over the slave trade by claiming that the city's wealth from trade "was firmly established before it began to dominate the slave trade".[37]

Anthony Tibbles' article,[38] published shortly after the slave gallery was opened, refers to the approach made by the Peter Moores Foundation in 1990/91 to Richard Foster, director of the National Museums and Galleries on Merseyside, an initiative that led to the Foundation granting nearly £550,000 for a permanent exhibition. Interviewed later, Peter Moores revealed that he had spent six years trying to find a museum in Britain prepared to have such a gallery: "A lot of people saw it as a hot potato".[39] The project was launched in December 1991, and an advisory committee met at the House of Lords at the end of the following month. The venue and the choice of members, predominantly black, but not Liverpool black, created initial local suspicion. The *Granby Toxteth Community Project Newsletter* referred to "white guilt" and the possibility that the Museum, which then charged entrance fees, would use the gallery to foster tourism and raise money at the expense of Liverpool's black community.[40] The advisory committee took immediate steps to repair the damage: its March 1992 newsletter promised "[to] continue to develop a consultation process with individual and community groups", and its membership was correspondingly supplemented with further representation from Liverpool 8.[41]

As an intent of its purpose, the advisory committee abandoned the gallery's provisional rather bland title and opted for the more purposeful present version mentioned above. When it finally opened on 24 October 1994, visitors could see that it had managed to address many of the concerns and views of the interests involved: even though health and safety regulations prevented an exact replica of conditions below decks, it captured the indignity and squalor of the Middle Passage; it provided an accurate historical record of West African society before and during the depredations of slave raiders; as its panel on the *Amistad* revolt indicated, it presented slaves as oppressed, but far from passive; it personalised the lives of a few of the twelve million slaves landed in the Americas and presented them as individuals, with names. Above all, it aimed at objectivity and avoided sentiment: to make a lasting impact, it had to be, in Moores' words, "factual, correct and non-emotive".[42] Apart from the slaves themselves, the gallery also addressed the less familiar, but potentially more controversial matter of the slave trade's contribution to the commercial development of Liverpool, from the streets named after slaving interests to its role in the growth of Liverpool banking sector. To some observers who had read their Eric Williams, it did not go far enough, and should have traced the story beyond the 1807 abolition into the development of industries in the Victorian age such as cotton manufacturing and sugar-refining.

Nevertheless, the gallery has attracted wide interest and a procession of famous visitors. Its outreach work, headed by Garry Morris, has generated a demand from local schools that has often taxed the resources of its educational staff.[43] In March 2005, the NMGM released a CD ROM, *Transatlantic Slavery: Facing Up*, designed for KS3 Citizenship and History pupils and their teachers, which includes a virtual tour of the gallery and the story of the young Ghanaian slave Kofi, told in cartoon form.

Towards an apology: the call for reparations

Preparations for the gallery took place during the first stages of an international campaign calling upon former slaving nations to make reparations to the victims of slavery, following recent precedents such as the payment of compensation to Japanese Americans interned after Pearl Harbour. The first International Conference on Reparations for slavery, held in Lagos in December 1990 was to be the first of many. Co-ordinating it, the African Reparations Movement (ARM) established a British chapter in 1993, headed by the black MP Bernie Grant. The questions of what form reparations should take, how much they should be, who should pay and who receive have remained contentious issues, and some of the more extreme demands have tended to undermine the credibility of the movement as a whole, giving cynics opportunities to make cheap jibes. The global, historical, character of the claim has brought into the equation a host of other consideration: the involvement of Africans themselves in the trade, the cost of its suppression up to and beyond the imposition of colonial rule, the related issue of "war crimes" committed by imperial powers against their subjects, and current Western initiatives to suspend/cancel African debt.

While these wider issues fall outside the remit of this chapter, one demand made by ARM spokesmen is directly relevant here: the call for an apology. This demand was highlighted in Lord Gifford's House of Lords motion of 14 March 1996, which *inter alia* called for "an apology at the highest level for the criminal acts committed against millions of Africans over the centuries of the slave trade". Here one should acknowledge the City of Liverpool's "emotionally and symbolically significant"[44] example of December 1999, when it became the first city in Europe to apologise and express regret for its role in the Atlantic slave trade. This was preceded by a ceremony on 23 August (corresponding with the start of Haitian revolt in 1791) when Bernie Grant unveiled a plaque outside the Museum of Liverpool Life. An annual commemoration at the Albert Dock, involving prominent black personalities, has occurred since then, while the TUC has added its voice to the suggestion that 23 August should be observed nationally. In the same month as Liverpool's apology, the President of Benin in West Africa apologised for his country's role in selling slaves to white traders. These are small gestures perhaps, but show that at least some international statesmen, to quote Marc Ferro, are willing to place "the ideology of human rights" over the "ideology of the nation state".[45]

The apology and Liverpool's black community

The Council's apology called upon Liverpool's black community to "forgive the past and claim its future"; in other words, to help in the forging of a new Liverpool in the next century. It was an appeal that led certain members of that community present in the council chamber to interject that it was "too little, too late", and protest that "not enough had been done for the black members of the community".[46] A balance sheet of what had, or not been done for the black community is a task beyond the limits of this chapter, but it is appropriate to set out briefly some of the historical events which may have contributed to the protest, and to take as an illustration the confrontation between the black community and Liverpool's Militant council in the early 1980s.

The black community (within the larger Liverpool 8 community) has been the subject of many studies and enquiries: indeed it could be argued that the number has been excessive, with correspondingly small results. Historically, the most notorious of these was Muriel Fletcher's report for the Liverpool Association for the Welfare of Half-Caste Children (1930), with its unacceptable comments about racial intermarriage under chapter headings like "History of the 'Colour Problem in Liverpool'", and "The Women Who Consort With Coloured Men".[47] Paul Rich notes that Fletcher's black interviewees felt they had been betrayed, despite their ready co-operation with her enquiries.[48] Sixty years later, suspicion of outside experts was registered by a team of researchers investigating black youth: "We have found that black Liverpudlians are closing ranks; they are refusing to participate in investigations which many now see as using black people as the topic of academic papers and reports which ultimately serve mainly to further the academic prestige of those who write them".[49]

Such responses were arguably the outward expression of an alienation from the majority white culture. Also, they represented a search for an identity[50] that had extended over a considerable period, but which had strongly manifested itself from the later 1960s onwards, with the increasing size of a locally-born black population that saw itself as a entity distinct from its immigrant parents, yet did not feel part of the majority culture and heritage. As a 1994 report authored by Liverpool 8- based professionals put it, "many young Black people have feelings of ambiguity towards a nation that played a major role in the dehumanisation of the African continent, even if it is the nation granting them citizenship".[51]

To this should be added the race attitudes of the dominant white culture from the later 1960s, and the mounting incidence of racist attacks, abuse and other forms of discrimination following the growth of far-right groups exploiting the fears and anxieties of the white majority. To take one example, a *Liverpool Daily Post* news item from 1980 describes how a mixed race schoolboy, born in Liverpool, was harassed over an 18 month period by National Front-influenced children at a school he attended outside Liverpool 8, harassment that included physical attacks on his home.[52] The effect was to create a virtually segregated society based in the Granby ward of Toxteth. As Pippa West, wife of a local vicar, remarked, Granby was a place "where young black people in particular feel at home; for some, the only place they feel comfortable in".[53] The overall effect was to generate a "them" and "us" attitude, with Granby (or "Toxteth", as it was more familiarly labelled) appearing as a "problem" area in official reports.

When left-wing groups such as the Liverpool Labour Party did take up black causes after World War II, they seem to have been ones removed from Merseyside: the extant minutes of the Toxteth Labour Party refer to South Africa after Sharpeville, the Notting Hill riots and the 1960 Congo crisis, but nothing on Liverpool's black population.[54] The increasing deprivation of Granby, a typical inner city area with decaying buildings and systemic unemployment merely added to the popular image of 'Toxteth'.

Case Study: the MCRC, the Black Caucus and Militant

The radicalisation of Liverpool 8 youth, growing anger about police harassment, and the economic downturn of the late 1970s and early 1980s, felt especially sharply on Merseyside, were contributory factors to the Toxteth riots, which involved white as well as black youth, in July 1981. However, the same period witnessed the development of a major social initiative, the Merseyside Community Relations Council (MCRC) which provided a vehicle for the expression of black and other non-white community groups. The MCRC was established in 1970, within the framework set by the 1968 Race Relations Act, and with Commission for Racial Equality and local authority funding. At first, it operated in accordance with the 'welfarist' context of earlier voluntary associations, which had worked with (or more often, for) the black community. Thus its first Object:

To advance the education of the inhabitants of Liverpool [after 1973, 'the Metropolitan County of Merseyside'] without distinction of sex or race or of political, religious, or other opinions and to provide facilities in the interest of social welfare for recreation and leisure time occupation with the object of improving the condition of life of the said inhabitants[55].

In practice, as the MCRC admitted, its resources could not encompass the 1½ million inhabitants of Merseyside, and its welfare efforts were concentrated in areas with sizeable black populations. The MCRC in any case soon found itself bursting free from its "welfarist" bonds. Its chief Community Relations Officer noted in the 1977 annual report that its focus had moved from the fostering of "racial harmony" to the more radical cause of campaigning for the equality of rights and opportunities, while adding that radical black people were becoming suspicious of the MCRC's role as spokesmen on their behalf.[56] It denounced the Merseyside police handling of the Toxteth riots,[57] an action that exposed the MCRC to the charge that it had forfeited its earlier role as "neutral" go-between. Its identification with the black cause provoked the Liverpool Council to add a warning tone to its usual foreword in the MCRC's 1981 annual report. Lord Scarman's report on the Brixton disorders (with some comment on Toxteth) echoed this, censuring CRCs in general for losing sight of their prescribed role of fostering, "not undermining", racial harmony.[58] While the MCRC attracted this type of official criticism, its reputation as a credible voice for the black community could only benefit: by the mid 1980s, it comprised 300 individual members and 60 affiliated organisations. Alongside it, another umbrella organisation with an overlapping membership, the Black Caucus, emerged in 1983. This body attempted to soften its Black Power image by adopting a logo stressing racial co-operation, two outstretched white and black hands in profile cupping its title, and listing its trade union, Labour ward branches, and senior churchmen supporters.[59]

The scene was now set for what was to become a famous controversy in Liverpool affairs, and served to intensify black suspicions, this time of the intentions of the Left in its local politics. Labour's success in at last winning a clear overall majority on the Council in 1983 brought to power an administration standing well to the left of Labour nationally in which Militant, advocating class-based, 'workerist' policies, had considerable influence. The new Council declared its commitment to anti-racist policies,[60] But as events were to show, Militant seems to have regarded racism as a by-product of capitalism, to be solved by the destruction of the class system.

Battle was joined in October 1984, with the appointment of Sampson Bond, a black surveyor from London and Militant member, to head a new Race Relations Unit reporting directly to the City Council's Chief Executive. The Black Caucus maintained that this was a political appointment, with the successful candidate chosen because he was prepared to toe the party line, even though he lacked the professional qualifications of the other candidates; and accordingly imposed a boycott on his activities plus those of volunteers brought in to work in Liverpool 8. Further outrage was expressed when the Council suspended its existing Race Relations Liaison Committee, on which black associations and their representatives had a powerful voice, and replaced it with an Equal Opportunities Committee in which race was placed alongside other forms of disadvantage such as gender and disability; the black voice was further diluted by an overall reduction of membership from voluntary organisations. Writing after Bond's dismissal by a post-Militant Council, Peter Taafe and Tony Mulhearn's defiantly Trotskyist *Liverpool- A City That Dared* (1988) condemned the Black Caucus as a group of mostly middle-class elements who mainly lived in the suburbs while claiming to be "community leaders in the Liverpool 8 area", and suggested that in ignoring the real possibility of a white working class background backlash against their policies, were simply serving capitalist interests.[61]

While a final verdict on the Sam Bond affair awaits the availability of relevant materials, its effect on the black community can be assessed. In the short term, it re-opened the historical fissure between immigrants and locally-born; it divided the community between those who rejected him and those willing to give him a chance; and it led to a revival of the Black Power "go it alone" spirit, especially amongst younger blacks. The Black Caucus began to disintegrate, resulting in the weakening of the MCRC, which was to disappear in 1993 when the CRE decide to end its funding on the grounds that it was not offering value for money. But above all, the affair seems to have convinced Liverpool's black community that Labour's Hard Left was no different from other political groups in white Britain, and had added insult to injury by denying Liverpool blacks their identity. In the 1985 Council elections a Black Caucus-supported candidate stood against the official Labour nominee in the Granby Ward.[62]

Conclusion

Post-Militant councils have moved some way towards repairing the damage caused by their predecessors. They set targets for the recruitment of black workers to its labour force, a policy Militant had rejected as divisive, but employment law, permitting no positive discrimination except in the case of posts in services specifically geared toward the needs of "ethnic minorities", has created a situation where black workers are trained but cannot be guaranteed employment at the end of that training. Nelson notes that the Council eventually set up departmental race equality units, though in parentheses it might be suggested that a central unit might have carried more weight, or-alternatively-pose more of a challenge to the city's bureaucracy. In the economic upturn of the late 1980s, a start was made to the re-development of Liverpool 8, including the Granby Toxteth Community Project.

The 1990s witnessed the emergence of housing associations, establishing new black icons for Liverpool, Steve Biko and Mary Seacole Houses, to set against streets named after slavers, though with the familiar criticism that a process of gentrification was not helping the really deprived members of the community.[63] A recent press report notes that 71.9% of children in the Granby ward currently live on benefits, the highest proportion in the North-West: this should be set against the national figure of 28%.[64] In the words of the Council chamber protestors, much more still needs to be done for Liverpool's black community.

On the main issue, recognising, apologising for and memorialising its historical legacy as a major participant in the slave system, Liverpool has taken the first few, albeit significant steps. Cynics may argue that the whole process had been driven by the needs of the tourist industry, launched with a flourish after the Toxteth riots and recently stimulated by the (ultimately successful) City of Culture bid. But it has made a start to a long process of restitution, an expression of guilt which in itself cannot be enough, and may say more about the oppressor than the victim. As Maya Angelou remarked when she opened the slavery gallery in 1994: "Guilt is about the most dangerous of emotions as it eats up the host but does nothing for the victim".[65]

Acknowledgements

My thanks to the staff of the Merseyside/Liverpool Record Offices, the Liverpool Central Libraries, the University of Liverpool libraries (including the Special Collections); to Anthony Tibbles, Garry Morris and Stephen Guy of the Merseyside Maritime Museum; to the Liverpool LEA for helpful advice; and to participants at the CLAMS Identities conference in March 2005 for comments on an earlier version of this chapter. Also, my thanks to Edge College of Higher Education for help towards travel expenses.

---

[1] "Children of Slavery Blast City's 'Quick-Fix' Apology," *Liverpool Daily Post*, 10 December 1999.

[2] Exclusion of the Liverpool Chinese and South Asian Communities from this chapter does not subtract from my view that all non-white people have experienced racial discrimination in Britain.

[3] *Land We Live In: a Pictorial and Literary Sketch of the British Empire, Vol 1.* (London: Charles Knight, 1847) 292, 302.

[4] James Aspinall, *Liverpool a Few Years Since: By an Old Stager* (London: Whittaker and Co, 1852) 152.

[5] "Dicky Sam", *Liverpool and Slavery: An Historical Account of the Liverpool-African Slave Trade* (Liverpool: A Bowker, 1884) 2.

[6] Gail Cameron and Stan Crooke, *Liverpool: Capital of the Slave Trade* (Liverpool: Picton Press, 1992) 65-70. Madge Dresser notes a similar reticence in Bristol (*Slavery Obscured:*

the Social History of the Slave Trade in an English Provincial Port (London: Continuum, 2001) 1-3.)

[7] (London: T Nelson & Sons, 1899).

[8] John Belchem, *Merseypride: Essays in Liverpool Exceptionalism* (Liverpool: Liverpool University Press, 2000) 18-19.

[9] Walter Rhodes, *A School History of Lancashire* (London: Methuen, 1907) 191.

[10] (Oxford: Clarendon Press, 1913) 220. Also, Hewitt gives the impression that there was no black community in Liverpool after the Mansfield judgement.

[11] *Lancashire Stories Vol 1* (London: T C and E C Jack, 1912) 348-50.

[12] (London: Sir Isaac Pitman and Sons, 1927 (2nd ed)) 174.

[13] Liverpool: Liverpool Daily Post, 1946, 36.

[14] Liverpool: Rondo Publications, 1972, 86.

[15] Robert Ballantyne, *Black Ivory; A Tale of Adventure Among the Slavers of East Africa* (James Nisbet and Co, 1873) Preface.

[16] William H G Kingston, *The African Trader or, Harry Bayford's Adventure* (London: Gall and Inglis, n d [1873]).

[17] As quoted in Gillian Klein, *Education Towards Race Equality* (London, Cassell, 1993) 171.

[18] John Mackenzie, *Propaganda and Empire: the Manipulation of British Public Opinion, 1880-1960* (Manchester: M[anchester] U[niversity] P[ress], 1984); John MacKenzie, (ed.), *Imperialism and Popular Culture* (Manchester, MUP, 1986).

[19] *Propaganda and Empire*, 176.

[20] Joan Blyth, *History in Primary Schools: a Practical Approach For Teachers of 5 to 11-Year Old Children* (Milton Keynes: Open University Press, 1989) 5.

[21] Norman Bridge, *My Liverpool Schools* (Portinscale: Kirkland Press, 1992) 36.

[22] L[iverpool] R[ecord] O[ffice], City of Liverpool, *Loan Collection of Lantern Slides: Catalogue*, 1928.

[23] LRO: City of Liverpool, *Reports of the Education Committee for the School Years 1950-51*, 16-17, and *1955-56*, 73-74.

[24] Andrew Scotland, *Modern Citizenship* (Edinburgh: McDougall's Education Co, n d [c1940-41]) 146ff.

[25] LRO, Liverpool Council Finance and General Purposes Committee, *The Story of Liverpool: an Exhibition Devised and Presented by the Liverpool Corporation and Liverpool University for the Festival Year 1951*, 34.

[25] Verlyn Klinkenborg, "Liverpool's Heart of Darkness", *Mother Jones*, July-August 2002, 66.

[26] Alison Yarrington, "Public Sculpture and Civic Pride" in Penelope Curtis, *Patronage and Practice: Sculpture on Merseyside* (Liverpool: Tate Gallery, Liverpool, and NMGM, 1989) 23-26.

[27] Herman Melville, *Redburn: His First Voyage* (New York: Russell and Russell, 1963 reprint) 198. Redburn also notes the "unhappiness" that discussions of abolition caused in Liverpool.

[28] e g, Liverpool Socialist Workers Party, *Socialism in Liverpool: Episodes in the History of Working-class Struggle* (Liverpool: Hegemon Press, 2000) 10.

[29] Terry Cavanagh, *Public Sculpture in Liverpool* (Liverpool: Liverpool University Press, 1997) 73.

[30] As illustrated in Quentin Hughes, *Seaport: Architecture and Townscape in Liverpool* (Liverpool: Bluecoat Press, 1992) 186-7, 103.

[31] Bob Dixon, *Catching Them Young 1: Sex, Race and Class in Children's Literature* (London: Pluto Press, 1978) 96.

[32] [M]erseyside [C]ommunity [R]elations [C]ouncil, *Black Linx*, June 1984, 2. The *Festival Guide*, written in prevailing optimistic Heseltinian spirit, has a jolly reference to "the greed of pirates and slave traders" (197), and also mentions William Roscoe, without saying anything about his abolitionist activities (200).

[33] Typescript n.d.[1973] in LRO, Hq 301.451 COM 2.

[34] Appendix 10 in Liverpool Education Authority, *Black Perspectives on Further Education,* June 1989, 101ff. Typescript in LRO HQ378.42753 HIG.

[35] *The Abolition of the Slave Trade.* Wakefield: Education Productions (Slide Set produced in association with the Historical Association), 1973. The last slide, "Cleaning up the Dark Continent" depicts, predictably, the inauguration of white rule in Africa.

[36] 1st ed, 1995; 2nd ed, 1997. The Williams quotation (p 40) comes from 178 of the 1964 (Andre Deutsch) edition. On Seymour Drescher, see his "Whose Abolition? Popular Pressure and the Ending of the Slave Trade," *Past and Present* 143 (May 1994) 136-66, and *Capitalism and Antislavery: British Mobilization in Comparative Perspective* (London: Macmillan, 1986).

[37] Anthony (Lord) Gifford, Wally Brown and Ruth Bundey, *Loosen the Shackles: First Report of the Liverpool 8 Inquiry into Race Relations in Liverpool* (London, Karia Press, 1989) 26.

[38] Anthony Tibbles, "Against Human Dignity: the Making of the Transatlantic Slavery Gallery," *IXth International Congress of Maritime Museums: Proceedings* (1996) 95-102.

[39] Simon Tait, "Chains of Shame," *The Times*, 20 October 1994.

[40] No 1, March 1992, 4. In LRO, Hq307 COM.

[41] NMGM, *Atlantic Slave Trade: Newsletter, Issue 2,* n d [March 1993]. In LRO Hq 380.144 ATL.

[42] Simon Tait, ibid. See also *Liverpool Echo,* 25 October 1994; *Liverpool Daily Post,* 25 October 1994; Jane Norrie, "Of Human Bondage," *Times Educational Supplement*, 21 October 1994; and "The Chains of History," *Sunday Times*, 30 October 1994, whose black author takes issue with some of its black critics.

[43] Garry Morris, interview, 10 February, 2005.

[44] Klinkenborg, ibid, 67. The information in this section has been drawn from the African Reparations Movement website, http://www.arm.co.uk. which at present is not being maintained; other internet links on reparations, and National Museums and City Council press releases kindly copied by Stephen Guy of the Merseyside Maritime Museum.

[45] Marc Ferro, *The Use and Abuse of History: or How the Past is Taught to Children* (London: Routledge, 2003 edition) ix.

[46] As reported in the *Liverpool Daily Post,* 10 December 1999. On Eric Lynch, named in this report, see Marie van Helmond, "Eric Lynch, a Very Active Life," *North West Labour History,* 20 (1995/96) 67-72.

---

[47] Muriel Fletcher, *Report of an Investigation Into the Colour Problem in Liverpool and Other Ports* (Liverpool: Liverpool Association for the Welfare of Half-Caste Children, 1930). For a typical reaction to Fletcher see Andrea Murphy, *From the Empire to the Rialto: Racism and Reaction in Liverpool, 1918-1948* (Birkenhead: Liver Press, 1995) 99. Fletcher's reference to the 'colour problem' echoes similar texts on colonial Africa written in the 1920s.

[48] Paul Rich, *Race and Empire in British Politics* (Cambridge: Cambridge University Press, 1986) 131.

[49] Michelle Connolly and others, *Black Youth in Liverpool* (Voorthuizen: Giordano Bruno Culemborg, 1992) 7.

[50] Diane Frost, "Ambiguous Identities: Constructing and De-constructing Black and White 'Scouse' Identities in Twentieth Century Liverpool" in Neville Kirk, (ed.), *Northern Identities: Historical Interpretations of the North and 'Northernness'* (Aldershot: Ashgate, 2000) 193-217.

[51] Educational Opportunities in Liverpool 8, *Explorations of Black Identity in the Granby Toxteth Area of Liverpool* [prepared by William Ackah and Ruby Dixon], n d [1994], Section 1.2. LRO Hq305.896042753, typescript.

[52] "Lessons in Hate For Our Schools", *Liverpool Daily Post,* 24 November 1980.

[53] Pippa West, *Down Granby Street: a Christian Family in Toxteth* (London: Triangle (SPCK), 1988) 62.

[54] Minutes of the Executive/Management Committee, 4 July 1958, 7 March 1960, 3 March 1961, LRO M331 TLP 1: Toxteth Constituency Labour Party, 1948-1966.

[55] As appearing in its 7th Annual Report, presented to the AGM on 22 September 1977 (LRO H301.34 MER).

[56] ibid, 9-14.

[57] A good introduction to this topic is provided by Phil Scraton's "Policing and Institutionalised Racism on Merseyside," in David Cowell and others, *Policing the Riots* (London: Junction Books, 1982) 21-38.

[58] HMSO, *The Brixton Disorders: report of an inquiry by the Rt. Hon. The Lord Scarman, OBE [Cmnd 8427],* 1981, 110.

[59] See reproduction on inside front cover of the MCRC Annual Report for 1984-85 (LRO H301.34 MER).

[60] See "Labour Council Moves to Combat Racism," *Liverpool News,* August 1984, 4.

[61] This account has been drawn from the MCRC's Annual Reports; MCRC: *Black Linx*; Taafe and Mulhearn's book (London: Fortress, 1988) and the text it attacks, Liverpool Black Caucus, *The Racial Politics of Militant in Liverpool; The Black Community's participation in local politics, 1980-1986* (Liverpool: Merseyside Area Profile Group and Runnymede Trust, 1986). Michael Parkinson, *Liverpool on the Brink* (Hermitage: Policy Journals, 1985) provides a relatively neutral account.

[62] For the later history of the MCRC, see William Nelson, *Black Atlantic Politics: Dilemmas of Political Empowerment in Boston and Liverpool* (Albany, NY: State University of New York, 2000).

[63] See ibid, 213-30.

[64] "Third of Children in North-West Live in Poverty," *Guardian,* 12 March 2005.

[65] Claire Stocks, "Focus on City's Slave Shame as Gallery Opens," *Liverpool Daily Post,* 25 October, 1994.

ECHOES OF LOSS: CONDOLENCE BOOKS AND COLLECTIVE MEMORY IN THE MOURNING FOR HILLSBOROUGH

MIKE BRENNAN

On 15 April 1989 95 supporters of Liverpool FC were crushed to death at an FA Cup Semi-Final match between Liverpool and Nottingham Forest at Sheffield Wednesday's Hillsborough stadium.[1] Many more were injured in what became Britain's worst ever football disaster.[2] In the public mourning that followed, and in the wake of hostile tabloid media criticism directed at Liverpool fans themselves,[3] a series of spectacular mourning events at once turned the city "in on itself for mutual support"[4] and galvanised local identity on Merseyside. Among these mourning events in the days following the disaster were the signing of public books of condolence at the city's two cathedrals; the Anglican and the Metropolitan. Other key events included the transformation of Liverpool's Anfield stadium[5] into a site of spiritual pilgrimage–a de facto third cathedral[6]; a symbolic "scarf-link" in which scarves of supporters of the city's two football clubs, Liverpool and Everton, were knotted together to form a mile-long bridge between their two respective stadiums, Anfield and Goodison Park;[7] and a number of ecumenical church services in which football and religion were seamlessly intertwined[8]–a feature made all the more remarkable for a city that has, historically, been characterised by religious sectarianism.[9] Drawing upon a variety of theoretical frameworks: social, semiotic and psychoanalytic, I want to suggest in this chapter that whilst the widespread public mourning after Hillsborough was clearly a mourning for the victims of Hillsborough–of 95(6) untimely and unspeakably tragic "bad deaths",[10] it was also a mourning for various other unmourned losses experienced at the personal, social and cultural level. Taking condolence books signed following Hillsborough as a point of focus, I suggest a number of key arguments. Chiefly, that the content of condolence books tells us much not only about the way contemporary culture mourns but about the social identities–identities in *historical transition*–of the people who signed them; that the way in which grief is languaged bears an intimate relation to unconscious fantasy, desire and the narrative imagination; and that throughout the condolence books, "Liverpool"–as a discursive sign system around which meaning is constructed–is productively drawn upon as a "text".[11] I begin, however, by sketching out an epistemological rationale for my choice of condolence books as a particular point of focus.

Why Look at Condolence Books?

In recent years public books of condolence have become a ubiquitous feature of the funerary landscape following high profile deaths or especially calamitous disasters involving the widespread loss of life. The Hillsborough disaster of 1989 was seemingly one of the first such events to inaugurate this trend in public mourning practices. Since then condolence books have been opened and signed by many millions of people world-wide for people to express their sympathies with the bereaved. Books of condolence were signed globally following the terrorist attacks on America on 11 September 2001 and, most famously, following the death of Diana, Princess of Wales on 31 August 1997–where people queued anything up to seven hours to sign them.[12] Since then they have been opened and signed following: the murders of popular television presenter Jill Dando in 1998 and Soham school-girls Holly Wells and Jessica Chapman in 2002; the deaths of Princess Margaret and the Queen Mother, also in 2002; and again in Liverpool following the death of former Beatle George Harrison in 2001. They were even signed following the announcement by Marks and Spencer that they were to close their stores in mainland Europe.[13] Yet despite their ubiquity, public books of condolence have, for the most part, remained hitherto unread, either by the bereaved or the wider public for whom they were presumably intended.

My own research in this area,[14] which considered condolence books signed following Hillsborough alongside a sample of condolence books signed following the death of Princess Diana, encountered peculiar problems of access in which the property rights of condolence books were thrown into sharp relief.[15] In the case of Hillsborough, the condolence books had seemingly been lost, with no record or trace of their whereabouts. Phil Hammond, of the Hillsborough Family Support Group claimed never to have seen the books, whilst Shelia Coleman of the break-away Hillsborough Justice Campaign and author of several reports into Hillsborough from a criminal justice perspective, was on record as saying that "if people took the time to write them, the least" that could be done is that they be kept "somewhere safe where people could have access to them". In neither case were condolence books openly on display for the public to read, nor were their contents recorded and logged for historical record.[16]

In addition, not only have condolence books been largely un-read by the wider public at large, they have at the same time remained largely un-researched by the academic community.[17] This lacuna in academic research is especially striking as the epistolary messages contained in condolence books provide a rich source of textual data that can be meaningfully mined from a number of perspectives: social, cultural, political, historical, psychological, philosophical.

Socially, condolence books tell us something about the social identities of people who mourned. Particular sentiments, and the ways in which they are expressed, can be indexed to the social structures of which people are a part, providing a "bottom-up" approach in which analysis begins with the individual and works outwards (in contrast to traditional varieties of sociology which, by definition, begin with society and work downwards or various incarnations of structuralism, in which the individual becomes a vanishing point or "blind spot" within social theory). They tell us something about the social significance of the people or "things" being mourned and the ways in which these are drawn upon and consumed as a resource in everyday life. In the case of the Hillsborough books of condolence, as we shall see, they provide a glimpse into the ways in which language is socially situated, reflective of local inflexions of language related to social, economic and geo-political currents sedimented in an historically evolved "habitus".[18]

Culturally, condolence books provide a site for understanding wider meaning-making processes through and by which the various "objects" being mourned are culturally invested. That is to say, for examining the "subjective or cultural forms" that condolence books realise and make available for analysis.[19] They tell us something about how contemporary culture mourns, about the discursive practices through which identity is performatively summoned, and society's relationship with death at the end of the twentieth century–a century characterised within Western societies by an ambivalence that has oscillated between death denial and public fascination.[20]

Politically, they reflect the distribution of power relations within society, helping to democratise and influence decision-making within the predominantly rationalistic public sphere from which various "subaltern counter-publics"[21] are, and have been, routinely excluded. To this extent, condolence books, are a "producerly" and "grass-roots" activity, which, as cultural theorist, Jim McGuigan puts it, represent an aspect of the cultural public sphere: a site of "affective communication and popular dispution over the conduct of life"; the "articulation of politics" as a "contested terrain through affective – aesthetic and emotional–modes of communication".[22]

Historically, condolence books provide an enduring documentary resource–of social, cultural and linguistic practices by which particular deaths, and the–often momentous–events that foreground them, are experienced, marked and personally understood. They provide an "empirical marker"[23]–of what has been and gone, allowing ordinary individuals the opportunity to play the role of social historian; to narrate historical events and their own role within them. In this way, personal identification with "the event" becomes a means of comprehending–because of its unexpectedness, size and scale–their seeming incomprehensibility. Moreover, as cultural historian Raymond Williams has noted, the surviving documentary evidence of any given culture provides us with an enduring source of recorded communication that allows access to the lived "structures of feeling"–and in this case, to the popular sentiments and sentimentality–of a particular community or collectivity.[24] Here Williams uses the said notion to refer to the largely intangible yet particular sense of life and "community of experience, hardly needing expression", characteristic of a specific time and place. This felt sense of life, as a "valued system of behaviour and attitudes" is, as Williams suggests, "as firm and definite as 'structure' suggests, yet it operates in the most delicate and least tangible parts of our activity".[25] Besides this, condolence books represent what historian Eric Hobsbawn might call an "invented tradition", a factitious "tradition" with seemingly no historical precedent other than the Victorian epistolary tradition of sending condolence cards.

Psychologically, condolence books tell us something about the ways in which language serves, often simultaneously, to articulate and deny the pain of loss. From this perspective, language sheds light on the psycho-dynamics of mourning, yielding-up (un)conscious investments in the people and "things" being mourned, reminding us of the intimate relationship that language shares within the unconscious. For as French post-structuralist and psychoanalytic theorist Jacques Lacan has famously suggested, the unconscious is itself said to be "structured like a language", from where particular utterances, slips or silences can be analysed to reveal the latent meaning buried deep within either its written or spoken forms.[26] In this light, Julia Kristeva, French feminist psychoanalytic theorist and leading exponent of "semanalyse" (the blending of psychoanalysis and semiotics), has argued that loss not only serves to summon a sense of identity[27] but that it triggers the narrative imagination in which semiotic (i.e. visual and aural imagery) and symbolic (i.e. written and spoken) aspects of language become "the communicable imprints of an affective reality".[28] Crucially, therefore, the contents of condolence books reflect the taking-in and transformation within the realm of psychic imagination of that which is socially "exterior", namely, culture, politics, people and society more generally.[29]

Philosophically, the injunction and compulsion to "do something" in the aftermath of catastrophic events such as Hillsborough–be it condolence book signing and/or the writing of poetry–reflects our moral responsibility for the Other; a responsibility, which, as social philosopher Zygmunt Bauman puts it, is "all the greater the weaker and more helpless the Other".[30] It is this recognition of the Other, according to American philosopher Emmanuel Levinas, which confirms and reaffirms our bonds to humanity. Such recognition of the Other's suffering, as a collective attempt to share the burden of loss, can be seen in the Latin etymology of the term "condolence", combining the words *"com"* (together) and *"dolere"* (to grieve).[31] Indeed, philosophically, the signature–as an attempt to mark in writing the "I-here-now" of enunciated speech–bears an uncanny relation to death, for by virtue of being detachable from its bearer it announces the death of its bearer; it is "the anticipated memory of a departure".[32]

Condolence books therefore can be seen, simultaneously, as serving a *social* as well as a *personal* or emotionally *interior* function, for they at once represent a public forum for a continued dialogue, not only with the self and with others, but with the deceased, with whom communication was abruptly and interminably interrupted by their sudden and unannounced death. At the same time, they provide an opportunity for the "working through" of emotions–of anger, blame, guilt and denial–routinely associated and unleashed by mourning; a process or "work" that must be seen through to completion.[33]

Mourning Hillsborough, Mourning Liverpool

Whilst the condolence books and wider public mourning events surrounding Hillsborough clearly reflect the grievous, in many ways un-grievable, and unnecessary loss of life in Sheffield, they are shot-through with a wider pathos–of loss–that outstrips the disaster's individual or collective victims. In his 1917 essay "Mourning and Melancholia", Freud extends the concept of mourning to include other "things", as the object of yearning, claiming it as "the reaction to the loss of a loved person, or to the loss of some abstraction which has taken the place of one, such as one's country, liberty, an ideal and so on".[34] In the remainder of this chapter, therefore, I want to argue that much of the mourning for Hillsborough was also a mourning for aspects of Liverpool that, in less exceptional everyday circumstances, had remained un-mourned; a mourning not only for the victims of Hillsborough (for many of those who mourned did not know the deceased or bereaved personally), but for the loss of selves and for people and places gone before, for these are inextricably intertwined.

Set against Liverpool's long-term social and economic decline, a decline that reached an unparalleled nadir in the 1980s–a decade begun by urban riots in the inner-city district of Toxteth, punctuated by the Heysel disaster, and culminating in Hillsborough, the condolence books signed following the Hillsborough disaster reflect a yearning for a proud and distinguished past long since congealed within local collective memory yet all but erased in wider contemporary pre-conceptions about the city which predominate elsewhere in the UK. Today Liverpool continues to conjure a range of images, most of them pejorative, and is a rare example of a city about which people throughout the UK have "definitive opinions", for whom Liverpool is perceived as "a city of problems where the people themselves are reckoned to be part of the problem".[35]

Mourning, as we have seen, is an attempt, in the first instance, to summon and resurrect in memory that which has been lost; "a repeated calling to memory of the lost object" in a process of reality-testing that unlike either nostalgia (as the antithesis of remembering) or melancholia (as mourning's pathological Other), "will end in letting go".[36] This mourning, can, then, be seen as a mourning for two distinct historical phases in Liverpool's history: the first, a period of unbridled economic expansion spanning almost a century from the end of the eighteenth to the beginning of the twentieth century, when Liverpool was a commercial and maritime powerhouse, second only to London and known globally as the "second city of Empire" or the "second metropolis". The second period, a cultural renaissance of sorts, especially prominent during the 1960s, in which Liverpool all but dominated popular cultural domains: of sport, show-business and music. Liverpool's status during this first period is reflected in a series of architectural statements and styles[37] which exude confidence and reaffirm its position as "world-city" rather than merely British Provincial—the New York of Europe.[38] Indeed, as Liverpool born novelist and journalist Linda Grant points out, many immigrants from Eastern Europe *en route* to New York thought that they had already arrived in the New World when they disembarked in Liverpool.[39] In the second period, the 1960s marked a cultural revolution or sorts, especially in music and the arts, but also in sport and popular culture. For as Andrew Ward and John Williams[40] write, not only were the Beatles the most famous group in the world, but in their "slipstream" came a host of bands whose trademark was the so-called "Mersey-Sound". Elsewhere, "Cilla Black was a big pop star" and a triumvirate of local poets such as Roger McGeogh, Adrian Henri and Brian Pattern "were creating a national stir". Comedians too, such as Ken Dodd and Jimmy Tarbuck were "household names" and the city "produced a string of boxing champions from Alan Rudkin to John Conteh". In football, Liverpool and Everton were "winning trophies regularly" and for several years during the 1960s and 1970s Labour Prime Minister Harold Wilson "ran Britain from the nearby Huyton consistency. All in all, the city had optimism, employment and good humour". "Culturally at least", therefore, "it was a relatively good time to be young, working-class and from Liverpool".[41]

Besides being a mourning for a Liverpool of yesteryear, and as we shall see in the messages I present below, the condolence books signed following Hillsborough are reflective of a sense of Liverpool exceptionalism in which the city is marked by a sense of Otherness from the rest of the UK. They are distinguished by subtle nuances and local inflexions of speech, as well as a certain irreverence, informality and verbal word-play characteristic of Liverpool's semi-Celtic and strongly communitarian ethic. It is these things in particular: distinctive patterns of speech; the seamless blending of football and religion; and a semi-Celtic and strongly working-class culture which give Liverpool a unique "structure of feeling".

Football, Religion and a Sense of Place

Various sociologists and social commentators have reflected upon the imbrication of football and religion on Merseyside–as mutually inseparable, providing focus and shape "in the lives of countless individuals and communities"[42]–in ways which were especially prominent in the days following the Hillsborough disaster.[43] Liverpool is also, "a city with an extraordinarily strong self-identity"[44] with a very definite sense of place[45] embodied in a series of landmarks, and geographical position which reinforces a perceived sense of isolation. We can see this in the messages I present below[46] which weave football and religion together in an unselfconscious and taken-for-granted manner reflective of the city's unique "structure of feeling".

> "Liver birds on their chest. God only takes the best".

> "L ive
> F or
> C hrist"

> "No cages! No turnstiles! Unlimited capacity – at the ground you have gone to now."

> "Oh please Lord. Please tell me why? Why did my friends have to die? To our 95 angels in the Kop in the sky. You will never be forgotten. Sleep peacefully fans. Goodnight."

We see this clearly in the first message, in which the Liver Birds, a key signifier or totem of local identity, are invoked[47] and rhymed with a religious enunciation that at once seeks to derive meaning and deny the possibility that the lives so needlessly claimed by the Hillsborough disaster might, after all, have been in vain. The Liver birds have, of course, since the time of Saint John the Evangelist and later King John, become synonymous with the city. The mythological nature of the Liver Birds relationship with Liverpool was given added impetus by the nineteenth century American novelist Herman Melville who in *Redburn* was inadvertently responsible for spreading the apocryphal story that Liverpool was itself named after this extinct stork-like creature. We see too this unusual admixture of football and religion in the second message presented here, which, expressed as an acrostic, spells out the initials of Liverpool FC in a vertical and descending order; and again in the third and fourth messages which conceive notions of an eternal hereafter in footballing terms, though these are clearly anthropocentric rather than theological in orientation.

And Here's to You, Bill Shankly...

In the Simon and Garfunkel hit "And Here's to You, Mrs Robinson" a lyrical stanza within the song begins "Where have you gone, Joe DiMaggio, A nation turn its lonely eyes to you" and finishes with "What's that you say, Mrs Robinson", "jolting Joe has left and gone away". The lyrical passage refers to the American baseball legend and American sporting hero of the 1930s and 40s, Joe DiMaggio.[48] In the years since then, nostalgia-soaked memories of an apparent age of American idealism and innocence have come to be embodied in the figure of DiMaggio, as the "Last American Hero". In similar fashion, condolence messages signed following Hillsborough look wistfully upon an era of unparalleled sporting success for Liverpool FC during the 1960s and 70s under the stewardship of former legendary manager Bill Shankly. Not only is Shankly famed with the dramatic turn-around of a club which having faced the ignominy of relegation from the old First Division into one which, in the space of five years, had delivered a League Championship and the club's first European trophy, the UEFA Cup in 1973,[49] but his resolutely "down-to-earth" approach to life, his roots in Scottish socialism and appreciation for traditional working-class values, of "hard-graft" and collectivism, apparently struck a chord and achieved a wider resonance with the spirit and people of 1960s Liverpool. It is in this particular light that the following messages can be read.

"Shanks' will be heart-broken to embrace so many. With him you will never walk alone."

"You'll Never Walk Alone. Shanks' is there."

"Shanks' only got it wrong once. He said football was about life and death—it shouldn't be."

"The brightest stars in heaven tonight are Shanks' boys saying goodnight. God Bless."

These messages, and many others like them in the condolence books signed following Hillsborough, convey the considerable purchase that Shankly continues to exert over the popular imagination on Merseyside. They are striking from a number of perspectives, not least a psychoanalytic one, from where Shankly appears in the guise of a totemic "father-figure" offering protection and comfort to the deceased and bereaved alike. In so-called "primitive" societies, the anthropological focus of much early psychology and sociology[50], totems were believed to offer a source of protection and self-representation of the community.

Here, then, the veneration of Shankly can be seen as the veneration of Liverpool itself.

There is undoubtedly an aspect of nostalgia at work here – itself an aspect of mourning–and it is not difficult to see why the 1960s should be looked back upon fondly as a "golden age" by Liverpudlians when set against the calamitous background of the 1980s, a decade when the city was "written to shreds"[51] by a hostile London-based print media. It is this retreat into the past, into fantasy–a theme that I take up in the messages below–that provides escape, albeit temporary, from the horrible reality of the present in which the Hillsborough disaster occurred.

Language, Fantasy and the Narrative Imagination

A further aspect of Liverpool exceptionalism identified by historians and social commentators is the Scouser's seeming proclivity for the verbal one-liner; a capacity exemplified in the verbal invention and word-play of one of the city's most famous sons, John Lennon, who in books such as *In His Own Write* and *A Spaniard in the Works*, makes an art of the verbal near-miss or malapropism, a linguistic pun known locally as the "Merseypropism" or "Malapudlianism".[52] Scouse dialect[53], as distinguished by structure, sound and propensity for humour from dialects of the neighbouring North-West, is perceived by John Belchem as a psychological response to Liverpool's economic hardship and relative marginalisation from the rest of the UK. Surreal word-play, a highly prized asset, especially among young men, can be seen here as a legacy of Liverpool's dock-based waterside casualism and "itinerant work culture", in which one established ones "credentials and comradeship" by accentuating the phonetics and humour of Scouse. It can also be seen as influenced by the large Irish presence in the city, a presence which mushroomed following the Irish potato famine of 1845-9 in what became known as the "hungry forties" of the nineteenth century.[54] This "gift of the gab" is reflected throughout the Hillsborough condolence books. It is manifested in a *poeticity*—where language does not simply refer indifferently to reality but where words acquire a weight and value of their own[55]—and creativity in which bereavement and loss "trigger the work of the imagination" as much as they threaten to spoil it.[56]

"God bless you all. Hope you get the ferry to heaven."

"Every red sky will remind us. Sleep in peace."

"I watched you drowning in a sea of silent sorrow. Walk on."

"Supporters of the world unite! God bless."

"And don't be afraid of the dark."

The first of these messages presented here seamlessly blends together the Birkenhead ferry—a key "signifier" of local identity which, since the 1960s, when popularised by the Merseybeat-Sound of Gerry and the Pacemakers, has become part of local folklore—with a spiritual wish for heavenly ascension. It can be read, psychoanalytically, as drawing unselfconsciously upon fantasy, an unconscious mechanism which compensates for loss[57] through the temporary suspension of external reality. For in this view, the retreat into fantasy is a wish-fulfilment that provides a defence against the painful reality of experience. Other messages draw semiotically upon the colour red as a signifier of Liverpool FC, whilst the third in this sequence of messages draws poetically not only upon the deafening and enveloping silence by which people met their deaths at Hillsborough[58] but on what it means to bear witness. Hillsborough, of course, was one of the first tragedies to unfold live on television. Nowadays everything is caught on hand-held camera and replayed endlessly from a variety of vantage points, from the events of 9/11 to the Asian Tsunami of 26 December 2004.

The remainder of the messages presented above draw, intertextually, upon texts—each inserted one within the other, whose meaning is inverted or deferred—already in circulation elsewhere. The first inverts Marx and Engels' rallying cry to the working-classes in the *Communist Manifesto*; while the second takes only part of the song "You'll Never Walk Alone", so synonymous and effortlessly understood by the Liverpool public with whom it resonates, that sociologist, Grace Davie, has described it as "Liverpool's 23rd Psalm".[59]

No Place like Home

The final sample of condolence messages I present in this chapter reflects the affective ties and emotional pull of home. Home, of course, is, according to popular proverb, where the heart is, and here it is clear to see that "familiarity, where it does not breed contempt"[60], breeds a "topophilic" affection for a sense of place. Elsewhere, Richard Hoggart[61] has written fondly of the lure of home and of homeliness as a characteristic feature of traditional northern working-class communities, whilst Freud relates the homely (*"heimlich"*) and native (*"heimisch"*)—as friendly, intimate and tame—to landscapes of predilection resonant of the maternal body.[62] These messages, signed by Liverpudlians from as far a field as South Africa, reflect a sense that in times of crisis there is a felt emotional need to be home, if not physically, then at least in spirit.[63]

"Even though I was far away, in my heart I was home that day."

"With love and sympathy to all the bereaved, from an ex-pat Liverpudlian."

"Just popped home to say you'll never be forgotten"

What is of course especially striking about these messages, especially the second, is that someone should refer to themselves as an "ex-pat Liverpudlian", for the term "patriot", from which "ex-pat" is derived, is ordinarily reserved to describe a person's loyalty, not to their region, but to their country. It is nevertheless a term repeated more than once in the condolence books, which reflects the passionate and extraordinary bonds of locality and tribalism characteristic of "structures of feeling" on Merseyside. Such messages are themselves reflective of a Liverpudlian diaspora within the UK and beyond. "Diaspora" comes from the Greek word meaning a scattering of seeds and Liverpudlians have for a long time been forced to leave home, often in search of a better life elsewhere. Between 1951 and 1986 the city haemorrhaged population at a rate of knots, in which the population was almost halved from 900,000 to 483,000.[64] There has long been an implicit recognition – especially among artists and musicians, from the Beatles onwards–that if you wanted to get on you needed to get out, preferably to London.

Conclusion

Throughout this chapter we have seen how condolence book signing following the Hillsborough disaster represents a "speech event": a "cultural salient event", which, like mourning itself, with its well defined boundaries of time and space, "rests upon the performance of some established and recognizable verbal routine".[65] If indeed condolence book signing was a "speech" or "communication event", then the "speech community" of interested parties that it summoned came together to participate in the circulation of shared meaning of *another* "text"–that of Liverpool itself. For in the cultural economy of signs upon which meaning and communication depend, "Liverpool" itself is a key cultural resource: a "discursive structure of potential meanings and pleasures"[66] through which social identity is both staged and narratively "performed". What is absolutely crucial about the many thousands of messages contained in condolence books signed following Hillsborough is that not only are they indicative of the ways in which people are subject to and "spoken by" prevailing discourses, but also the ways in which people actively insert themselves within, and contribute to, the circulation of discourse. For we have seen how the past, both recent and distant, permeates popular memory and consciousness in ways which, triggered by loss, help to summon and shape collective social identity.

---

[1] 95 became 96 when in 1993 a land-mark legal ruling by the House of Lords decreed that doctors no longer need artificially preserve the life of Tony Bland, who had remained in a coma from injuries sustained in the 1989 disaster. Most of the fans who died at Hillsborough did so from asphyxiation, crushed against the "crash-barriers" designed to protect them, their escape further prevented by 12 ft high perimeter fences erected to prevent pitch-invasions.

[2] In all, 766 were injured, many of them young Liverpool supporters who had entered the ground early to soak-up the atmosphere and ensure an optimal view of the match (Taylor, the Rt Hon Lord Justice Taylor, *The Hillsborough Stadium Disaster, Interim Report*, London: HMSO, 1989).

[3] For a detailed account of the tabloid media's wilful manipulation of actual events at Hillsborough–fabricated stories whose provenance lay with attempts by senior South Yorkshire Police officers on-duty that day to shift responsibility for the ensuing disaster, see Phil Scraton, *Hillsborough: The Truth* (Edinburgh: Mainstream Publishing, 2000) esp chapter 6.

[4] John Williams, "Kopites, 'Scallies' and Liverpool Fan Cultures", in John Williams, Stephen Hopkins and Cathy Long (eds), *Passing Rhythms: Liverpool FC and the Transformation of Football* (Oxford: Berg, 2001) 112.

[5] Over a million people, twice the population of the city, filed through Anfield in the week following the Hillsborough disaster, leaving floral tributes that transformed the pitch into a carpet of flowers. For discussion of the transformation of Anfield into a sacred site, and as invoking a sense of "place(ness)", see Ian Taylor, "Hillsborough, 15 April 1989: Some Personal Contemplations" *New Left Review*, 177 (1989) 89–110; John Bale, "Playing at Home: British Football and a Sense of Place", in John Williams and Steve Wagg (eds), *British Football and Social Change: Getting into Europe* (Leicester: Leicester University Press, 1991).

[6] Grace Davie, "'You'll Never Walk Alone': The Anfield Pilgrimage", in Ian Reader and Tony Walter (eds), *Pilgrimage in Popular Culture* (London: Macmillan, 1993).

[7] For further discussion of this and other public mourning events following Hillsborough, see Tony Walter "The Mourning after Hillsborough" *Sociological Review*, 39(3) (1991) 599–625.

[8] See ibid, 608.

[9] For a comparative discussion of religion and football, including religious sectarianism, in Liverpool and Glasgow–as arguably Britain's most "Celtic" cities, see Raymond Boyle, "Football and Religion: Merseyside and Glasgow", in Williams *et al*, *Passing Myths*, 39–52.

[10] "Bad deaths" are typically those that occur in the prime of a person's life in either tragic or violent circumstances and involving some degree of pain or suffering. In contrast to the "good death", which is seen as occurring at the end of a person's "natural" life-span, "bad deaths" are perceived as complicating the work of mourning by shattering the expectations and assumptions of the bereaved. Accordingly, the spontaneous mourning events following the Hillsborough disaster can be seen as "a public response to the unanticipated, violent

deaths of people who do not fit the categories of those we expect to die, who may be engaging in activities in which there is a reasonable expectation of safety" (C. Allen Haney and Dell Davis, "America Responds to Diana's Death", in Tony Walter (ed.), *The Mourning for Diana*, (Oxford: Berg, 1999) 236.

[11] From a cultural studies perspective, "text" refers to any aspect of culture—be it a Madonna video or a pair of jeans: as providing a system of signification in which meaning(s) is embedded, contested and/or produced through its popular consumption.

[12] D. Francis, G. Neophytou and L. Kellaher, "Kensington Gardens: From Royal Park to Temporary Cemetery", in Walter, *Mourning for Diana*, 113–134.

[13] "Books of condolence as Paris mourns the end of M & S", *Independent*, 7 April 2001, 13.

[14] M. J. Brennan, "Mourning Identities: Hillsborough, Diana and the Production of Meaning" (Ph.D diss., Warwick University, 2003). In all I examined over 7,000 messages contained in seven books of condolence using a method of what I have termed "textu(r)al" analysis: a focus that was at once a materially grounded insistence upon the *textual* character of messages whose *texture* lay not only with wider cultural and structural practices that helped produce them but was itself referential of the social and historical identities of the people who wrote them.

[15] For further discussion see Brennan, "Mourning Identities", 190–200. For more on the apparent "disappearance" of the Hillsborough books of condolence which my research uncovered, see "Hillsborough books are missing", *Liverpool Echo*, 25 May 2000, 2; "Found: Now books may go show to public", *Liverpool Echo*, 27 May 2000, 1,2.

[16] The advent of electronic media has, in recent years, greatly facilitated the storage, access and transmission of oral and written testimony. See, for example, Stephen Spielberg's *Survivors of the Shoah Visual History Foundation* (www.vhf.org) which has sought to videotape and preserve the testimonies of Holocaust survivors and witnesses. Since its establishment in 1994 Spielberg's Visual History Foundation has collected over 50,000 eyewitness testimonies in 57 countries and 32 languages.

[17] The exception is Bethan Jones' research into a sample of condolence books signed following the death of Princess Diana. See Bethan Jones, "Books of Condolence", in Walter, *Mourning for Diana*, 203–214.

[18] "Habitus" refers to the particular personality and behavioural traits of any given social group which, over time and through repeated iteration, become "second nature" so as it to be hardly recognisable by the people performing them. Etymologically, the concept derives from a combination of "habit" (the repeated performance of an action) and "habitation" (the social environment in which the habit is given shape). In sociology the term has gained widespread currency through the work of French social theorist Pierre Bourdieu who uses it, as a collective social psychology, to describe "the durably installed generative principles" that help (re)produce the social practices of a class or class fraction (see, for example, Pierre Bourdieu, *Outline of a Theory of Practice*, Cambridge: Cambridge University Press, 1977). The concept has a longer provenance in German sociology where it was in widespread usage during the 1930s and was first used by the historical sociologist, Norbert Elias, in the preface to the 1939 edition of *Über den Prozeß der Zivilisation* – a work widely regarded as his magnum opus – to describe the ways in which "the fortunes and experiences of a nation (or of its constituent groupings)" become sedimented, as a form of "embodied social

learning", within the social practices of its individual members. For a discussion of Elias's use of the concept and differences between his and Bourdieu's usage, see Eric Dunning and Stephen Mennell, Preface to *The Germans: Power Struggles and the Development of Habitus in the Nineteenth and Twentieth Centuries*, by Norbert Elias, trans., and ed. Michael Schröter (Cambridge: Polity, 1996).

[19] Richard Johnson, "What is Cultural Studies Anyway?", *Centre for Contemporary Cultural Studies, Stenciled paper*, No.74 (Birmingham: University of Birmingham, 1983) 35.

[20] The corpus of literature on a purported tendency towards death denial within Western societies is immense and too numerous to list here. Seminal texts in the burgeoning field of "death studies", however, include: Philippe Ariés, *Western Attitudes Toward Death: From the Middle Ages to the Present* (Baltimore: Johns Hopkins University Press, 1974); Ernest Becker, *The Denial of Death* (New York: Free Press, 1973); Norbert Elias, *The Loneliness of the Dying* (Oxford: Blackwell, 1985); Geoffrey Gorer, *Death, Grief and Mourning in Contemporary Britain* (London: Cresset Press, 1965); Michel Vovelle, *Mourir autrefois: attitudes collectives devant la mort aux XVII et XVIII* (Paris: Gallimard, 1974).

[21] Nancy Fraser, "Rethinking the Public Sphere–A Contribution to the Critique of Actually Existing Democracy", in *Habermas and the Public Sphere*, ed. Craig Calhoun (Cambridge, Mass: MIT Press, 1992).

[22] Jim McGuigan, "British identity and 'the people's princess'", *Sociological Review*, 48(1) (2000) 1–18.

[23] Paul Alberts, "Sublime and Corporeal Diana'", in *Planet Diana: Cultural Studies and Global Mourning*, eds. Ien Ang, et al (Kingswood, New South Wales: Research Centre in Intercommunal Studies, University of Western Sydney, Nepean, 1997), 97–101.

[24] Raymond Williams, *The Long Revolution* (Harmondsworth: Penguin, 1984). As a cultural historian whose work was an antecedent of contemporary cultural studies, Williams identifies aspects of popular culture, from "poems to buildings and dress-fashions", as vital elements worthy of historical investigation. Here we can add condolence books to the various aspects of popular, recorded and documentary culture that Williams sees as providing reliable access to the social character of any particular time and place within any given historical period.

[25] Ibid, 63, 64

[26] Freudian psychoanalysis, thus conceived as the "talking cure", in which the analysand is asked to narrate one's (childhood) memories and experiences in an uninhibited movement of "free-association", is, from the very beginning, concerned, inter alia, with teasing out meanings ordinarily policed by the conscious, controlling and rationalistic part of the brain.

[27] In psychoanalytic theory, loss is the process through which the individual establishes a sense of self and relationship with others. It can be seen first and foremost in the infant's separation from its mother, wherein the child is forced to recognise its difference and separateness from its mother. In this at first terrifying experience, in which the child fears abandonment, the child fantasies her presence in the imagination. Not only therefore, according to Freud, is the child's desire for its mother created by her absence but it is in the child's capacity for imagination that it has "created an object out of the mother" (Sigmund Freud, "Inhibitions, Symptoms and Anxiety", in James Strachey (ed and trans) *The Standard*

Edition of the Complete Psychological Works of Sigmund Freud, (1966; reprint, London: Hogarth Press, 1986) 20:170. The *Standard Edition* is hereafter cited as SE.

[28] Julie Kristeva, *Black Sun: Depression and Melancholia*, trans., Leon. S. Roudiez (New York: Columbia University Press, 1989) 22. The indexical relationship between language and loss can again be seen in the child's separation from its mother; a loss which, according to Kristeva, causes the him (*sic*) "to try to find her… along with other objects of love, first in the imagination, then in words" (Kristeva, *Black Sun*, 6).

[29] In more socially inflected aspects psychoanalysis, such distinctions between "inner" and "outer" worlds can, to all intents and purposes, be seen as reified concepts. This is best exemplified in the school of "object-relations" theory pioneered by Melanie Klein, in which various "objects" external to the individual become internalised, worked upon and transformed within the unconscious and fantasised realm of human interiority; in which there is a "continual shuttling of inner and outer worlds, from which a sense of self emerges" (Anthony Elliott, *Psychoanalytic Theory: An Introduction* (Oxford: Blackwell, 1994) 26. The social implications of psychoanalytic theory are provocatively drawn out by Elliott, who, by reference to Freud's 1924 essay "A note upon the 'mystic writing pad'", usefully illustrates the "deep impressions" made upon the repressed unconscious by society itself (Anthony Elliott, *Subject to Ourselves: Social Theory, Psychoanalysis and Postmodernity* (Cambridge: Polity, 1996).

[30] Zygmunt Bauman, "What Prospects of Morality in times of Uncertainty?" *Theory, Culture and Society,* special issue on Zygmunt Bauman, 15(1) (1998), 19.

[31] L. M. Zunin and H. S. Zunin, *The Art of Condolence: What to Write, What to Say, What to do at a time of Loss* (New York: Harper-Collins, 1992).

[32] Geoffrey Bennington and Jacques Derrida, *Jacques Derrida* (Chicago: University of Chicago Press, 1993) 148.

[33] Eric Lindemann, "Symtomatology and Management of Acute Grief", *American Journal of Psychiatry*, CI, 1944, 141–8. Whilst Freud refers repeatedly to mourning as "work", Lindemann's paper is significant for the trend it initiated towards psychoanalytic "stage-theories" of grief—later popularised in the work of psychiatrists Elizabeth Kübler-Ross and Colin Murry Parkes—ranging from denial and intense guilt to anger and disorientation. It is perhaps not surprising, given the circumstances in which people died at Hillsborough, and the scurrilous lies perpetuated by the tabloid press about the behaviour of some Liverpool fans, that anger should be a major component of the mourning after Hillsborough.

[34] Sigmund Freud, "Mourning and Melancholia", *SE*, 14, 243.

[35] Tony Lane, *Liverpool: City of the Sea* (Liverpool: Liverpool University Press, 1997) xiii.

[36] Annette Kuhn, "A Journey Through Memory", in *Memory and Methodology*, ed. Susannah Radstone (Oxford: Berg, 2000) 188.

[37] From the "three graces" on the city's water-front (a testament to the profligacy and excess of the latter days of the British Empire), to the rows of Georgian terraces (which outnumber those in the Regency city of Bath) built to accommodate the city's expanding class of eighteenth century merchants, to the Albert Dock (the world's first and largest non-combustible dock warehouse system), Liverpool was clearly a city to be reckoned with.

[38] "Liverpool: Port, Docks and City", *Illustrated London News*, 15 May 1886, cited in John Belchem, *Merseypride: Essays in Liverpool Exceptionalism* (Liverpool: Liverpool University Press, 2000) xiii.
[39] See Linda Grant, *Still Here* (London: Little, Brown, 2002) 151. See also "History broke Liverpool, and it broke my heart", *Guardian*, 5 June 2003.
[40] Andrew Ward and John Williams, "Bill Shankly and Liverpool", in Williams *et al, Passing Myths*, 73.
[41] John Williams, "Kopites, 'Scallies' and Liverpool Fan Cultures", in *ibid*, 101.
[42] Davie, "You'll Never Walk Along", 211.
[43] See *ibid.*, 1993; Walter, *Mourning for Diana*.
[44] Walter, *Mourning for Diana*, 621.
[45] Social geographer Edward Relph has coined the term "placeness" to capture the unconscious interiorisation of place; "of being inside and belonging to *your* place as an individual and as a member of a community, and to know this without reflecting on it" (Edward Relph, *Place and Placeness* (London: Pion, 1965).
[46] In the interest of research ethics and good practice, I have anonymised the messages presented here as they are reproduced without the permission or consent of the people who signed them.
[47] For more on the popular mythology surrounding the tall and graceful cormorant known as the Liver Bird, see Peter Aughton, *Liverpool: A People's History* (Preston: Carnegie Press, 1990).
[48] As if DiMaggio's on-field sporting successes were not enough to guarantee his status as an "All American Hero" (in his first four years with the New York Yankees the team won consecutive American League pennants and World Series Championships) off-field, and following his retirement from baseball, he married another quintessentially American icon, Marilyn Monroe.
[49] From taking charge of Liverpool in 1959, who at the time were a Second Division club, Shankly quickly steered Liverpool to the Second Division Championship (1961–2), followed by three league Championships (1963–4, 1965–6, 1972–3), two FA Cups (1965 and 1974) and the UEFA Cup in 1973.
[50] See, for example, Sigmund Freud, "Totem and Taboo", *SE*, 13 (1913; reprint, London: Hogarth Press, 1957); Emile Durkheim, *The Elementary Forms of Religious Life* (1912; reprint, London: Unwin, 1954).
[51] Bob Gill, chairman of Liverpool FC Supporters Association, cited in John Williams, "Football and Football Hooliganism in Liverpool", Research Report, Sir Norman Chester Centre for Football Research (Leicester: University of Leicester, 1987) 7.
[52] Belchem, 2000, 53.
[53] "Dialect", as socio-linguist Peter Trudgill suggests, refers to "differences between kinds of language which are differences of vocabulary and grammar as well as pronunciation". "Accent", on the other hand, refers only to differences of pronunciation (Peter Trudgill, *Sociolinguistics: An Introduction*, Harmondsworth: Penguin, 1979) 17.
[54] Irish immigration to Liverpool was both rapid and steep. In the space of just three months Liverpool's Irish population had grown by 90,000, which, within a year, had swelled to 300,000 (P. H. Williams, *Liverpolitania: A Miscelleny of People and Places* (Liverpool:

Merseyside Civic Society, 1971) 11). By 1851 22.3 per cent of the city's population were Irish-born (Belchem, 2000, 203).

[55] Roman Jakobson, "What is Poetry?" in Roman Jakobson, *Selected Writings*, trans. Christian Hubert (Cambridge: Cambridge University Press, 1983) 750.

[56] Krsiteva, 1989, 9.

[57] Elliott 1999, 59.

[58] This is a feature of Hillsborough drawn upon both by those who were present as well as those who watched events from afar. See, for example, the comments of Trevor Hicks, whose daughters Sarah and Victoria died at Hillsborough, in Rogan Taylor, Andrew Ward and Tim Newburn, *The Day of the Hillsborough Disaster: A Narrative Account* (Liverpool: Liverpool University Press, 1995). See also American novelist Don Delillo's book *Mao II* in which one of the story's main characters watches the disaster unfold silently on television; Don Delillo, *Mao II* (London: Jonathan Cape) 32–34.

[59] For a discussion of the various transpositions "You'll Never Walk Alone" has undergone since its origin in the Rodgers and Hammerstein musical *Carousel*, see Davie, 208 211.

[60] Yi Fu Tuan, *Topophilia* (Englewood Cliffs: Prentice Hall, 1974). Put simply, "topophilia", combining the Greek word for place ("*topos*") with a particular fondness or inclination towards an activity or "thing" ("*philia*"), describes a condition that "couples sentiment with place".

[61] Richard Hoggart, *The Uses of Literacy* (Harmondsworth: Penguin, 1957)

[62] Sigmund Freud, "The Uncanny", in *SE*, 17: 217–52.

[63] C.K. Alsop, "Home and Away: Self-Reflexive Auto/Ethnography", *Forum: Qualitative Social Research On-Line*, 3(3), September 2002. Available online at http://www.qualitative-research.net/fqs-texte/3-02/3-02alsop-e.htm.

[64] Sara Cohen, *Rock Culture in Liverpool: Popular Music in the Making* (Oxford: Clarendon Press, 1991) 2.

[65] Martin Montgomery, in O'Sullivan et al, *Key Concepts in Communication and Cultural Studies*, 2nd ed (London: Routledge) 295.

[66] John Fiske, *Understanding Popular Culture* (London: Routledge, 1990) 27.